DRUG POLICY CONSTELLATIONS

The Role of Power and Morality in the Making of Drug Policy in the UK

Alex Stevens

First published in Great Britain in 2025 by

Bristol University Press
University of Bristol
1-9 Old Park Hill
Bristol
BS2 8BB
UK
t: +44 (0)117 374 6645
e: bup-info@bristol.ac.uk

Details of international sales and distribution partners are available at bristoluniversitypress.co.uk

© Bristol University Press 2025

British Library Cataloguing in Publication Data
A catalogue record for this book is available from the British Library

ISBN 978-1-5292-3132-8 hardcover
ISBN 978-1-5292-3142-7 paperback
ISBN 978-1-5292-3143-4 ePub
ISBN 978-1-5292-3144-1 ePdf

The right of Alex Stevens to be identified as author of this work has been asserted by him in accordance with the Copyright, Designs and Patents Act 1988.

All rights reserved: no part of this publication may be reproduced, stored in a retrieval system, or transmitted in any form or by any means, electronic, mechanical, photocopying, recording, or otherwise without the prior permission of Bristol University Press.

Every reasonable effort has been made to obtain permission to reproduce copyrighted material. If, however, anyone knows of an oversight, please contact the publisher.

The statements and opinions contained within this publication are solely those of the author and not of the University of Bristol or Bristol University Press. The University of Bristol and Bristol University Press disclaim responsibility for any injury to persons or property resulting from any material published in this publication.

Bristol University Press works to counter discrimination on grounds of gender, race, disability, age and sexuality.

Cover design: Liam Roberts Design
Front cover image: iStock/ blackred

For Vida, Grace and Georgia

Contents

List of Figures and Tables		vi
About the Author		vii
Preface		viii
1	An Introduction to Drug Policy Constellations	1
PART I	**Contexts, Concepts and Methods for Studying Drug Policy Constellations**	
2	Facts and Narratives of the UK Drug Policy Context	11
3	Power and Morality in Policy Making	20
4	Policy Constellation: A Critical Realist Approach	33
5	Studying Policy Constellations in the Real World	42
PART II	**Morality and Power in UK Drug Policy Constellations**	
6	Moralities in Action: The Ethico-Political Bases of UK Drug Policy	61
7	Mapping UK Drug Policy Constellations	76
8	Power in UK Drug Policy Constellations	93
PART III	**Cases in Drug Policy Making in the UK**	
9	The Limited Legalisation of Medical Cannabis	109
10	Responses to the Drug Deaths Crisis: Explaining Differences at UK and Scottish Levels	125
11	The UK's Ten-Year Drug Strategy	145
12	A Retroductive Conclusion	160
Notes		177
References		180
Index		215

List of Figures and Tables

Figures

2.1	Drug-related deaths in Great Britain, 1996–2020	16
3.1	The circumplex of basic values (adapted from Schwartz and Boehnke, 2004)	29
6.1	The modified circumplex of ethico-political bases in UK drug policy	62
7.1	Sociogram of policy actors (grey) and policy positions (black) in the UK drug policy field (with ethico-political bases in italics)	78
7.2	Sociogram of the UK drug policy field showing overlapping policy constellations	91
10.1	Sociogram of the Scottish drug policy field (with relevant ethico-political bases in italics)	131
10.2	Sociogram of the Scottish drug policy field showing policy constellations	132

Tables

5.1	Interviewees	45
5.2	Documents purposively selected for discourse analysis	47
5.3	Parliamentary debates and meetings selected for discourse analysis	48
6.1	Comparison of how ethico-political bases relate to ideological narratives (Haidt et al, 2009) and philosophical underpinnings of drug policy (MacCoun and Reuter, 2001)	74
7.1	Selected members of the conservative policy constellation	80
7.2	Selected members of the public health policy constellation	81
7.3	Selected members of the drug policy reform constellation	82
10.1	Selected members of the reformist policy constellation	133
10.2	Selected members of the abstentionist policy constellation	134

About the Author

Alex Stevens is Professor in Criminal Justice at the University of Kent. He is also a board member of Harm Reduction International and chair of the Drug Science Enhanced Harm Reduction Working Group. He was formerly president of the International Society for the Study of Drug Policy (2015–2019) and a member of the UK Advisory Council on the Misuse of Drugs (ACMD, 2014–2019). Professor Stevens holds a BA in French in the School of European Studies from the University of Sussex, an MA in Socio-Legal Studies from the University of Sheffield, and a PhD in Social Policy from the University of Kent. He is the author of *Drugs, Crime and Public Health: The Political Economy of Drug Policy* (Routledge, 2011) as well as numerous articles on related topics. He lives with his family in Whitstable, where he was for 14 years a member of the crew and helmsman of the RNLI lifeboat.

Preface

Explaining drug policy is not an easy task. As Alison Ritter (2022, p 79) puts it, drug policy 'often seems to occur without much logic'. Explanation requires the discovery of some underlying logic, even if it is not particularly rational. As this logic is underlying, it cannot be directly observed. But we can use a variety of research methods to improve our understanding of how it works, of the mechanisms that combine, in some situations, to produce particular drug policies.

There are some excellent books that point the way towards such explanations. I have learnt a lot from Ritter's short but magisterial monograph on *Drug Policy*. Another is Susanne MacGregor's (2017) book on *The Politics of Drugs*. People who are interested in the history of British drug policy will gain a lot from it, as they will from Virginia Berridge's (2013) *Demons*, Harry Shapiro's (2021) *Fierce Chemistry* and Jock Young's (1971) *The Drugtakers*. They might also be interested in my previous book on *Drugs, Crime and Public Health: The Political Economy of Drug Policy* (Stevens, 2011a).

When I read MacGregor's book, I was impressed by the depth of her description of drug policy fields at UK and international levels. But I was left unsatisfied by the conceptual tools she used to explain these policies, which are mostly based on methodological individualism. So I set out to provide an account which assumes that policy making is a *collective* endeavour. Policy outcomes are not just the aggregation of discrete, individual actions. To understand social processes, we need explanations that operate at the level of social groups. The theoretical precepts of critical realism provides such an understanding (Bhaskar, 1975; Archer, 2000). I present the policy constellation as a critical realist concept that I have developed to explain policy outcomes.

I developed this policy constellations approach in order to explain policy making in one field in one country. That field is drug policy. The country is the UK, which is made up of four separate nations with their own histories and relationships with controlled drugs. I try to reflect some of that national diversity by giving attention to drug policy in Scotland as well as at UK level. I hope that the policy constellations approach can also be applied to other policy fields and in other places.

I am a criminologist by background and have had to teach myself about theories and methods to use in policy analysis. Paul Cairney has been an invaluable guide, especially his books on *Understanding Public Policy* and *The Politics of Policy Analysis* (Cairney, 2019, 2021). Professor Cairney is such a prolific writer that I am bound to have missed or skimmed over some of his useful insights. Apologies to him and all the other authors that I cite in this book for the moments where I may have traduced their work.

The book has benefited hugely from discussing its ideas with people in the field, and especially those I interviewed in the run-up to writing it. They are listed in Chapter 5, with thanks. Others who, even if they did not know it, have helped me to develop these ideas include my partner Jo Tonkin, my father Geoffrey Stevens, Niamh Eastwood, Peter Reuter, Caroline Chatwin, Fiona Measham, Harry Sumnall, Clara Musto, Pat O'Hare, Gerry Stimson, Mark Monaghan, Jack Spicer, Matt Bacon, Jack Cunliffe, Luis Eslava, Tim Leighton, Bernie Pauly, Alissa Greer, Naomi Zakimi, Mark Hill, Alex Betsos, Colleen Daniels, Karen Joe Laider, Marie Jauffret Roustide, Kat Smith, Esben Houborg, Caitlin Hughes, Carl Hart, Ethan Nadelmann, Sheila Vakharia, Kassandra Frederique, Tony Duffin, David Nutt, Gavin Irwin, Karl Wilding, Campbell Rodd, Kathryn Oliver, Annette Boaz, Geoff Monaghan, Tim Rhodes and Kari Lancaster. I learned a lot from discussions of my use of critical realism with Tim, Kari and others of a more post-structuralist bent, even if we have failed to persuade each other of the superiority of our ontological assumptions.

I also learnt from the PhD students I have supervised in the last ten years. Especial thanks go to Giulia Zampini for sharpening my interest in the role of morality in understanding drug policy and for working with me on the first iteration of the policy constellation concept (Stevens and Zampini, 2018). Greg Los pioneered the international application of this concept in his comparative study of drug policy in the UK and Poland (Los, 2023a, 2023b). Bisi Akintoye taught me about the less visible effects of racially unjust drug law enforcement, as well as the application of critical realism to ethnographic research (Akintoye et al, 2022).

In recent years, we have lost friends and colleagues from whom I learnt so much about drugs, drug policy, and how to reduce their harms and enhance their benefits. They include Paolo Pertica, Gill Bradbury, Sara McGrail, Mark Kleiman, Franz Trautmann, Kevin Molloy, Tomáš Zábranský and Ambros Uchtenhagen. Far too many others have died drug-related deaths that could have been prevented. We miss their love, wit and wisdom.

My colleagues in the School of Social Policy, Sociology and Social Research at the University of Kent have provided an excellent (let's not say four-star) intellectual environment for learning and trying out new ideas, including in our Thursday evening research seminars and on the picket line. My colleagues at the Medway campus – including Dawn Lyon, Tara Young,

Balihar Sanghera, Ellie Jupp, Kate Bradley, Phil Hubbard, Simon Shaw, and Annikki Laitinen – have been particularly inspirational and supportive, as has my current boss, Iain Wilkinson, and our magnificent occupational health manager, Brenda Brunsdon.

This book could not have been written without the support of two beautiful institutions; the National Health Service and my family. In 2014, I was diagnosed with a brain tumour. I doubted I would be able to write again. The superb care provided by the NHS through three craniotomies has so far protected the mysterious parts of my brain that do the writing. I am immensely grateful to Mr Francesco Vergani and the rest of the neuro-oncology team at King's College Hospital for saving my life.

My family dealt with all this with huge love and great humour. I sometimes think that coping with my selfish concentration on book writing has been more of a trial for them than the tumour. It was not easy for my daughters Vida, Georgia and Grace to face these vicissitudes – and a global pandemic – over their teenage years. They overcame every challenge with aplomb. They have grown into marvellous, insightful and entertaining young women. They are my greatest inspiration. It is to them that this book is dedicated, with love.

Alex Stevens
Whitstable
March 2023

1

An Introduction to Drug Policy Constellations

This book is about how policy is made. It uses examples of British policies on illicit drugs to develop and illustrate a new approach to understanding policy making. It is born of a mixture of fascination, curiosity, frustration, sadness and anger, with occasional moments of dark humour.

Drugs are fascinating. The range of pleasures and pains they produce, the lengths some people will go to get them, and the effects of their use on our social and cultural lives have inspired a huge range of academic and artistic work. As a committed drug policy geek, I also find myself fascinated by the process of policy making. Out of the wide range of harms and pleasures that people experience, how do we come to focus our attention on some and not others? From the myriad proposed policy responses, how are some selected for legislation and funding while others are left on the intellectual scrapheap? Why do 'zombie ideas' – which have long since been discredited – continue to be so influential (Peters and Nagel, 2020)?

In economics, undead ideas include that markets are inherently efficient, that they tend to equilibrium, that wealth trickles down, and that the economic advantages of the global North are solely the product of the ingenuity and hard work of White men and have nothing to do with the legacy of slavery and colonisation (Keen, 2001; Quiggins, 2010; Hope and Limberg, 2022; Berg and Hudson, 2023). In drug policy, still walking among us are the supposedly inherent difference between licit and illicit drugs, that it is possible to achieve a 'drug-free society', and that there is a winnable 'war on drugs' (or even a war on drugs at all). Why are these ideas so influential? This is a question I get asked a lot. It was expressed well by one of the people I interviewed for this book, Dr Ed Day, the UK's national Drug Recovery Champion: "I really struggle with ... criminalising drugs as an issue because it just doesn't seem to work. I can't see evidence it's worked ever, and it just causes massive harm. And so why do we do it?"

My inquisitive urge to answer such questions is tinged with frustration. I have spent the best part of my career trying to find out which drug policies work best. Time and again, I have toiled for months on a project, produced a report to the best of my ability and discussed it in detail with colleagues and policy makers, only for the next policy announcement to ignore all that hard work or even to run directly contrary to it.

I am hardly the only researcher to have observed the failure of governments to 'follow the science' on a controversial issue (Smith, 2017; Cairney, 2020; Stevens, 2020b). The COVID-19 pandemic provided many examples, and they also abound in drug policy. My colleague David Nutt, for example, once lost his post as chair of the Advisory Council on the Misuse of Drugs (ACMD) for failing to toe the government line (Nutt, 2021). I myself resigned from the ACMD over my concerns that ministers were not protecting its independence (Stevens, 2021).

This is not just about the bruised egos and thwarted hopes of researchers like me. The recommendations we make are intended to achieve some good. In 2015, I initiated work (with Annette Dale-Perera, Tim Millar and other members of the ACMD) on a report on *Reducing Opioid-Related Deaths in the UK* (ACMD, 2016e). We had noticed that such deaths were rising. We collated evidence on how they could be prevented. The practical results – or rather non-results – of our work are reported in Chapter 10. The fact that thousands of people have since died who could still be alive if better policies had been adopted makes me both sad and angry.

The absurdities of drug policy occasionally provide flashes of grim humour. I get a hollow laugh whenever a politician who has acknowledged their own use of controlled drugs says that we need to punish other people for doing the same. Former UK Prime Minister Boris Johnson is a prominent example of this darkly comic hypocrisy. Anger and cynical amusement are not particularly helpful in working out how we can improve matters. My own frustrations made me want to understand why it is that policies do not meet the needs of the people they are supposed to help and so led me to the analysis of public policy making.

This is a rich and fertile field (Colebatch, 2009; Hill, 2009; Dunn, 2017; Cairney, 2019, 2021). Reading these and other guides has enriched my understanding of how policy is made, and why it is inadequate to think of policy making as 'authoritative choice' (Colebatch and Hoppe, 2018; Ritter, 2022), a technical process of fitting effective means to rationally justified ends. But in studies that applied these ideas to drug policy, I found there were some things missing. Specifically, not enough attention is paid to the influences of two important drivers of drug policy outcomes: power and morality.

The first of these issues is addressed in nearly all policy analyses. The ability to achieve desired policy goals is included in several definitions of what power is. But in the theories that are most often applied to the analysis of drug policies, power takes on curiously nebulous forms. This is true for both the mainstream, neo-pluralist approaches and their more radical, critical alternatives. In the former camp we can place the advocacy coalitions framework (ACF) of Jenkins-Smith and Sabatier (1993), the multiple streams approach (MSA) of Kingdon (1984), and Baumgartner and Jones' (2009) punctuated equilibrium theory (PET), as well as R.A.W. Rhodes' (1990) ideas on 'policy networks'. In the latter camp, we find post-structuralist forms of policy analysis, including applications of Foucauldian critical discourse analysis, actor network theory and other developments of science and technology studies, such as Tim Rhodes and Kari Lancaster's 'evidence-making interventions' approach (Howarth, 2000; Mol, 2002; Law, 2004; Latour, 2005; Bacchi, 2009; Rhodes and Lancaster, 2019). There is not enough space in this book to go into the details of the strengths and weaknesses of these approaches. I cover some of them in Online Appendices 1.1 and 1.2 (on pluralist and post-structuralist policy theories). In the book itself, I present a new approach which builds on the strengths and – I hope – avoids some of the pitfalls of these existing attempts to explain policy stability and change.

There is growing interest in 'the role of normative ethics and meta-ethics[1] in public policy analysis' (Dunn, 2017, p 325). There are some interesting studies that address such normative concerns in drug policy (Scheerer, 1993; Keane, 2003; valentine, 2009; Euchner et al, 2013; Ferraiolo, 2014; De Saxe Zerden, O'Quinn and Davis, 2015; Rogeberg, 2015; Musto, 2018; Zampini, 2018; Christie et al, 2019; Ritter, 2022; Lerkkanen and Storbjörk, 2023). However, as Zampini (2018) and Ritter (2022) have argued, too little attention has generally been paid to the role of morality in shaping drug policy.

The use of morality in policy is an inherently inter-personal process. Kathryn Oliver and Moira Faul (2018, p 369) have argued that policy 'is significantly shaped by who is included, the conversations they have, how they are connected (or not), and the dynamics of their relationships. … Knowing who is taking part and how they are connected is vital to decoding, and ultimately influencing, evidence and policy processes'. In this book, I build on this insight by showing how who is involved and how they relate to each other is crucial for understanding drug policy making. The book also builds on three other insights that are assembled in Paul Cairney's practically essential manual on *The Politics of Policy Analysis*. These are: that policy making is a complex process which cannot be understood as a linear sequence of events that is directed solely from the centre of government; that normative, moral concerns play an important role in deciding what policies get made; and that people draw on emotions as well as cognition to make policy choices (Cairney, 2021). I also answer the call for more use of sociometric analysis of the networks through which drug policies are made (Zakimi et al, 2023) by using social network analysis to explore the policy constellations which operate in the UK and Scottish drug policy fields.

This all adds up to a sociological analysis of the processes involved in drug policy making. Back in 2011, I wrote an editorial which called for sociological analyses of 'how drug policies are the outcomes of specific conjunctures of political, socio-economic and cultural factors that are spatially and temporally specific and are open to change through social action' (Stevens, 2011d, p 402). This book provides such an analysis for recent drug policy in the UK and a critical realist approach for analysing other policies in other times and places: the policy constellations approach.

The rest of this chapter lays some necessary groundwork for the whole book. The spiky issue of what certain terms mean – always a source of conflict in drug policy debates – is addressed here after a short note on reading this book. I then summarise the argument and structure of the rest of it.

A note on reading this book

I set out to write this book in a slightly self-mocking tone, which invites the reader to take all the claims in it – mine and everyone else's – with a pinch of critical salt. The book revels in the richness of academic language, but I have also tried to make it clear. If your sense of humour sometimes makes you smile while reading, so much the better. If my use of complex sentences and arcane terms makes it difficult for you to understand, that is my fault, not yours.

Academic writers need to give up our illusions that readers pay close attention to every one of our carefully crafted phrases, especially in the age of the digitally searchable text. Much as we hope our work will escape academia, our readers are mostly students looking for quotes, ideas and facts to use in essays, or fellow researchers who want concepts, methods and data to turn to their own use. So it behoves us to enable people to find and digest what they need. I have tried to make this book easy to skim.

Readers who are particularly interested in theories and methods in public policy analysis may focus their attention on Part I. Those who want to know specifically about drug policy will find Parts II and III most rewarding. Within these parts, I start each chapter with an introductory summary of the ideas it presents, followed by a longer justification so that readers can learn more if they want to. It may even be possible to gain a rudimentary understanding of the arguments of this book just by reading its chapter headings and sub-headings. I hope you, dear reader, will be inspired to follow me into a little more depth.

You will see that I have used both single and double inverted commas for quotes. Single ones indicate text that I have taken from written documents. Double ones are used for direct quotes from the interviews I carried out for this book.

The book raises many theoretical and technical issues which it does not have space to cover in detail, so I have created online appendices for readers who want to explore them further. These can be found at https://drugpolicyconstellations.pubpub.org/.

Titular, descriptive concepts

Let's start with the four concepts in the book's main title.

- In this book, the term *illicit drugs* refers to those substances of which uses are controlled under the sections, classes and schedules of the Misuse of Drugs Act 1971 and the Misuse of Drug Regulations 2001. I will sometimes use 'drugs' for short, but we should remember that this is a category that also includes alcohol, tobacco, tea, coffee and – in some usages – medicines, and even sugar (Shapiro, 2021).
- A *policy* is 'a set of interrelated decisions … concerning the selection of goals and the means of achieving them within a specified situation' (Jenkins, 1978, p 15; Hill, 2009, p 15). In the UK, the term 'drug policy' is applied to decisions about illicit drugs and the people who use them. As some of the interviewees for this book noted, drug policies operate at different levels; local, national and international. The focus of this book is on national-level decisions taken by the UK and Scottish governments. When I refer to policy outcomes in this book, I mean the decisions that are made as the end result of policy processes, not the effects that these policies eventually have on the outside world when they are implemented.
- A *policy constellation* is a set of social actors (individuals and organisations) who come together in deploying various forms of socially structured power to pursue the institutionalisation in policy of shared moral preferences and material interests (Stevens and Zampini, 2018, p 62). So a drug policy constellation is such a set whose members focus their efforts on drug policy. See Chapter 4 for more details. There are two key differences between a policy constellation and one of the ACF's advocacy coalitions. One is that a coalition is coordinated (Jenkins-Smith et al, 2018), whereas a constellation is decentralised (Feldman, 2011). The other is that the constellation concept explicitly links the groups who are involved in making policy with the social and cultural structures that enable them (or constrain them) in choosing and achieving policy goals, rather than following the 'modified methodologically individualist' stance of Jenkins-Smith et al (2018, p 140). A policy constellation brings policy

actors together in ways that make them more than and different to the sum of the constellation's parts.²
- The *UK* is the United Kingdom of Great Britain and Northern Ireland. When I use 'British', I am referring to things that happen on the island of Great Britain, within a geographical rather than constitutional space. I try to avoid the criminological 'tendency to treat the somewhat disparate collection of states that comprise the United Kingdom as a single political entity' (Brewster, 2023, p 172). Drug law is made centrally by the UK government in London, primarily in the bomb-proof office of the Home Office on Marsham Street, and in the Houses of Parliament at the pretend-Gothic Palace of Westminster. This level of policy making is my main focus. Policy-making processes in Scotland, Wales and Northern Ireland, and at local authority level, are different. They have divergent moral influences and flows of power. I have tried to show some of this diversity by discussing distinctly Scottish policy constellations, especially in Chapter 10.

Sub-titular, explanatory concepts: power and morality

The concepts in the subtitle of this book help to explain how policy is made. They raise some even more thorny issues and will be discussed in more detail in Chapter 3. For now, I briefly define them.

- *Power* is the capacity to act in concert to get things done (Arendt, 1970; Allen, 1998). In the case of this book, the people who are potentially acting in concert (policy actors) are people who want to see their preferences and interests reflected and advanced in policy decisions. For them, getting things done means making sure that a policy is what they want it to be.
- *Morality* refers to the complex, multiple sets of norms – involving reasons, conventions, dispositions, affective emotions and moods – that social groups apply in judging what is right or wrong, good or bad. These apply not just to practices of consumption, but also to issues of who will be treated as a fully human being and who will be denied this status by processes of exclusion, stigmatisation and othering. It also relates to issues of rights: who bears them, to what do they entitle us, and what responsibilities do they bring? Morality is crucial to the explanation of all human action. 'To understand why people act as they do, we must first know what they value' (Bruce, 2013, p 37).

The policy constellations approach that I introduce in this book is based on the theoretical presuppositions of *critical realism*. This is a philosophy of science developed by Roy Bhaskar and others (Bhaskar, 1975; Collier, 1994; Archer, 2000; Sayer, 2000; Elder-Vass, 2012). Critical realism offers an alternative to two common sets of theoretical assumptions that are used in drug policy analysis. The first is positivist and empiricist work which cannot account for the deep underlying structures and mechanisms that produce observable reality. The second is post-structuralist and constructionist analysis which cannot offer a solid footing for policy action (Danermark, Ekstrom and Karlsson, 2019; Stevens, 2020a). The key features of critical realism that are used in this book are its ontological realism, epistemological relativism, judgemental rationality and cautious ethical naturalism. These are briefly explained at the start of Chapter 4 and in more detail in Online Appendix 4.1.

I also make particular use of the concept of a *field*, as in the UK drug policy field. This is a social and ideational space. It is populated by policy actors who share an interest in similar problems, even if they differ about how to define and solve them. In Chapters 7 and 10, I present maps of the social and ideational networks of the UK and Scottish drug policy fields in the form of social network sociograms.

Explaining drug policy with policy constellations: the structure of this book

The rest of the book is laid out in three parts. The first discusses the contexts, concepts and methods of the policy constellations approach. The second provides an over-arching analysis of the operation of morality and power in British drug policy constellations. The third applies the policy constellations approach to three specific cases in drug policy making.

Before we get to grips with the concepts that I will use to explain drug policy making, we need to share some knowledge of their specific contexts, which is the social world of illicit drugs and drug policy in the UK. This is described in Chapter 2. Chapter 3 provides some theoretical tools for thinking about drug policy, in the form of concepts of power and morality. It will explain why we need to think about the ethical and political underpinnings of policy preferences, which I call their ethico-political bases. Chapter 4 will present the policy constellations approach and show how it offers a critical, coherent and useful understanding by incorporating social and cultural structures of power and morality into the analysis of drug policy making. It uses concepts from critical theory and critical realism in doing so. In Chapter 5, I will show how these ideas can be developed and tested through a mixture of research methods. These include ethnography and auto-ethnography, elite interviews with policy actors, critical realist discourse analysis of policy documents, and social network analysis of policy actors and the policy positions they support. This first part of the book will be of use to policy scholars, no matter what area of policy they are interested in.

The three chapters in Part II focus on the moralities, constellations and powers that operate in the field of UK-level drug policy. Chapter 6 describes the particular forms of morality – the ethico-political bases – that animate drug policy making at UK level. Chapter 7 shows how these ethico-political bases bring policy actors together in policy constellations that circulate around shared policy positions. Chapter 8 will discuss the forms of power that flow through these policy constellations. This flow of powers through policy constellations is what explains which policy preferences prevail and so make it into officially accepted policy.

Part III presents the case studies which inform and illustrate the arguments made in Parts I and II. Chapter 9 explains the 2018 legalisation of cannabis-based medical products. Chapter 10 covers the belated response to the unrelated rise in drug-related deaths. It focuses on Scotland for two reasons. One is that I have covered the non-response to drug-related deaths in England in a previous publication on the 2017 UK drug strategy (Stevens, 2019). The other is that this provides a useful opportunity to show how the policy constellations approach deals with differences between national contexts and ethico-political bases. Chapter 11 examines the development of the ten-year drug strategy for the UK which was published in December 2021. It will again show the interplay of policy actors and policy preferences with the social and cultural structures of power and morality, and how these influence the outcomes of policy debates.

Finally, Chapter 12 will provide what critical realists call a retroductive summary. It will link the key concepts of the book with the key findings of its case studies. It will show how the policy constellations approach provides a useful and coherent framework for understanding the outcomes of policy processes.

Conclusion: drug policy as a testing ground for the policy constellations approach

Drug policy is an important and fascinating topic for developing theory on public policy. It mixes moral, political, legal, health, economic, geographical and geopolitical concerns. It is central to the operation of the criminal justice and health systems which affect us all.

We need a theory of how people interact with social structures of power and the cultural structures of morality in creating constellations of people and ideas that circle around policy issues. The operations of these policy constellations ensure that policies are decided on the basis of these actors' preferences and power, not on purely rational deliberation or on transactional negotiations between interest groups. This book provides such a theory and applies it to particular cases on the island of Great Britain.

PART I

Contexts, Concepts and Methods for Studying Drug Policy Constellations

2

Facts and Narratives of the UK Drug Policy Context

Our choices of how to measure and describe the illicit drug phenomenon are themselves moral and political. These forces shape the narratives on which we draw when making policy, which are known as 'policy narratives' (Roe, 1994; Hajer, 1995; Rhodes, 2018). Narratives string together ideas that frame the problem in a particular way and so suggest a certain response (Jones and McBeth, 2010; Wolton and Crow, 2022). They often include recurring tropes, the elements that are used to construct the story, like the big bad wolf, the dark forest, the innocent child, the heroic woodcutter and the evil baron. They represent the problem (Bacchi, 2009), but they also relate to actual events and real causal processes (Flatschart, 2016; Stevens, 2020a).

Some narratives and their tropes have been a consistent feature of drug policy discussions for decades. An example is the idea that opioid maintenance prescribing for people who are dependent on heroin is just like prescribing insulin to people with diabetes. I found this trope in a book published in the 1960s (Laurie, 1967) as well as in recent discussions. Other long-standing examples include the ideas that there is a 'war on drugs' or that cannabis is a 'gateway drug'.

We need to place these narratives in their broader contexts. In my interview with him, Professor Keith Humphreys reminded me of the importance of previous decisions and other policy fields in influencing current drug policy. What he called "decision accretion" – the set of decisions that have built up over time – influence what any policy actor can do now. Humphreys linked this to another point about drug policy, which is that it hardly exists in its own right. In a saying that he attributed to our mutual friend Peter Reuter, he said "drug policy is a sort of analytical convenience that doesn't actually exist. You know, a lot of it is about other things". Another academic, David Best, told me something similar about the dependence of drug policy on other fields, like health and economic policy: "You could have whatever drug policy you like. If those other areas aren't moving in a similar direction, it's irrelevant really."

From his American perspective, Humphreys reported:

> 'my view is that in post-war Britain, there's only two hugely consequential Prime Ministers. Atlee and Thatcher. And they are the most important drug policy officials in British history, right? You have an NHS [National Health Service]. It was definitely not created to deal with Britain's drug problem. OK, but that's just a hugely consequential thing.'

Clement Atlee's socialist building of the welfare state took place in the 1940s. Forty years later, Margaret Thatcher partly dismantled it in her anti-socialist pursuit of free markets. Both of these morally informed political missions continue to affect how drug policies are made in the UK.

In the period of research for this book, there were two particular issues which influenced drug policy making that had nothing to do with illicit drugs. One was the interminable wrangling over the UK's relationship with the rest of Europe. The other was the global pandemic of COVID-19. Both of these sucked up huge amounts of political attention, leaving little space for other policy developments. The collateral effects of the UK's decision to leave the European Union included the elevation to Prime Minister of both Theresa May and Boris Johnson, who had very different approaches to policy making in general, and drug policy in particular. May is famously straight-laced. Her greatest reported vice was 'running through fields of wheat' (McCann, 2018). Johnson has a rather different approach to personal morality, with a well-known past of infidelity and illicit drug use (Morgan, 2019) and a reputation for incessant dishonesty (Stewart, 2020). May was also much tighter in controlling the policy process, while Johnson took a more haphazard approach, described by one former adviser as being 'like a shopping trolley smashing from one side of the aisle to the other' (Stewart and Walker, 2021).

Brexit also enshrined a more insular view of Britain's place in the world, which may have helped to insulate the UK from the major changes that happened in drug policy in the 2010s. First Uruguay, then several US states and then Canada legalised the sale of cannabis for recreational use (Musto, 2018; Decorte, Lenton and Wilkins, 2021). In response to rising numbers of drug-related deaths, spaces where people could use drugs more safely – known as drug consumption rooms, or overdose prevention centres – spread around the world (HRI, 2022). Such signs of divergence from the 'Vienna consensus' of prohibitionist international drug policy (named after the Austrian seat of the United Nations Office on Drug Control) increased the perception that this consensus was 'fractured' (Bewley-Taylor, 2012).

These developments were often mentioned in UK policy debates but were not followed, except in the limited ways described in Chapters 9 and 10.

This book will explain why the UK did not pursue other countries down the path of reform. But first we need to gain some familiarity with British forms and narratives of drug control, harms and use.

Medical and penal control in UK drug policy

The more specific context of British drug policy was heavily influenced by two earlier drug policy officials: Sir Humphrey Rolleston and Sir Malcolm Delevingne. Rolleston was a medical doctor and, incidentally, grand-nephew of the chemist who discovered that nitrous oxide could be used as 'laughing gas', Sir Humphry Davy. Rolleston led the committee which recommended that heroin should be prescribed to people who became dependent on it (Departmental Committee on Morphine and Heroin Addiction, 1926). This came to be known as 'the British system' of heroin prescription (Spear, 2002). While Sir Humphrey represents the strain of British thinking which sees drugs as a problem that should be dealt with medically, Sir Malcolm represents the agencies of more punitive and penal social control. He believed in the need to restrict drug supply in order to combat the 'evil' of drugs. In a remarkable career, spanning nearly 40 years at the Home Office and then a further 14 in international diplomacy, Delevingne was deeply involved in the birth of both the British and international drug control systems (Collins, 2017). Thanks to his and others' efforts, the Rolleston report was not a simple triumph for medicalisation. Rather, it led to a 'gentlemanly compromise' between the doctors and the Home Office (South, 1998, p 88). The medics got their prescriptions, but the Home Office remained in control. It is this balance between Home Office officials and medical professionals that the historian Virginia Berridge (2013, p 131) has dubbed the 'hybrid medico-penal framework'. She shows how this hybrid between the medical and criminal justice systems has run British drug policy since its inception. I argue in this book that the medico-penal framework is still the dominant force in UK drug policy making.

In the UK, illicit drugs are now controlled under the Misuse of Drugs Act 1971. This legislation was controversial when it was introduced. A contemporary, critical criminological account saw it as the endpoint of a moral panic (Young, 1971). A deviancy amplification spiral had taken place during the cultural changes of the 1960s. Emerging patterns of youthful drug consumption were highlighted in the media, followed by increasing publicity and calls for control, followed by increased use and round the spiral again. The new Act continued the prohibitive approach which already dominated UK and international drug laws. It should be noted, however, that the people behind the Act saw it as a more liberal approach (Seddon, 2022). Previous legislation had not, for example, made a distinction between drugs with different effects; sentences for cannabis offences were the same as for heroin. Since 1971, controlled drugs have been placed in three classes – A, B and C – with different maximum sentences for possession, cultivation, production and sale of the drugs that are placed in each class.

Which drugs are in which class is set by the Home Secretary passing decisions through Parliament. According to the 1971 Act, she has to seek the advice of the Advisory Council on the Misuse of Drugs (ACMD) when doing so. This Advisory Council was set up by the Act with the remit to advise ministers on 'measures (whether or not involving alteration of the law) which in the opinion of the Council ought to be taken for preventing the misuse of such drugs or dealing with social problems connected with their misuse'.

For watchers of British drug policy, there is a familiar cycle of ministers referring substances for consideration by the ACMD and then taking their advice if it is to impose tighter control or ignoring it if the Council advises a more liberal approach. Fiona Measham and I (both former members of the ACMD) call this the 'drug policy ratchet', because it only turns in one, ever-tightening direction (Stevens and Measham, 2014). A rare exception was made for cannabis in 2004, when it was moved from Class B to Class C. This was soon corrected following much media discussion of harms related to cannabis, especially the effect on young people's mental health. Cannabis was put back in Class B in 2009 (Nutt, 2021).

The coincidence in 1971 of the enactment of the Misuse of Drugs Act with US President Nixon's launching of his 'war on drugs' has often tempted people to apply that martial term in the British context, despite it being both 'nonsensical and sinister' (Shapiro, 2021, p 9). Some have argued that it is inappropriate because there has been no war on drugs in the UK and that drug possession has already been effectively decriminalised (Hitchens, 2012). This ignores the fact that thousands of people still get criminal records every year for drug possession. In the ten years to March 2020, nearly 162,000 court cases in England and Wales where drug possession was the most serious offence ended in conviction. Of these, over 10,000 received immediate custodial sentences, out of a total of 87,000 drug offences that led to a prison term. On 30 September 2020, 18 per cent of people in prison in England and Wales were there for a drug offence (MoJ, 2021b). The overall number of people sucked into the criminal justice system for drug offences has dropped – with policing resources – over the last ten years. Imprisonment, however, has grown. The number of years given in prison sentences for drug offences went from 24,839 in 2010 to 27,684 in 2020 (calculated from data tables in MoJ, 2021a).

This is in addition to the thousands of cautions that have been given for drug possession in that period. In 2020/21 in England and Wales, 19,226[1] formal cautions were given for drug offences (Home Office, 2021).² Many arrests, cautions and charges resulted from stop and search activities, most often carried out under Section 23 of the Misuse of Drugs Act. People who are classed as Black are massively over-represented in these figures, being nine times more likely to be stopped and searched for drugs than White people (based on the proportions of Black and White people in the population census). They are also eight times more likely to be imprisoned for drug offences (Akintoye et al, 2022). Debate continues about the causes of this disproportionality, with some attempts to mask it behind misrepresentation of the existing research. For example the report of the government's Commission on Race and Ethnic Disparities tried to explain it away, partly by giving a misleading summary of a study on the effects of stop and search (Tiratelli et al, 2018; CRED, 2021). A more recent study showed more detailed evidence of 'officer bias' in stop and search, with Black people being searched more often than would be predicted by their presence among crime suspects, not just in the residential census (Vomfell and Stewart, 2021).

Others have argued that there is a war but that it is a war on people, not drugs (Buchanan and Young, 2000), especially if they are poor and Black. It is these groups who suffer the consequences of failed drug policies, including damages to their livelihoods, family relations and mental health through incarceration and the stigma of criminalisation.

I prefer to avoid such belligerent metaphors in discussing drug policy. The image of war conjures up the state leading the citizenry in regimented action to destroy an external enemy. In drug policy, we are largely fighting each other. The conflict often gets hot in the places where coca and opium are grown, with deployment of military and paramilitary force in Colombia, Afghanistan and other countries of the global South. This is also a battle of ideas. Actors compete for supremacy in drug policy by seeking to win legitimacy for their conceptions of drugs, however factual or coherent, absurd or irrational they may be.

Drug-related harms: public health crisis or crime epidemic

There may not be a war on drugs, but there is collateral damage from these ongoing disputes. One of the many ongoing discussions is over how to frame the harms that are related to drugs. On one side, there are public health experts who emphasise the ongoing crisis of opioid-related deaths (Kimber et al, 2019; Rae, Howkins and Holland, 2022). On the other are those who present drugs first and foremost as a problem of crime (for example, Johnson, 2021).

The public health narrative now focuses on the increasing numbers of people who have died with drugs since 2012 and their concentration

Figure 2.1: Drug-related deaths in Great Britain, 1996–2020

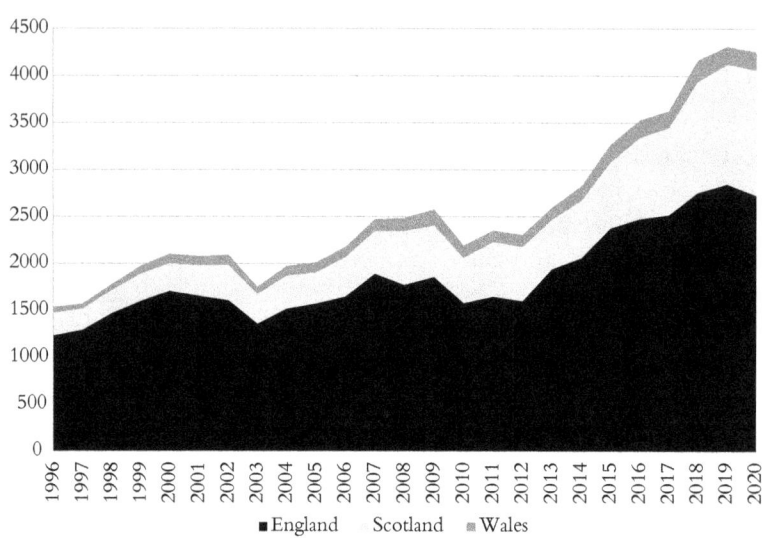

Sources: NRS, 2021; ONS, 2021

in the poorest areas. In 2012, the age-standardised rate of drug-related mortality was 29 deaths per million in England. By 2020, this had risen by 51 per cent to 52 per million, with a total of 2,994 people dying that year (ONS, 2021). The rise was even steeper in Scotland, where these deaths have affected a larger proportion of the population. In 2020, 1,339 people were reported as having died in Scotland with illicit drugs. The rise in age-standardised mortality was from 109 to 245 per million between 2012 and 2020, an increase of 125 per cent (NRS, 2021). The overall figures for Great Britain are shown in Figure 2.1. A death is recorded as drug-related if the coroner records an underlying cause of drug poisoning or drug abuse and the drug involved is controlled under the Misuse of Drugs Act. The most commonly mentioned drug is heroin, but many deaths also involve other substances, with alcohol being the most common. In Scotland especially, a large portion of these deaths also involve benzodiazepines.

At UK level, it is not these deaths that have garnered most policy attention. The main narrative that sets out what the problem is, and so what solutions we should use, focuses on drug use as a cause of crime. This crime control narrative became particularly salient decades ago when Tony Blair presented drugs as a cause of crime on which we should be tough, first as Shadow Home Secretary, and then – from 1997 – as Prime Minister. I covered this 'criminalisation of drug policy' and its exaggerated claims on the drug–crime link in a previous book (Stevens, 2011a).

The New Labour focus on crime reduction via opioid substitution treatment was replaced, for a while, by a shift to promoting abstinence and recovery, first in Scotland (Scottish Government, 2008), then England (HM Government, 2010). Some called this approach 'new abstentionism' (Ashton, 2008). One of my interviewees called it the "lurch to recovery". Berridge (2012) noted that it revived older tropes of temperance and cure. But the most recent UK drug strategy renews the presentation of crime as the main problem posed by drug use and punishment as the obvious solution. In his foreword, Prime Minister Boris Johnson repeated an estimate that 'illegal drugs' cost society £20 billion per year, largely as a result of 'drug-driven crime'. He stated that the strategy 'is all about a new approach to the problem that will reduce crime and improve people's lives' (Johnson, 2021). So the strategy promised more punishment and 'tough consequences' for people who use drugs. As I will show in Chapter 11, this approach is not particularly new. It reprises familiar narratives and factoids about the link between drugs and crime; a narrative that continues the stigmatisation and blaming of people who use drugs for society's ills.

Other narratives are available about drug problems and solutions, as we will see in later chapters. Claims are made, for example, that the primary cause of drug problems is prohibition itself, with the obvious solution therefore being to legalise drugs. Others argue that the problem of drugs is a problem of poverty, and so the solution is to improve the lives of the poorest. This book will show that the relative success of these competing conceptions in becoming the dominant interpretation of the drug problem – their epistemic power – is a crucial influence on how policy is made.

Drug use in the UK

A central element of narratives around drug policy is the tale of what is happening to drug use. The idea that drug use is rising is useful to many policy actors. They can use it either to call for tougher action or to argue that the existing policy has failed. But what has actually happened to illicit drug use in recent years? As drug use is a private and criminalised activity, we have no direct access to the actual levels of use. There are, however, traces of this use in high-quality surveys, like the Crime Survey for England and Wales (CSEW, formerly the British Crime Survey).

In reported fact, the rate of drug use among all adults has remained remarkably stable over the last 25 years. Every year from 1995 onwards, about 10 per cent of 16–59-year-olds in the CSEW's sample have reported using an illicit drug in the past year. There has been more volatility among younger people. Reported use of any illicit drug in the past year by people aged 16 to 24 peaked at 32 per cent in 1997, falling to 7 per cent in 2013, before rising again to 20 per cent by 2020 (ONS, 2020).

The most commonly used illicit drug is still cannabis. Among 16–59-year-olds, 83 per cent of all self-reported past-year illicit drug use in 2019/20 involved cannabis, with only 36 per cent of people who used any illicit drug reporting use of a Class A drug, such as cocaine, MDMA/ecstasy or – more rarely – heroin.[3] The pattern of stability among all adults with more volatility among young people holds for both cannabis and Class A drugs.

There is no obvious link between trends in illicit drug use and changes in law or practice in drug law enforcement. The downward trend in young people's cannabis use continued both when cannabis was downgraded to Class C in 2004 and when it was put back in Class B in 2009. There was no legal change in 2013 that could explain the apparent increase in both cannabis and Class A drug use since that year (I am currently working on a project with colleagues, led by Harry Sumnall at Liverpool John Moores University, to examine reasons for this upward trend). The apparent increase in Class A use among young people is mostly related to use of cocaine; use of MDMA has increased since 2013, but to a lesser extent than cocaine (ONS, 2020).

There are also interesting – and fairly stable – patterns in who uses these substances. Looking only at income, it is people in the lowest income group (earning less than £10,400 per year) who are most likely to report illicit drug use. But this may be largely a product of that being the income group which contains students and young people, who have higher rates of drug use. When taking such factors into account, drug use is actually more common among more affluent groups (Stevens, 2011a).

Drug use is also more common among people living with chronic and other medical conditions. Some find that cannabis helps relieve their suffering. This ranges from children living with severe epilepsy to older people suffering cancer and treatment side effects. Cannabis is also used by some people who suffer anxiety and chronic pain. A poll by YouGov has been used to suggest that there are about 1.4 million people using cannabis for medical purposes (Couch, 2020). As will be discussed in Chapter 9, only a small fraction of them have benefited from the change to the scheduling of cannabis-based medical products. In 2018, these were moved from schedule 1 of the Misuse of Drugs Regulations 2001 to schedule 2. In law, this legalised cannabis products for medical use, enabling specialist doctors to prescribe them. In practice, the number of people receiving such prescriptions remains relatively small. NHS prescriptions are even rarer, with most people still having to pay for their cannabis, whether prescribed or illicit.

Use of especially stigmatised substances, like heroin and crack cocaine, is poorly captured by household surveys, which omit two particularly important groups from their samples; people who are homeless or in prison. Estimates have been made using capture–recapture rather than survey methods. These estimates are ageing and not very robust. They do, however, accord with estimates derived from drug-related mortality data, which may be a superior method (Jones et al, 2020). And, again, they suggest a relatively stable picture. The figure of about 300,000 users of opiates and crack has been in use in English policy circles for over a decade.

Overall, the available data present a picture of remarkable stability in levels and patterns of illicit drug use, despite stories to the contrary and a century of efforts to eliminate illicit drug use from British society. Drug use trends continue to fluctuate in young people, with new substances joining the illicit menu, especially since the boom in new psychoactive substances from 2008 (Evans-Brown and Sedefov, 2017). Although recent use of illicit drugs is only reported by a minority of Britons, millions of us have personal experience of it, including some recent Prime Ministers. Like them, most of us have never had a health or criminal justice problem related to illicit drug use, despite the dominant narratives of illicit drugs presenting them as pathological, criminal or both.

Conclusion: the abundance of drug-related facts and narratives

It is impossible to provide a fixed understanding of what a drug is, who is using it, and with what effects. This impossibility creates multiple opportunities for the construction of various policy narratives. This is because we have no direct access to the underlying realities of drug use and must rely on imperfect empirical indicators of the actual events of drug use and control (Bhaskar, 1975; Stevens, 2020a). Perceptions of drugs and drug policies are inevitably bound up with the viewpoints and morals of the perceivers. As I will show in later chapters, the epistemic power to control what is known about illicit drugs is a major avenue for influencing drug policy outcomes.

This book could itself be seen as an exercise in epistemic power-grabbing. It attempts to establish a particular way of thinking about drug policy making. In line with the book's critical realist underpinnings, I argue that this is justified by the practical adequacy[4] of the accounts I give here of illicit drug use and policy making. These accounts help us not only to understand these phenomena but also to take actions that may change them for the better: to reduce suffering and enhance human flourishing (Sayer, 2011).

3

Power and Morality in Policy Making

In this chapter, I will lay the groundwork for a coherent, critical theory of policy making by more deeply describing the explanatory concepts that I introduced in Chapter 1: power and morality. I will explain the different forms of political power and social power that help explain how policy is made. Forms of political power include institutional, legal and coercive. These come from the winning of political power, whether by democratic election or military force. Forms of social power come from relationships between social groups inside and outside the formal government. They include economic, media, epistemic and affective power. In studying the UK drug policy process, I developed a new concept of power to explain what I observed. This is savvy social power.

In studying the influence of morality in policy, it is useful to use a framework that identifies the different positions that people may hold (Lerkkanen and Storbjörk, 2023). The normative bases for human thought and action tend to cluster together. People who hold traditionalist views tend to hold a set of beliefs which include respect for authority, a desire for conformity with the rules of established religion, and belief in moral purity and sanctity. On the other hand, people who believe in progressive social justice tend to be more concerned with fairness in the form of equality of outcome and the avoidance of discrimination on grounds of race, gender, class or other distinctions. Compassion for the suffering of other people is shared across these groups, although it may be directed at different targets. When compassion combines with a belief that the relief of suffering requires the state to control the actions of citizens, this is known as paternalism. When people take the opposite view, that the state should leave it to citizens to make their own decisions, their priority is liberty. Drawing on previous moral typologies and my observation of the drug policy field, I identity the ethico-political bases for UK drug policy making. These combine moral and political beliefs. A supplementary discussion of the usefulness of moral foundations theory and the value of truth is provided in Online Appendix 3.1.

Both power and morality are 'essentially contested concepts' (Lukes, 1974, 2013). There is no one, inherently correct way of describing either of them (Haugaard, 2020). What matters is that the concepts we use enable us to produce ideas about power and morality that explain and influence how they operate in the social fields we study.

Political and social power and its stratifications

Power is the capacity which enables policy actors to influence both the making and the taking of decisions.[1] It includes the ability to block things from happening as well as to order action (Bachrach and Baratz, 1962). To understand drug policy, we need to pay attention to the way that power is distributed among the people who make it and are subject to it (Friedman, 1998; Klein, 2008; Stevens, 2011a). And to understand power, we need to recognise that it has different forms and stratifications.

Forms of political power: institutional, legal and coercive

Power can take different practical forms. Different people and groups – even within ruling elites – will hold diverse forms of power (Pahl and Winkler, 1974). Jürgen Habermas (2006) made a distinction between political power and social power. Political power is born from what the feminist scholar Amy Allen (1998) called 'power-over'. This is the power to control the actions of others and comes in three forms; institutional, legal and coercive.

Institutional power accrues to actors who occupy positions in official hierarchies that enable them to decide on other people's choices. Legal power is the ability of a social group to force others – or empower themselves – to act in a certain way by enshrining it in law or using existing laws to achieve desired goals. Coercive power involves the use of force to ensure that desired ends occur; for example, by deploying the police, prisons or military forces.

Forms of social power: economic, epistemic, affective, media and savvy

Economic power is the ability of social actors to get what they want by paying for it. Such economic advantages also offer opportunities to influence decisions in ways that would not occur through unfettered, democratic deliberation. '[T]he best resourced policy advocates' have the capacity to 'shape the information environment in which policies are made via the funding, conduct and promotion of research' (Hawkins and Oliver, 2022, p 202). Some policy actors in the cases I studied had more financial resources than others, and this affected their capacity to influence policy.

Policy analysts are well used to considering inequalities of gender, class and race but have 'paid little attention to the specific difficulties caused by inequalities in knowledge and expertise' (Pamuk, 2021, p 109). According to Alfred Archer et al (2020, p 28), epistemic power is the ability 'to influence what people think, believe, and know'. An example in my interviews came from Catriona Matheson. When I asked her what kept harm reduction services going in Scotland during the years in which the government's policy turned towards abstinent recovery, she said "it happened because everybody knows that you've got to have harm reduction services". When a concept is so widely accepted that everybody knows it, then its proponents have epistemic power.

This form of power can come from the 'epistemic authority' that is held by professionally trained experts. But this is not some pure form of power into which academics can tap, as if drawing clear water from a limpid pool. The authority of experts is 'always contingent, historically situated, and grounded in practice' (Jasanoff, 2003, p 392). And academics and scientists are not the only holders of epistemic power. Archer and his colleagues (2020) note that there are often more influential holders of epistemic power, such as celebrities. They worry that this may be 'unwarranted'. Academics have to do 'credibility work' to become trusted as authorities in our field by 'performing trustworthiness' (Baumberg-Geiger, 2021). But people working in the drugs field know that some organisations, such as the Royal College of Physicians, have more epistemic authority than others, such as think tanks that are known for advocating particular policy positions.

If epistemic power is the capacity to influence what people believe, affective power is the capacity to influence what they feel. I may be the first person to use the phrase 'affective power' explicitly in policy analysis, although I am certainly not the first to examine the role of affect in politics and policy making (Pedwell, 2014; Padley and Gökariksel, 2021; Zembylas, 2022). I came up with the phrase 'affective power' while reading one of the documents I analysed for this book: the report which the novelist Boris Starling (2016) wrote for the Adam Smith Institute on how to achieve the legalisation of cannabis. Starling suggested that people who want to see cannabis legalised should change the languages they use in order to change the way people respond to ideas at an emotional level. Affective power is particularly likely to play a role in debates on drug policy. As a participant in the policy debates I analysed put it, 'the issue evokes strong emotions in different quarters' on which 'there is no settled demand for any specific legislative change' (Anne McLaughlin MP in Hansard, 2015). Affective power can also provide access to more powerful policy actors in a way that epistemic power may not. Steve Rolles of Transform told me, "If you say 'I'm a bereaved mother', politicians won't ever deny you a meeting. If you say 'I'm a nerd from an advocacy group that wants to legalise drugs', they just won't meet you."

Media actors (for example, journalists and editors or television, internet and publishing companies) have power because 'they select and process politically relevant content and thus intervene in both the formation of public opinions and the distribution of influential interests' (Habermas, 2006, p 414). There are obvious overlaps between all these forms of power, perhaps especially between epistemic, affective and media power. As sources of knowledge multiply along with media outlets and people increasingly get what they know via short, emotive videos on platforms like TikTok, YouTube and Facebook, academics lose any grip we used to have on knowledge production, and media stars use their epistemic, affective and media power to access political power.

In this book, I develop the concept of 'savvy social power'. This brings together epistemic and affective power with a canny, tacit, engaged knowledge of how to use institutional systems to effect change. The US National Institute of Health defines 'political savvy' as the 'ability to exhibit confidence and professional diplomacy, while effectively relating to people at all levels internally and externally'. It lists a range of attributes that make up savvy, including 'develops and maintains professional relationships' and 'uses knowledge of the organizational culture in making decisions' (NIH, 2022).

Being savvy is a characteristic that is needed by successful 'policy entrepreneurs'. But to call these policy actors entrepreneurs is to place too much emphasis on their individual attributes. '[W]hile the literature on policy entrepreneurship often places the focus on specific individuals, how they collaborate with others is always fundamental to explaining the development and promotion of policy innovations' (Mintrom, 2019, p 308; see also Online Appendix 1.1). In using the concept of savvy social power, I want to emphasise the relational aspects of this form of power. It is best deployed by people who are already recognised by others as having it. This will depend not only on the qualities of the individual but on their fit with the institutional context within which they operate. It can align with use of media power but is often used without it; for example, in behind-the-scenes persuasion within government circles. The key feature of my concept of savvy social power is the ability to bring together the various other forms of power that flow through policy constellations to effect change. It is therefore not just an individual aptitude, like entrepreneurialism, but a form of power that is shaped and constrained by social and cultural forces.

This abductively derived concept comes from my theoretically informed observations of how policy change was actually made in two instances that I discuss in this book: the legalisation of medical cannabis and the development of the 2021 drug strategy (see Chapters 9 and 11).

Stratification and reproduction of power: the unequal distribution of the ability to influence policy

Power is always both structured and relational. It does not exist in a 'social void' (Bourdieu, 1998, p 12). It depends on the previous existence of social structures in which individuals and organisations can act to reproduce or transform the social positions that enable and constrain their agency. Margaret Archer (2000) goes so far as to state that agency itself is a collective rather than individual property. She argues that it is only by becoming aware of their shared interests, and acting jointly on them, that a social group (a 'primary agent') can effectively transform its opportunities and choices by becoming a 'corporate agent'. Archer (2000, p 265) gives the examples of 'self-conscious vested interest groups, promotive interest groups, social movements and defensive associations'. In common with other social theorists, including Pierre Bourdieu and Anthony Giddens, Archer produces a theory of how social structures are reproduced and transformed through social action, a process she calls 'morphogenesis' (because it relates to the generation of social forms). Giddens (1984) called a similar process 'structuration', while Bourdieu (1977) described it in his 'theory of practice'. These are cyclical processes. How people act within and work on the structures they are faced with reproduces and modifies these structures and so the set of opportunities and limits that are faced by the next generation.

These social structures include the classic sociological trinity of class, race and gender, which also shape social networks and how they interact with each other (Fuhse, 2009). Actions across each of these dimensions of stratification arrange people into groups who tend to have (but do not always have) different levels of the various forms of power listed in the previous sections of this chapter. As a critical realist, Archer is committed to the idea that these social structures have a real existence. They cannot be directly observed, but they leave their traces in the data that can be collected about consistent disparities in access to material goods, services, and social recognition and respect (Byrne, 2011). The linkage of these social structures to the forms of power that networks of actors are able to deploy in policy making is a central feature of my policy constellations concept. The actions of people in these constellations tells us part of the story of how these social structures influence social action and so are reproduced in their turn.

Moral foundations, bases and narratives for understanding policy making

The journalist Peter Hitchens and the former academic Neil McKeganey both argue that people's views on illicit drugs are 'rooted in a moral view of the world' (McKeganey, 2010, p 165; Hitchens, 2012, p 249). I agree with them on this, if little else. It is important to unearth the moral assumptions that underlie people's preferred drug policy positions. This applies not just in drug policy but across a wide range of policy issues. Moral values are 'the criteria people use to select and justify actions and to evaluate people (including the self) and events' (Schwartz, 1992, p 1). They provide the lens through which people judge what is right to do in a wide range of situations, including policy making. In their seminal analysis of drug policy, Rob MacCoun and Peter Reuter called these moral positions 'philosophical underpinnings'. These 'are not always explicit in the policy debate, but they nevertheless shape the politics of drug policy formation' (MacCoun and Reuter, 2001, p 56).

The ethico-political bases of policy action are themselves collectively structured, not individually chosen. As forms of power are shaped and stratified by the social structures of class, race, gender and so on, ethico-political bases are produced and reproduced through the real cultural structures through which beliefs and attitudes flow in a cyclical process of learning and transmission (Archer, 2000; Elder-Vass, 2012).

The effects of morality

Normative views affect people's other beliefs and behaviour, including their policy preferences (Smith, 2017; Jenkins-Smith et al, 2018). People's social position – for example, their occupation, education, class, gender and race – also affect the values they hold (Schwartz, 1992). And the unequal distribution of power that results from structured inequalities mean that some forms of morality are given more weight than others in shaping policy. This is not an original insight of mine. It is central to work by authors as diverse as Antonio Gramsci, Michel Foucault and Pierre Bourdieu (Schmidt, 2008). It goes back at least as far as Marx and Engels' (1998 [1845], p 67) famous statement that 'the ideas of the ruling class are in every epoch the ruling ideas', and their less famous corollary that these ideas are then taken as 'eternal laws'. We have since moved on to more sophisticated models of ideology (see Thompson, 1990; Stanley, 2015; and the discussion of ideology in Online Appendix 4.2). There is no longer – if there ever was – a hegemonic, unified ruling class that gets its way on every issue (Gidden, 1975). But it remains useful to think about the conceptions of right and wrong that help to maintain the power of the most advantaged social groups, and about how they converge with the moral notions that are most powerfully expressed in policy. From a critical realist perspective, it is also important to recognise that 'though moralities do indeed tend to be shaped by systems of power they are never wholly reducible to such legitimations' (Sayer, 2011, p 15).

One of the many things that have changed since Marx and Engels wrote *The German Ideology* is the fragmentation of moral notions. Just as there is no one homogeneous ruling class, there is no longer one uniform set of ruling ideas as given, for example, by one national religion. The increased diversity of moral ideas is a defining feature of 'high modernity' (Archer, 2000). There has been religious disenchantment, post-colonial mass migration and various social revolutions, including successive waves of feminism and campaigns for the civil rights of ethnically and sexually diverse groups. Such fragmentation has been accelerated by the digital revolution of the 21st century (Archer, 2010). The success of these revolutions is only partial, and they are still hotly contested, as can be seen in current discussions of 'wokeness' and other 'culture wars'.

There has also been a partial social revolution in our attitudes towards illicit drug consumption. In the UK, some forms of drug use have been 'normalised' (Parker, Aldridge and Measham, 1998; Aldridge, Measham and Williams, 2011), at least among some 'bounded social groups', including young people who attend nightclubs and festivals (Measham and Shiner, 2009). Various studies have found a move away from explicitly moralistic positions in drug policy debates (Euchner et al, 2013; Ritter, 2022). For example, in their study of moral framing in Australian political debates about drug testing welfare recipients, Ritter and her colleagues were surprised to find so few statements of the idea that drug use itself is immoral (Curchin, Weight and Ritter, 2022). Politicians made much more use of consequentialist arguments over the effects of the proposed policy. Ritter (2022) reports that discussions of drug use as inherently wrong (for example, that it is sinful) have largely been replaced by arguments that drug use has bad consequences (that it is harmful).

Traditional moral positions on drug use continue, nevertheless, to influence attitudes, as well as voting patterns on drug policy issues. This was seen in the failure of the 2020 referendum to legalise cannabis in New Zealand. Believing that cannabis use is immoral was strongly associated with voting against legalisation (Wilkins et al, 2022). In California, voters who held strongly negative, moralistic beliefs about drug use were less likely to support Proposition 36, which sought to divert drug offenders from punishment and into treatment (Murphy, 2017). In Pennsylvania, police officers who hold traditionalist views were less likely to support treatment and harm reduction (in the form of naloxone) and more likely to endorse punishment for drug offenders (Murphy and Russell, 2020). Moral beliefs affect a wide range of other attitudes and behaviours that influence the outcomes of drug policy debates.

The contents of morality

Participants in these debates hold to moralities with particular contents. These are sometimes explicitly stated as deontological rules and sometimes lurk behind consequentialist arguments about policy effects. MacCoun and Reuter (2001), in their analysis of US discourse, including essays published in US newspapers, found four 'philosophical underpinnings' for arguments on drug policy. These were legal moralism, legal paternalism, Millian liberalism and libertarianism.

Another interesting contribution to the study of moral positions comes from evolutionary psychology. This is known as 'moral foundations theory' (Haidt and Joseph, 2004). It was popularised by Jonathan Haidt (2012) in his bestseller on *The Righteous Mind*. Haidt and his colleagues suggest that 'a person's moral intuitions may underlie, motivate, and unite ideological positions across a variety of issues' (Koleva et al, 2012, p 184). The idea that there are some basic moral intuitions which are predictably different between people with different political orientations is an attractive one. It is also presented in Shalom Schwartz's (1992, 2012) theory of basic values, which presents ten foundational values: power, achievement, hedonism, stimulation, self-direction, universalism, benevolence, tradition, conformity and security.

I have used these ideas myself in describing how conservative politicians take sides in policy debates and use moral positions to 'sidestep' the evidence. They tend to resist policies that they see as going too far to the left on Haidt and Joseph's dimension of liberty/oppression, and favour policies which stick to the right side of the subversion/authority and degradation/purity dimensions (Stevens, 2019). The other three of the six moral foundations that are measured by the Moral Foundations Questionnaire (Graham et al, 2009) are care/harm, fairness/cheating and ingroup loyalty/betrayal.

Value orientations differ measurably between countries (Inglehart and Welzel, 2005; Piurko et al, 2011). A recent study found that answers to the Moral Foundations Questionnaire can actually be reduced to only three foundational constructs – rather than six – for British respondents. These are traditionalism, compassion and liberty (Harper and Rhodes, 2021). According to Harper and Rhodes, people on the political right in the UK tend to value tradition more highly than compassion, whereas American studies tend to show more evenly distributed support across the moral foundations among political conservatives (see Christie et al, 2019). The political distribution of support for the moral foundation of liberty was nuanced in Harper and Rhodes' sample. Support for it was strongest among those people who supported leaving the European Union, rather than those of a more general right-wing orientation.

Similar to MacCoun and Reuter's linking of drug policy positions to their 'philosophical underpinnings', Haidt et al (2009) linked specific moral foundations to four recurrent 'ideological narratives'. The first is secular or progressive liberalism. This links political beliefs in humanistic progress and social justice to the moral foundations of care and fairness. It also tends to involve opposition to religious or political domination, and with that comes low valuing of the moral foundations of purity and authority, foundations that group together in the British moral foundation of traditionalism (Harper and Rhodes, 2021). The second of Haidt et al's narrative clusters is libertarianism. This links a political belief in individual freedom to a relatively low regard for the moral foundations of care, fairness, authority and purity. The third cluster is formed around the group Haidt et al call 'the religious left'. The stories these people tell themselves and others to make sense of the world include biblical imperatives to right wrongs, heal the sick, love one's neighbour, respect one's father and priest, and to believe in the one true God. The fourth and final of these ideological narratives is social conservatism. The narrative of this cluster, as presented by Haidt et al, is particularly American. It presents the federal government as the enemy of an inherently righteous and God-fearing people, forcing them to pay taxes on their earnings to subsidise 'welfare queens', a position summed up by Handley (2007, p 1) as 'blame welfare, ignore poverty and inequality'. In the US, people with more conservative political orientations are less likely to support drug harm reduction measures such as the provision of naloxone (Agley et al, 2022).

The meaning of fairness changes between its support by liberal progressives and by the two religious clusters. In the former, fairness is linked to equality of outcome, in the latter to getting your just deserts. This distinction between two modes of fairness was included in *The Righteous Mind* and was further developed by Haidt's more recent study of moral foundations. Atari, Haidt et al (2022) distinguished between proportionality and equality. Proportionality relates to concern that people should receive rewards in proportion to their merit or contribution. Equality relates to concerns about equal treatment and equal outcomes. This distinction is relevant for the analysis presented in this book, as one of the policy constellations that I found in the UK-level drug policy field (the progressive social justice constellation) is more concerned with a version of fairness that stresses equality rather than proportionality. The difference between valuing equality of outcome rather than equality of opportunity is also important for understanding the Scottish policy field.

Using Schwartz's (1992, 2012) theory of basic values alongside moral foundations theory adds two useful concepts. One is the value of 'universalism'. This involves 'understanding, appreciation, tolerance, and protection for the welfare of *all* people and for nature' (Schwartz 1992, p 12). This tends to be found more commonly, alongside the value of benevolence, in people who are politically on the left (Piurko, Schwartz and Davidov, 2011, p 539). Universalism is missing from tests of moral foundations theory, including that by Harper and Rhodes (2021) in the UK. My analysis of drug policy making shows that we need to consider it when thinking about moral influences on UK drug policy, especially in Scotland. It also suggests that while compassion is a value that is espoused across the political spectrum, it is targeted at different recipients by people who take different positions on drug and other policies. People who hold traditionalist views tend to condemn, rather than express compassion towards, people who take drugs, especially if they do not agree that this requires either treatment or punishment. It is tempting to believe that people with more libertarian and universalist moralities are more compassionate than these traditionalists, but they may still condemn some behaviours and policies. As we will see, libertarians tend to condemn public health professionals who attempt to place strict regulations to protect health, sometimes referring to this as the 'new puritanism' (Truss, 2019). And there is tendency among some people with socially progressive views to cast their opponents as heartless fools, without offering them the 'hermeneutic charity' (Dunn, 2017, p 380) of attempting to understand their viewpoint before condemning them for holding it.

Another useful concept from basic values theory is that of the 'circumplex' (Schwartz and Boehnke, 2004). This places the ten basic values at the rim of a circle, according to respondents' value preferences. Values that are commonly shared by the same people are placed close together on the circle. Those that are not commonly shared are placed further apart. Indeed, values that are placed on opposite sides of the circle may be directly opposed to each other. Schwartz's circumplex is illustrated in a simplified form in Figure 3.1. Schwartz placed the ten basic values in four groups. Values that express 'openness to change' (stimulation, hedonism and self-direction) are directly

Figure 3.1: The circumplex of basic values (adapted from Schwartz and Boehnke, 2004)

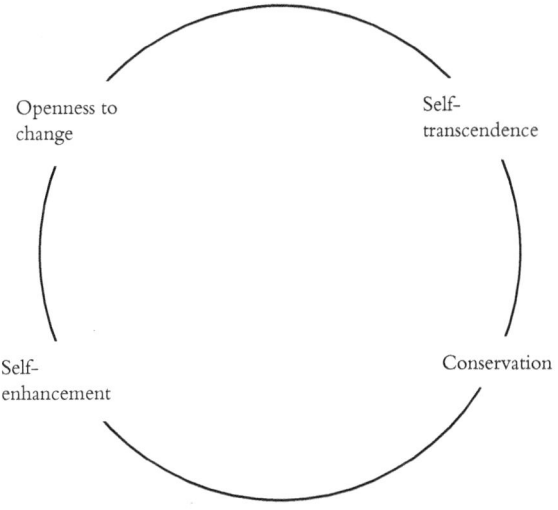

opposite to those which prioritise 'conservation' (security, conformity and tradition). Those which express 'self-transcendence' (universalism and benevolence) are directly opposed to those which prioritise 'self-enhancement' (hedonism, achievement and power).[2] The idea that values cluster together and can also be directly opposed is very useful in explaining drug policy outcomes, as I will show in Chapter 6.

Overlapping moral, material and affective imperatives

There is overlap between people's moral and political concerns. Indeed, the measurement of moral foundations involves asking people about their political beliefs (Haidt et al, 2009). This is why I describe the foundations of people's policy preferences as reflecting ethico-political bases, rather than beliefs that are *either* moral *or* political in nature.

It is crucial to the argument of this book that some moral beliefs coincide with the material interests of the people who hold them. For example, culturally traditionalist respect for the authority and sanctity of existing institutions legitimates and secures the structural advantages of people who already benefit from the inequalities which these moral positions maintain. Freedom is politically and economically – as well as morally – threatening to the status quo, which is why authoritarian governments try so hard to oppress it. In the study of racial politics, it has been observed that morally justified changes that progress the interests of dominated groups (for example, the abolition of slavery and the de-segregation of education) may occur only when it is also in the material interests of the powerful (Williams, 1944; Bell, 1980). This is known as 'interest convergence', another concept that will help us understand when and why stability and change occur in drug policy (see also Online Appendix 4.2).

An overly rationalist or instrumental view of morality would risk ignoring the complex role that affect plays in moral judgements. Combinations of emotions and moods may range from empathy, sympathy, compassion, pride and love to pity, guilt, regret, resentment, anger, fear, hatred and disgust. The role of emotions in policy making is under-explored in academic research (Wang, 2020). They surely play a part in shaping our preferences, as they do in other forms of decision-making (Lerner et al, 2015). Affect may be mobilised for both normative and political purposes. For example, Carolyn Pedwell has shown how even an emotion as positively regarded as empathy has multiple roles in structuring social relations. Calls for empathy can 'turn away from political and economic structures and towards an individualist politics of feeling' (Pedwell, 2014, p 121).

Moralities rest on a complex mix of intuition, reason, affect and power. All of these shape our normative commitments and so how people work in making policy.

Conclusion: all policy is morality policy

Drug policy is often classed as an example of 'morality policy'. This is a label given to policies that engage controversial moral issues, including abortion, the death penalty, euthanasia and stem cell research. Ritter (2022, p 73) suggests that this label is 'not helpful' in studying drug policy, as moral discourses and framings change over time and other framings also play a part in drug policy debates. She suggests we 'eschew' the term 'morality policy' in discussions of drug policy.

I go further by suggesting that we avoid using the label of 'morality policy' in any policy discussion. This label implies that there are some areas of policy making that engage moral issues and so – by implication – there are others that do not. As if it were possible to decide some policies on purely technical grounds, without regard to normative concerns. This position may still have some advocates among those who wish to give themselves a 'veneer of steering clear of value judgements' (Kothari and Smith, 2022, p 61). But it is not sustainable, either theoretically or empirically. Theoretically, the positivist separation of fact from value falls at the first hurdle of asking *why* we pursue the creation of facts, which must be because we value them and so must value the conditions in which they can be created (Collier, 1994). Empirically, studies too numerous to reference individually here have found that peoples' values play a role in determining what they believe to be a fact. As Justin Parkhurst (2017, p 137) put it, '[u]ltimately people and their representatives make decisions based on what they feel to be right rather than what experts tell them is optimal'.[3] This is why people who aspire to influence policy are advised to pick their moments wisely and to avoid challenging people's deeply held beliefs without first establishing trust; this may be counter-productive and be met with 'premature rejection' (Cairney and Kwiatkowski, 2017, p 5).

If we reject the separation of fact from value, then technical issues cannot be separated from normative judgements. The decision of where to set the minimum wage or to place a new airport involves moral decisions, as does at what stage it is legal to terminate a pregnancy or who is allowed to consume what substances. In interviews for this book, I asked interviewees whether they saw a role for morality in drug policy making. One of them said, "couldn't you argue that there is a moral element in everything?" My answer to this question is yes. There are normative dimensions to all policy debates, even if they are more or less explicitly referred to. This is a question of degree rather than there being a clear distinction of kind between policies that do or do not engage morality.

This means that the ideas in this book may be applicable across a broad range of policy issues. To ignore such moral problems would be to go along with the idea that there is some 'eternal law' which rules them out of discussion in a particular policy area. In drug and other policy areas, moral debates are increasingly presented in technical forms. My argument is that we need to account for the interplay of power and morality if we are to understand how policy is made, even if issues of power stratification and related moral positions are not openly discussed in that policy field.

4

Policy Constellation: A Critical Realist Approach

The policy constellations approach brings together social theory with concepts from the study of policy processes and a 'social network perspective' to 'focus on how the constellation of relationships in networks may facilitate and constrain' the resources that policy actors bring to the policy process. Such a perspective 'move[s] from a primary focus on the individual and the attributes of that actor, to understanding the more dynamic supports and constraints of the larger social infrastructure' (Finnigan et al, 2021, p 131). This infrastructure includes the social structures of power and wealth, as well as the cultural structures of morality.

I built the policy constellations approach using the theoretical tools of critical theory and critical realism. I do not want to take readers too deeply into these conceptual labyrinths, but I provide short guides to them in Online Appendix 4.1 (on critical realism) and 4.2 (on the critical study of ideology). Here I give even shorter summaries of these theoretical frameworks.

The policy constellations approach is distinct from the most commonly used, neo-pluralist theories of the policy process because it provides a critical framework which avoids methodological individualism. It identifies the forms of power and morality that operate at the level of social and cultural structures and uses them to explain how policy making works. It is not a revolution in thinking about these processes which seeks to repudiate all existing accounts. Rather, it incorporates many of the ideas that have been developed in previous research on the topic and brings them into a new theoretical framework. This creates more powerful explanations by bringing a wider range of phenomena into its scope and going deeper towards an understanding of the generative mechanisms that underlie the actual events and actions that occur in policy making.

Critical frameworks for policy analysis: a very brief introduction

In developing the policy constellations approach, I used four key features of critical realism (Bhaskar, 1975; Collier, 1994; Sayer, 2000, 2011; Archer et al, 2017). These are:

- Ontological realism: the belief that there is a real world that exists before we come to study or apprehend it. This is the opposite of ontological constructivism, which suggests that there is no reality that exists before we perceive it, that reality is constructed through our perceptions of it.
- Epistemological relativism: the belief that people's knowledge of the world depends on the position in place, time and society from which they perceive it. This is the opposite to the view that knowledge is a direct reflection of reality, that we can be positively sure of what it is and how it works.[1]
- Judgemental rationality: the belief that some accounts of what is in the world and how it works are superior to others. One way of choosing between competing depictions of the world is to consider their practical adequacy, the extent to which these depictions help us achieve worthwhile goals.
- Cautious ethical naturalism: the belief that it is possible to make rationally justified judgements about what is right and wrong while leaving space for people to differ on these issues. Critical realism rejects the idea that facts and values are in completely separate realms of thought. For example, if we value facts, that is already a judgement of value.[2] In Sayer's (2011) version, ethical naturalism involves valuing human flourishing and so the social conditions which enable people to thrive.

The policy constellations approach also learns from critical theory, as indicated by my references to Habermas in the previous chapter. A key Habermasian insight for the study of policy making is that these processes operate through constellations of power, knowledge, morality and the strategic and communicative action of policy actors in interaction with each other (Habermas, 1986, 1995, 1996). These two theoretical frameworks are highly compatible. 'Critical realism and critical theory are complementary parts of a single project: to develop a critical theory of society that is able to analyse, diagnose, criticize and transform society' (Vandenberghe, 2019, p 334).

What are policy constellations?

> And the suspicion is only too justified that in the clash of value preferences incapable of further rationalization, the strongest interest will happen to be the one actually implemented. This explains,

moreover, why the outcome of judicial proceedings can be so well predicted in terms of interests and power constellations. (Habermas, 1986, p 241)

In this quote from Habermas, he discusses why there is a consistent pattern of judicial processes ending in decisions that favour the most powerful interests, despite the purported impartiality of the law. In this book, I extend this idea to the outcomes of policy processes. Habermas saw that these decisions rest on normative value preferences. These principles are sometimes incompatible. There will be occasions, for example, in which a policy cannot reflect both a traditionalist preference for abstinence and a compassionate desire to reduce the suffering of people who use drugs, such as when there is a public health crisis of HIV or drug-related deaths. There will be clashes. To understand the outcome of these clashes, we need to understand the operating constellations of interests and power.

A policy constellation is a set of social actors (individuals within organisations) who come together in deploying various forms of socially structured power to pursue the institutionalisation in policy of shared moral preferences and material interests. By institutionalisation, I mean that policy actors hope to establish their preferences as the ones that get accepted as the basis for the actions of governmental and other institutions, such as parliaments, ministries, police forces, health services and even charities, businesses and other bodies that operate outside the state. Even if they cannot hope that everyone always agrees with them, policy actors try to win the assent of enough powerful supporters, and at least enough acquiescence from opponents, to ensure that their preferences are put into action. One way of doing this is through influencing policy decisions.

Constellations are not stable groups with fixed rules or memberships. They are made up of fluid sets of actors who gravitate towards each other on the basis of shared preferences and norms. Their actions are not necessarily directed or coordinated. Rather, actors in a constellation tend to align their actions through creating connections of mutual recognition and support. They do so in contest and collaboration with the members of other constellations, who have different interests and norms (although there may be overlap between the memberships, interests, preferences and norms of some policy constellations). Constellations are not actors in themselves. Rather, the connections between actors that constitute the constellation serve to amplify the influence of each individual actor in an emergent process which builds the power to act in concert to achieve desired policy goals. The degree of amplification will depend on the power of other actors in the same constellation.

The concept of the policy constellation builds on previous analysis of the way networks operate in policy making. 'That policy emerges from relatively stable clusters of organised participants has long been part of the experiential knowledge of practitioners' (Colebatch, 2018, p 207). There is now a long tradition of researchers – on both sides of the Atlantic – studying the activities of networks of policy actors. These are variously known as 'policy communities', 'issue networks' or 'policy subsystems', as well as 'policy networks', 'advocacy coalitions' and 'discourse coalitions' (Heclo, 1978; Rhodes, 1990; Hajer, 1993; Munro, 1993; Sabatier and Jenkins-Smith, 1993; Richardson, 2018; Nichols, Malenfant and Schwan, 2020).[3]

Policy actors come from both inside and outside government. They include officials (for example, ministers and civil servants) and external actors such as businesses, academics, campaigning groups, and directly affected people and their families. In the policy constellations approach, power can flow in both directions, to and from the state.

From the critical realist and Habermasian perspectives, actions can be enabled and constrained by forms of power and morality that actors hold, which are at least partly explained by their position in social structures (for example, of class, gender and race) (Stanley, 2015). This is an approach that explains both the relative influence of competing policy actors and the preferences they bring to these contests. In this way, the policy constellations approach can provide a more powerful explanation of why some policy outcomes – which may not appear to be rational – emerge. It helps explain, for example, why 'evidence is necessary but not sufficient in public-health decision making' (Kothari and Smith, 2022, p 62). This explanatory power is drawn from the ability of the policy constellations concept to bring in socially and culturally structured powers and normative preferences into a coherent analytical framework. This leaves the policy constellation as a distinctive – but not revolutionary – concept for analysing and explaining policy making.

Morality as "shared mission"

In Habermas' (1976, p 161) terms, members of distinct policy constellations share a particular 'background consensus' of normative beliefs. This theoretical understanding was confirmed by one of my interviewees:

> '[W]e're part of a shared mission. We might think about it in different ways. We might use different language to conceptualise it. We might have different sets of priorities and our individual and organisational and institutional missions don't all completely coalesce and overlap 100 per cent. Of course they don't, but I'd like to think that, broadly, we all feel like we're on the same side, but we've just got different vantage points within the system.'

It is this "shared mission" which brings policy constellations together. As another of my interviewees told me, when trying to emphasise that his research group did not have a corporate view, "if you pushed me and said, 'Well, hold on, isn't there a likelihood that a lot of your views would coalesce because you wouldn't have got together as a group if you conflicted too much?' Yeah, that would be correct, but there isn't a central machine".

In the presence of a "shared mission" based on a 'background consensus', there may be no need for a "central machine" to bring a policy constellation together. Actors with diverse methods and understandings may all be on "the same side". This implies that there are other actors who are not on that side. There is no need for total convergence of language and aims for actors to be considered to be part of "a shared mission".

These quotes also illustrate the reflexivity of policy actors, who are aware of the contingency of the particular "vantage point" that they and other actors have and of the likelihood of this being viewed differently from the outside than the inside. These quotes also show how understandings of policy action are driven not just by a need to describe it but also by a desire for it to operate in certain ways. For that policy actor, having a shared mission was important for "driving people together, not apart". This shows a recognition of the forces of attraction and repulsion which animate policy constellations.

The people I interviewed, and the policy documents I read, gave me very clear examples of who policy actors saw as being their allies and opponents. People who support progressive reforms, including more liberal drug policies and the achievement of racial justice, tend to see people who prioritise social conformity and the continuity of the established order with suspicion, if not downright hostility. And the feeling is obviously mutual. Similarly, people who prioritise individual and commercial freedom, including the freedom to profit from the selling of drugs, tend to disparage the people who seek to control these activities in the name of public health. In turn, public health professionals often attempt to limit the freedoms of businesses to profit from trades that they see as health-harming. It is therefore possible, as I show in Chapter 6, to create a modified moral circumplex for the drug policy field. This shows which policy actors and policy positions can work alongside each other and which cannot, on the basis of shared and conflicting ethico-political bases.

Policy constellations and forms of power

Power must also be analysed in relation to 'the social and economic environments within which it is embedded' (Habermas, 1977, p 15). Power to affect policy is produced through the actions of people who come together in constellations to which they bring pre-existing resources, capacities and commitments, which are shaped by existing social and cultural hierarchies and cleavages. Success in achieving their goals will in turn enhance their capacity to influence future policy debates. Policy constellations produce power, as well as deploying it.

So the political institutionalisation of social actors' preferences is fundamentally influenced by socio-economic inequality (Volk, 2016). Policy constellations draw from the powers held by the sets of actors of which they are formed. These powers are always socially situated and stratified. Different actors may be able to bring different forms of power to the pursuit of aims that are shared by members of a constellation. Some will have legal power, others may have media power, still others economic power, and so on. The different combinations of these powers will influence how influential that policy constellation is likely to be.

For example, a policy constellation may form around the shared preferences of actors who have the political power to convene policy discussions, with actors who have the media power to create salience and support in the public sphere, with other actors who have the economic power to buy advertising or expensive lawyers. Such a well-endowed constellation is likely to be more influential than constellations which have only one of these forms of power or none at all. In some constellations, it may be the same actors who have all these forms of power, as in the case of a rich family that includes politicians and owns media outlets. In other constellations, different actors may bring different types of power.

Policy constellations may be more influential if their members can deliberately amplify the influence of their members by close coordination. But this is not a feature of all policy constellations. Some may not have members with the power to bring the various actors together. Others may be fissiparous, in that they have a tendency to split. This is often because they share some social positions or normative commitments but are divided by other preferences or material interests. This may particularly be the case of social groups which are stuck in what Archer (2000) calls 'primary' rather than 'corporate' agency. This is to say that they have not yet achieved the capacity to articulate their interests, in two ways: their common interests are not clearly understood or communicated, and they are not joined together with the interests of other people who might share these interests.

As I will describe in Chapter 8, this has been the situation of people who avowedly use drugs. They may share interests (for example, in ending police interference in their lives, or getting access to treatment), but they have not yet articulated them by developing a shared language or set of goals (Askew et al, 2022), or by creating stable structures for joint action. This may be changing, as groups like the International and European Networks of Drugs develop their institutional capacities and their expression of shared goals, including 'full decriminalisation' of drugs (Madden et al, 2021).

It is the forms of power that policy constellations amplify by both types of articulation (communicating interests and joining together) that gives their members the ability to influence policy outcomes in concert with each other.

Constellations and reflexivity: where you stand affects your view

As expected by the epistemological relativism of critical realism, the labels we choose to place on actual events influence how we view them and so how we act on them. The metaphor of astral constellations implies dynamism. Stars are born, move across the universe in relation to each other and eventually die. It also implies structure. There are forces of attraction and repulsion which put stars in these dynamic relations to each other. We should not push such metaphors too far. One of my interviewees warned me that the metaphor of a constellation implies stable and predictable orbits, which are not necessarily present in policy making. Things can shift quite unpredictably.

A constellation is an essentially reflexive concept. The identification of a constellation depends on one's own physical, social and cultural location. Each constellation of stars would look very different if viewed from different points in the universe. On Earth, different cultures have placed the same stars into different constellations. It is possible to spy groups of stars within astral constellations (like the Great Square within Pegasus). Such asterism may link stars in more than one constellation (as the Great Diamond includes stars that straddle the constellations named Boötes, Virgo, Leo and Canes Venatici).

With policy constellations, the identification of the constellation and its members also depends on the viewpoint that one takes. Similarly, there may be links within or across the policy constellation that circle around particular policy beliefs, just as the astral constellations of the northern hemisphere circle around Polaris. The concept of the policy constellation is therefore compatible with both a realist understanding of the causation of social reality by underlying generative processes that are not directly observable and the critical idea that the observer plays a crucial role in the construction of our perceptions of social reality.

Conclusion: the advantages of the policy constellations approach

The policy constellations approach avoids focusing solely on rationalist, individualist motivations. Individuals' actions in policy making may involve self-interested maximisation of utility. But they also involve complex – often unwitting – interactions of interest, preference and affect. Policy constellations are, to borrow a phrase from Jorge Luis Borges (1999 [1927]), 'networks of sympathies'. People form constellations by accident as well as design. They do so on the basis of emotions, sentiments and mutually recognised moral affiliations, as well as strategic planning. Constellations help to shape people's moralities and the forms of power they can deploy, as well as providing arenas for discursive contest and political transaction.

This enhanced understanding comes from empirical observations of the drug policy process, as filtered through the four key aspects of critical realism that I presented in the introduction to this chapter. These allow us to coherently understand the epistemological relativism of policy narratives and our accounts of them, while consistently claiming that there is some ontological depth – an underlying reality to which these narratives refer, and which they can go on to influence. Critical realism also provides grounds for choosing between competing accounts of both policy problems and policy processes through its judgemental rationality. Cautious ethical naturalism provides a coherent way of thinking about the harms that can be done through bad policies or inadequate accounts of policy making.

A full analysis of the policy process will incorporate some aspects of the previous approaches that I mentioned in Chapter 1 and discuss more fully in Online Appendices 1.1 and 1.2. The policy constellation approach can account for the tendency of policy to remain stable for long periods between shifts that are difficult to predict, which was described by Baumgartner and Jones (1993) as punctuated equilibrium. It incorporates the interest in problem framing and agenda setting that are also features of the advocacy coalition framework and the multiple streams approach (Kingdon, 2013; Jenkins-Smith et al, 2018). It inherits an interest in the normative 'core beliefs' of policy makers from Sabatier and Jenkins-Smith (1993) and enhances it by linking it to the critical realist explanation of the production and reproduction of ethico-political bases as cultural structures (Archer, 2000).

The critical realism of the policy constellations approach overcomes the methodological individualism of these neo-pluralist accounts of the policy process. Its epistemological relativism enables it to cast a critical eye on the framing of policy problems and how these are constructed in ways that favour the most powerful social groups. Critical realism's ontological realism enables judgemental rationality to choose between competing accounts of policy problems – and processes – on the basis of their practical adequacy and their potential contribution to human flourishing.

Uncritical accounts still offer an over-simplistic vision of policy making as linear, sequenced and rational (Cairney, 2021). The policy constellations approach replaces this with one that is a complex, multi-cyclical mixture of motivations, path dependencies, happenstance and strategic, moral and political communication. In the policy constellations approach, reasoning is not just bounded, it is motivated by the ethico-political bases of policy making as well as the material interests of policy makers. These influences on policy making operate through complex combinations of contexts, actions and underlying mutable mechanisms. This produces an explanation of policy making that is more powerful than the approaches on which it is built, in that it can explain a wider range of the events and decisions that are observed in the field of action (Lawson, 1997), in this case, the UK drug policy field.

5

Studying Policy Constellations in the Real World

This chapter describes the methods I applied in studying drug policy making in the UK. I am interested in how people's interpretations of reality affect their actions, interactions and outcomes, a task for which ethnography (including auto-ethnography) is suited (Hammersley and Atkinson, 2007; Ellis et al, 2011). I am interested in other people's perspectives on these processes, so I interviewed people with particular relevant positions in the policy field. I am also interested in how ideas and narratives operate in the making of policy, so I used discourse analysis. As I have adopted critical realist presuppositions, this had to be a critical realist form of discourse analysis (Flatschart, 2016). I am also interested in how policy actors and ideas operate through the networks of connections between them. I found social network analysis (SNA) to be a valuable tool. Combined, these methods enable me not only to identify the motivations and actions of individual policy actors but also to assess the shared, generative mechanisms of policy action.

Data analysis is – in the critical realist tradition – a cyclical process. It moves between tentative, plausible explanations which are developed inductively from available data to fallible, deductive, empirical testing and refinement of developing explanations. In critical realist analysis, this is known as abduction (Danermark et al, 2019). It is compatible with the adaptive approach of Derek Layder (1998), which I also drew on in planning my analysis.

Here, I describe how I applied this approach in carrying out ethnography, elite interviews, discourse analysis and SNA in studying drug policy constellations in the UK. I also discuss some of the ethical issues involved in each method. My approach to these issues was approved by my university's research ethics process.

Casing and sampling for ethnography, interviews and documents

It is not possible to encompass the entirety of any policy field in one book. Choices must be made of the cases and samples to observe. Casing is a crucial step in all social science. 'Science studies cases which [are] instances of a particular situation or set of circumstances' (Byrne, 2009, p 1). For this book, I chose to study the parts of the policy field that I found to be most illuminating of the processes of policy making in the UK. I focused my study on the period between the UK general election of May 2015 and the publication of the UK's ten-year drug strategy in December 2021. This gives a sufficiently long period to observe policy development, but not so long as to swamp the analysis with too much data. Significant changes occurred during this period. New UK drug strategies were announced in both 2017 and 2021. The medical use of cannabis-based products was legalised in 2018. Drug-related deaths rose across the UK, with varying responses in Scotland and England. Much also stayed the same in this period, with no reform to the Misuse of Drugs Act 1971.

Ethnography of policy work

The choice of these cases enabled me to use ethnography and auto-ethnography. I have observed the process of policy making at first hand for over 27 years. The contexts in which I directly participated in policy processes include meetings of policy advisory and parliamentary committees. For example, I was a member of the Advisory Council on the Misuse of Drugs (ACMD) from 2014 to 2019, a period during which it advised the government on drug-related deaths and the legalisation of cannabis-based medical products. I was the lead author of the ACMD's (2016e) report on opioid-related deaths and its (2019c) report on custody–community transitions. I was a special adviser to the House of Commons Health and Social Care Committee for its 2019 report on drugs, and an oral witness to the Scottish Affairs Committee for its concurrent inquiry on drug-related deaths in Scotland. For these committees, I wrote policy documents, met politicians and officials, and discussed these issues with a wide range of stakeholders. I also took part in several national and regional conferences on drug policy. I observed other policy-making contexts by reading and watching their proceedings in reports and video recordings. These included other policy conferences, parliamentary speeches and debates, and media articles and appearances by politicians and other people involved in drug policy processes. I have regularly written about these processes, both in published articles and in private fieldnotes.

My mixture of overt and covert observation involves complex ethical issues. The people I interviewed for this book were all directly informed that

I would be carrying out observation and gave their consent to be observed. Others were observed more covertly, in that they may not have known I was writing a book on my observations of the policy field. In this book, I only use observations of people when they were working in public places as part of their public role (for example, making a public speech). I made it very clear to all and sundry that I was writing a book about drug policy making, including in a Tweet that I pinned to the top of my Twitter feed. I have not named any people I observed covertly, or made their actions identifiable, unless they gave explicit consent to be named, or when I am referring to a document they published or a public speech they gave under their own name.

Elite interviewees

I carried out semi-structured interviews with a purposively stratified sample of 22 people, as listed in Table 5.1. Interviewees were selected for their capacity to inform me of particular aspects of the British drug policy field. Creating the sample was not a straightforward task. David Best told me about his own experience of trying to find interviewees to talk to him about drug policy:

> 'It was like talking to a suspect in a police custody suite in Glasgow. The first three answers were typically, "It wasnae me. I wasnae there. Nae comment." It's like everybody just wanted to deny that drug policy was anything to do with them. We couldn't find anyone who would own up to saying that they had any responsibility for it.'

In my purposive sampling, I wanted to create a balance of people with diverse political and moral commitments from across the policy field. So I made deliberate efforts to contact interviewees who did not have direct contacts with each other. I was less successful in securing interviews with people from within government, despite repeated efforts, although I did interview one MP, two civil servants and a serving minister in the Scottish government.

The sample was heavily skewed towards people in middle age and beyond. The oldest interviewee was in their eighties and still very active in the field. The youngest were in their late twenties. One of them admitted to being more of an "observer", rather than being "at the coalface" of policy making. Many of the interviewees, like myself, got into working in policy after developing experience and expertise through more direct forms of research or practice. So it is unsurprising that their average age was late on in the usual working career. The coalface of policy making tends to be mined by older workers.

As the interviewees included people with high levels of power (for example, the Scottish drugs minister and Professor Dame Carol Black, who was very influential on the 2021 UK drug strategy), this could be

Table 5.1: Interviewees

Name	Description
Angela Constance	Scottish drugs minister, Scottish National Party
Carol Black	Professor and Dame, adviser to government
Catriona Matheson	Professor, former chair of the Scottish Drugs Death Taskforce
Chris Snowdon	Head of Lifestyle Economics, Institute of Economic Affairs
Crispin Blunt	MP and chair of Conservative Drug Policy Reform Group
CS1	Civil servant in Department of Health and Social Care
CS2	Civil servant in Department of Health and Social Care
Daniel Pryor	Head of Research, Adam Smith Institute
David Best	Professor, Leeds Trinity University
David Liddell	Chief Executive, Scottish Drugs Forum
Deirdre Boyd	Director, DB Recovery Resources
DTP	Director, residential drug treatment provider
Ed Day	Psychiatrist, National Drug Recovery Champion
John Strang	Professor at King's College London
Keith Humphreys	Professor at Stanford University, US
Mat Southwell	Drug user organiser, European Network of People who Use Drugs
Matthew Lesh	Researcher, Institute of Economic Affairs
Mike Trace	Chief Executive, Forward Trust
Oliver Standing	Director, Collective Voice
Paul North	Director, Volteface
Steve Moore	Founder, Volteface and Association for the Cannabinoid Industry
Steve Rolles	Senior Policy Analyst, Transform

considered an exercise in 'elite interviewing'. To anonymise or not in elite interviewing is a tricky topic (Ellersgaard et al, 2022). I left it to the interviewees to decide. All of them asked to be named, except for the two civil servants and one director of a residential drug treatment provider. Some interviewees were happy to be named except in relation to comments that they made about other individuals. Some told me that they did not want a specific section of the interview to be used or attributed to them. I have respected these requests in reporting my findings in this book. Where an interviewee requested to be named, you will usually find their name beside the quotes that I have used. Where they did not, I have kept them anonymous. I have erred on the side of caution in not naming people when I judged that the interviewee would rather not be named alongside a particular quote. This means that some interviewees are sometimes quoted alongside their name and sometimes anonymously. The interviews took between 55 and 87 minutes. They were carried out and transcribed in online video meetings.

Documents for discourse analysis

In sampling documents, I purposively collected those that were relevant to UK and Scottish-level drug policy making in the chosen period, with a focus on the three topics of medical cannabis, drug-related deaths and the UK drug strategy of 2021. I did this by downloading documents that I knew to be relevant from my close involvement in these policy discussions. Others were mentioned by interviewees or referred to in other documents. I also downloaded reports published by organisations that were mentioned in interviews. For parliamentary discourse, I used the official online record of the proceedings of the UK and Scottish parliaments to search for relevant debates. For explicitly political statements, I downloaded the 2019 UK and 2021 Scottish election manifestos presented by the Conservative, Labour, Liberal Democrat, Scottish National, Green and ALBA parties. I also collected relevant reports from parliamentary groups and select committees, which can be important venues for the shaping of policy proposals (Hawkins and Oliver, 2022).

A list of the 134 policy documents I analysed is included in Table 5.2. Most of these documents were publicly available online, but one (Victoria Atkins' letter to the ACMD requesting advice on 2,4-dinitrophenol (DNP) was not, and so I requested and got it from the Home Office under the Freedom of Information Act.

I also selected 42 parliamentary debates and meetings for analysis, as listed in Table 5.3.

Some policy actors were frequently present in my coding of these documents. For example, former Liberal Democrat MP Norman Lamb spoke in most of the Commons debates that I analysed and also appeared in some of the other documents. By contrast, there were many people who appeared only once in the data. For example, Maggie Throup MP was appointed as a junior health minister in September 2021. It fell to her to give the government's response in a debate on the Black review (Hansard, 2021a), despite her having shown little interest in the issue of illicit drugs prior to – or even since – her appointment. Some people strive to be a drug policy actor. Others have it thrust upon them.

Coding and analysis of fieldnotes, interviews and documents

My analytical coding of interviews, fieldnotes and policy documents followed the adaptive process described by Layder (1998).[1] I created a list of provisional

Table 5.2: Documents purposively selected for discourse analysis

Policy documents by government ministers and departments
Atkins, 2018; Brine and Newton, 2017; Churchill, 2019; DHSC, 2018; HM Government, 2021; Home Office, 2022; Javid, 2018a, 2018b; Javid and Hancock, 2018; Malthouse, 2020a, 2020b, 2021; MHCLG, 2019; MoJ, 2019; Patel, 2020, 2021; PHE, 2016, 2019; Scottish Drug Deaths Taskforce, 2020; Scottish Government, n.d., 2018, 2020; UK Government, 2021
Policy documents from political parties
ALBA, 2021; Conservative Party, 2019; Green Party of England, 2019; Labour Party, 2019; Liberal Democrats, undated; Ross, 2021; Scottish Conservatives and Unionists, 2021; Scottish Greens, 2021; Scottish Labour, 2021; Scottish Liberal Democrats, 2021; Scottish National Party (SNP), 2019, 2021
Policy reports by quangos, advisers and advisory committees
ACMD, 2015a, 2016a, 2016c, 2016e, 2016f, 2018a, 2018b, 2018c, 2018d, 2019a, 2019b, 2019c, 2019d, 2019e, 2019g, 2020a, 2020b, 2020c, 2020d, 2021; ACMD Recovery Committee, 2017; CRED, 2021; Lammy, 2017; NICE, 2019b; SDDTF, 2020, 2021b, 2021a
Reports and statements by parliamentary committees
APPGDPR, 2016; Health and Social Care Committee, 2019; Scottish Affairs Committee, 2019; Webster, 2017
Speeches by ministers
Javid, 2021; Sturgeon, 2021
Media articles, press releases and blog posts
ACMD, 2015b, 2016d, 2019f; Daily Record, 2019; Davidson, 2021; Drug Science, 2019b; English and Doughty, 2017; Garavelli, 2020; Hutcheon, 2019; Jones et al, 2018; LCDPR, 2018; McGarvey, 2019; McKeganey, 2017; Phillips, 2018; Pryor, 2018, 2020; Rudd, 2017; Silke, 2021; Transform, 2018c; Worstall, 2019
Documents from non-governmental organisations
Ahmun et al, 2016; Bartle, 2019; Bhatarah et al, 2021; Carre and Ali, 2019; CSJ, 2018a, 2018b; Drug Science, 2016, 2019a; FAVOR UK, 2021; Fisher and Measham, 2018; Garius and Ali, 2022; Keeling, 2021a, 2021b; King et al, 2021; King and Moore, 2020; MCCS and Drug Science, 2021; McCulloch, 2017a, 2017b; McCulloch et al, 2018; McCulloch and Furlong, n.d.; Moore, 2019; Moore et al, 2021; North, 2017a, 2017b; Nutt, 2022; Power, 2017; Pryor, 2018, 2020; Pryor and McCulloch, 2019; Release, 2018, 2019; Rolles et al, 2016; Rucker et al, 2020; Scottish Drugs Fourn (SDF), 2018, 2021; SDF and Scottish Government, 2019; SFAAD, 2022; Shiner et al, 2018; Scottish Recovery Consortium, 2022; Starling, 2016; Stevens, 2017; Transform, 2015, 2017a, 2017b, 2018a, 2018b, 2020, 2022

codes from previous research and my own knowledge of the field, set them up in QSR Nvivo software for qualitative data analysis, and then added additional codes that I created from repeated readings of these transcripts, fieldnotes and policy documents. I highlighted particularly useful pieces of text as I went along to assign them to particular codes. I then read and re-read the final lists of codes and their contents and reorganised them into

Table 5.3: Parliamentary debates and meetings selected for discourse analysis

UK House of Commons
- Misuse of Drugs Act 1971 (14 December 2021)
- Medical cannabis (access) bill (10 December 2021)
- Ten-year drug strategy (6 December 2022)
- Medical cannabis: alleviation of health conditions (4 November 2021)
- Dame Carol Black's independent review of drugs report (27 October 2021)
- Misuse of Drugs Act and health outcomes (8 September 2021)
- Medicinal cannabis (6 September 2021)
- Misuse of Drugs Act (17 June 2021)
- Problem drug use (29 September 2020)
- County lines drug gangs (28 October 2019)
- Drug consumption rooms (Glasgow) (24 July 2019)
- Drug treatment services (16 July 2019)
- Dangerous drugs (3 July 2019)
- Medical cannabis under prescription (20 May 2019)
- Drug policy (23 October 2018)
- Cannabis-based products: medical use (11 October 2018)
- Drug-related harm (24 July 2018)
- Cannabis-based medicines (19 June 2018)
- Medical cannabis (20 February 2018)
- Drug consumption rooms (17 January 2018)
- Drug addiction (20 November 2017)
- Drug policy (18 July 2017)
- Cannabis (12 October 2015)

UK House of Lords
- Drugs: Black review (19 October 2021)
- Drugs: methadone (28 October 2019)
- Cannabis: medical use (16 July 2018)
- Cannabis (12 March 2018)
- Cannabis (7 September 2017)
- Drug policy: departmental responsibilities (7 February 2017)
- Drug Policy (21 November 2016)
- Drugs (4 February 2016)
- Drugs: cannabis (17 June 2015)

Scottish Parliament
- Joint committee meeting: reducing drug deaths in Scotland and tackling problem drug use (2 February 2022)
- Criminal Justice Committee: misuse of drugs and the criminal justice system (27 October 2021)
- Health, Social Care and Sport Committee: session 6 priorities (drug policy) (14 September 2021)
- Drug policy (20 January 2021)
- Health and Social Care Committee: drug policy (9 March 2021)
- Drug-related deaths (7 January 2020)
- Supervised drug consumption facilities (5 November 2019)
- Drug strategy (22 May 2018)
- Safer injecting facilities (19 April 2018)

core and satellite codes. The core codes form the basis of the main themes in the analysis presented in the following chapters.[2]

Narratives and tropes

In this analysis, I found various narratives about illicit drugs and drug policy. Such narratives have often been found in policy analysis, of various types (Hajer, 1989; Roe, 1994; Jones and McBeth, 2010; Stevens, 2011c; Boswell, Geddes and Scholten, 2011; Crow and Jones, 2018; Rhodes, 2018; Fadlallah et al, 2019). In the data I analysed, these stories did not come complete with the full list of narrative components identified by Jones and McBeth (2010). Rather, they were often presented in fragmentary fashion, through the tropes that add up to the full story. In my interview with him, Steve Rolles gave me a list of a few of the narrative tropes that he observed in the media: "drug-related outrage, and moral panics, and imperilled youth type narratives, and reefer madness type narratives, and 'cocaine ruined my life' type narratives, and gangster stories, and street violence, and all these things that are fodder for not just the tabloids, I mean the media generally".

Factoids

Alongside such narratives and tropes, I often came across what can be called factoids. These are statements, often in the form of numerical claims, about the nature or size of a particular problem or solution. They circulate in the policy field between actors who use them in supporting their preferred policy positions and narratives. Just as in my reference to narratives, I do not mean to imply that all such statements are always inaccurate or fictional. Rather, I want to imply that these mini knowledge claims are stripped from their context and used like shuttlecocks that are batted back and forth between policy actors.

An example of a factoid that commonly popped up in the data related to the social cost of drug use in the UK: in her ministerial speech on the 2017 drug strategy, Sarah Newton MP put this figure at £10 billion per year (Hansard, 2017a). By the time of the 2021 drug strategy, this estimate had doubled to £20 billion (HM Government, 2021). In both items of discourse, it was claimed that acquisitive crime accounted for about half of the figure. The implication that such crimes had also doubled in four years is not supported by any other crime data. What matters to the discursive use of a factoid is not its accuracy but its capacity to convey a certain picture of the policy problem; in this case, that drugs are a huge problem, and that problem is largely to do with crime.

Most people who used these factoids displayed little knowledge of – or interest in – where they came from. An interesting exception was Russell

Findlay MSP. In a session of the Scottish Parliament's Criminal Justice Committee, he used the factoid that organised crime costs Scotland £2 billion per year. He had the grace to acknowledge, 'this is a much-quoted figure, although I am not entirely sure where it comes from' (Scottish Parliament, 2021).[3] Most of the people who bandied about such factoids presented them without such a disclaimer, as if they were settled, well-evidenced fact.

Policy positions

I also created codes for the policy positions that people expressed in interviews, the public events I observed, and the documentary discourse I collected. I coded policy positions from statements that specifically expressed support (pro) or disagreement with (anti) a particular practice or proposal in policy on illicit drugs. In doing the coding, it became clear that I also needed codes to record statements that reflected ambivalence about a policy. An example of such ambivalence came when I asked Dame Carol Black about what motivated her work on drug policy. Part of her answer was, "am I prepared to spend my time arguing for whether we'd be better off with drugs decriminalized or legalized? No, because I work with the system at the moment to try and bring about change". She did not come out against either of these options, but nor did she support them, so I coded her as being ambivalent on both.

Some of the policy positions I coded were very specific (for example, being in support of a specific legal amendment, or of providing a particular form of drug treatment). Others were more general (for example, being in support of 'a public health approach', or a general preference for free markets for drugs, or for drug prohibition). A full list of all the 195 policy positions I coded is given in Online Appendix 5.1.

Policy actors

In Nvivo, I also categorised the policy actors I observed in my ethnography and discourse analysis as 'cases' and classified some of their attributes. This included whether they were individuals or organisations, and the polity in which they worked (UK or Scottish). Those with an avowed political party affiliation were classified to that party. A text that was authored by a person for an organisation (for example, Liz McCulloch for Volteface) was coded as belonging to both these cases (for example, both Liz McCulloch and Volteface). Where a policy document had a foreword by another policy actor, data in the foreword was coded to the publishing organisation, the document author/s, and the foreword's author. I assumed that the authors of a document would share the positions expressed by the foreword author but not necessarily vice versa.

Coding

Some sections of data included more than one type of discursive element. For example, a parliamentary debate was closed by the late Labour MP Paul Flynn, a long-time campaigner for cannabis legalisation. His peroration included the following statement:

> We are throwing 2 million or 3 million of our young people into the hands of irresponsible gangsters. We should ensure that these drugs are controlled so that they are kept out of the hands of people with mental ill health and others whose health might be threatened, such as pregnant women. (Hansard, 2015)

In just this short data segment, there is: a factoid (borrowed from the Crime Survey for England and Wales) on the millions of people who use illicit drugs, a policy position (pro cannabis legalisation) and four narrative tropes. These narratives are: that prohibition creates crime by handing the drug market to 'irresponsible gangsters'; that legalisation would improve public health by increasing control of the drugs people are using; that drug use can exacerbate mental health problems; and that women need special protection from the harms of drugs. I coded this segment to each position, factoid and narrative trope.

My sampling gave me a lot of material to work on. Luckily, politicians – like academics – tend to repeat themselves. It was not necessary to code every segment of text in the documents I analysed, as they often repeated the same ideas. Politicians also share with academics a tendency to be verbose. Large portions of the texts I analysed were not directly relevant to drug policy. To avoid suffering the law of diminishing returns by coding every single speech and intervention in parliamentary debates, I focused my efforts purposively on those that were most relevant to the cases that I studied, as well as on speeches by parties' front bench spokespeople, and the MPs who intervened in these speeches.[4]

Ethico-political bases

Analysing the ethico-political bases which informed policy actors' discourse and policy positions posed a particular challenge. There were frequent references in policy documents and political speeches to the need for compassion, particularly in the form of 'saving lives'. The inherent value of knowledge was invoked in frequent calls for 'evidence-based policy' and for more research to be done. Other moral positions were less frequently and directly stated.

When I asked interviewees about the role of morality in policy making, they told me that it is rarely openly discussed. Ed Day said that in his private discussions with civil servants and junior ministers, they would sometimes tell personal stories which reflected moral positions: "It's like a lot of things in addiction. If they're close to people that this has affected, they get that and the morality part of it would be larger". But, more generally, morality itself was, according to Day, "not on the agenda". Drug policy, he said, is "discussed more as a functional risk reduction type problem rather than anything bigger than that". I got the impression from some interviewees that it would have been rather un-British to discuss policy in terms of morality, that it was both more convenient and more convivial to avoid opening up disputes about underlying values. So policy discussions concentrate on the surface-level issues of means, rather than deeper questions of ends. Of course, even if morality is not openly discussed, it is present. The choice of which risks to reduce, and which people facing such risks should be prioritised, is inevitably moral.

An interviewee or political speech can tell you straight that they are driven by a moral position that promotes social justice or the respect of religious belief. But they can also show you that position by supporting a policy which leads towards more equal outcomes or to respect of religious traditions. Narrative tropes often contain ethico-political assumptions and so provide clues about the moral positions that underpin policy preferences. For example, the trope that drugs are the root cause of social ills reflects a moral position that drug use is inherently wrong. On the other hand, the narrative trope that currently illicit drugs can be beneficial often accompanies a normative judgement that people should be free to use these substances. I coded texts and speech to particular moral positions when it was clear that a segment of text – such as a trope, a factoid or a policy position – was linked to a moral position in which its speaker or author believed.

The policy positions that people support – and the narrative tropes and factoids that they use – can both reveal and reinforce the ethico-political commitments that underlie their policy preferences. This reflects the critical realist assumption that there are real causal structures which generate social reality (Elder-Vass, 2012) and that these include cultural structures, including moralities (Archer, 2000). In the subsequent chapters of this book, I show how I used the data I gathered to identify the ethico-political bases that underlie the different policy constellations of the actors and ideas that animate British drug policy.

Analysis of policy constellations with SNA

To analyse the complex 'networks of sympathies' that make up policy constellations, we need a method that 'conceptualizes a policy-making process as a network of policy actors and allows empirical measuring of [actors'] positions in this policy network' (Varone et al, 2016, p 322), and

SNA provides that method. It creates a visual diagram of the interactions of policy actors to help us understand how particular policies came to be. SNA draws on many years of work on statistical and graphical techniques (Moreno and Jennings, 1938), as well as on compatible developments in studying social systems as having a network structure; for example, Granovetter's (1973) work on 'the strength of weak ties'. Because links in a network carry meaning and networks are socially and culturally structured, examining networks of policy actors can help us understand how power operates in a particular field (Fuhse, 2009).

SNA relies on the mathematical and topographic processing of data on how components of a social system are linked together. It shows how 'nodes' are connected by 'ties' (otherwise known as 'edges'), which nodes have ties to each other, and which do not. It can present these networks in the form of mathematical matrices or – more usefully for my purposes – diagrams of the social network, known as sociograms.

This is, as far as I know, only the second study to use SNA to analyse drug policy making. A recent scoping review (Zakimi et al, 2023) found only one previous example. This was a chapter in Clara Musto's (2018) PhD thesis on the legalisation of cannabis in Uruguay, which used SNA alongside the advocacy coalition framework (Sabatier, 1993). This was carried out at the universities of Kent and Utrecht as part of the Erasmus Mundus Doctorate in Cultural and Global Criminology, which I helped to lead.

Two-mode SNA

Musto's was a one-mode SNA, using only the ties between policy actors, so mine may be the first two-mode SNA that has been done in this field. In one-mode SNA, the nodes of the network are of the same type. The network can consist, for example, of nodes that represent people, publications or ideas, but not more than one of these types at a time. A one-mode sociogram could show, as Musto's does, the network of people who work with each other on a particular policy. In two-mode SNA, the network diagram brings together nodes of two types, such as people and their ideas (Hansen et al, 2011). I chose to use two-mode SNA because of its ability to visualise how policy actors and policy positions come together in clusters (which I call constellations) that share similar ethico-political bases.

I based my SNA on lists of the policy actors (individuals and organisations) and policy positions which I developed through my ethnography, interviews and discourse analysis. The organisations included government departments, parliamentary committees and groups, charities and think tanks, campaign groups and their funders, as well as some private companies. The individuals included politicians, academics, writers, lawyers, campaigners and experts-by-experience (people who have their own direct experiences of issues around illicit drugs). The second mode of nodes in the network is made up of the policy positions that I coded from these actors' speech and discourse, and from my ethnographic knowledge of their views.

To carry out the SNA for the UK-level drug policy field, I excluded policy actors that were only active at the Scottish level (for example, Scottish charities and members of the Scottish Parliament). For the SNA of Scottish drug policy making, I excluded actors who were not active at the Scottish level (for example, members of the UK Parliament and London-based think tanks that did not get involved in Scottish drug policy debates). Some policy actors had a presence in both Scottish and UK policy processes, and so were included in both the UK and Scottish analyses. Examples included the UK Home Office, the then Scottish First Minister, Nicola Sturgeon, and Dave Liddell, who was a member of the ACMD as well as being head of the Scottish Drugs Forum.

Nodes and ties

My full process for converting the Nvivo coding into sociograms in Gephi, via reverse pivot tables in Excel, is described in Online Appendix 5.2. In brief, I ran queries in Nvivo to cross-tabulate policy actors against the policy positions that I had coded them to in the data; one cross-tabulation for the UK and one for the Scottish policy field. From each of these two cross-tabulations, I created two lists. The node list contained a row for each policy actor and each policy position that I coded in the data. The edge list had a row for each bilateral tie between a policy actor and a policy position they supported. These lists were refined after preliminary analysis in order to correct errors and to highlight connections between actors and positions that I knew to be connected from my ethnographic participation in the field. The organisations that I coded as policy actors, as well as the policy positions in each of the UK and Scottish level datasets, are listed in Online Appendix 5.1.

In the UK-level SNA, there were 333 policy actors (88 organisations and 245 individuals) and 173 policy positions in the node list. The edge list contained 1,901 bilateral connections between policy actors and policy positions; that is, coded mentions of a policy actor supporting a policy position in the policy documents, fieldnotes or interviews. If an actor mentioned supporting that position multiple times, or in multiple documents, they were still only counted once as a supporter of that position in the SNA.

The average policy actor was connected to (was coded as supporting) six policy positions. The average policy position was connected to (was coded as being supported by) 11 actors. The distributions were highly skewed, with a few policy positions being supported by large numbers of the policy actors (for example, support for funding drug treatment, harm reduction and the use of cannabis for medical purposes), while many were mentioned only by one policy actor. Similarly, some policy actors were coded to only one position (for example, MPs who made only one point relevant to drug policy in the analysed parliamentary debates), while others were coded against many policy positions. This tended to be the case for ministers who spoke a lot about drug policy in Parliament or in policy documents (for example, Kit Malthouse, in whose remit was drug policy), or the interviewees who told me about the positions they supported (and opposed).

For the analysis of Scottish drug policy constellations, the node list contained 130 policy actors (38 organisations and 92 individuals) and 145 policy positions. The Scottish edge list contained 822 ties based on my coding of the support of policy actors for policy positions.

Creating sociograms

On the basis of the data in these lists, I used Gephi software (version 0.9.5) to analyse policy actors' connections to policy positions, so mapping the networked, ideational structure of the UK and Scottish drug policy fields.

As is usual in two-mode SNA, the only direct ties in the analysed networks were between nodes of one mode (actors) and another (positions). Actors are clustered closely together in the sociograms if they support the same policy positions or policy positions that are not far away in the network (with a small number of steps through connections to other actors and policy positions). Similarly, policy positions are placed close together in the sociogram not by direct ties between them but by being supported by the same policy actors, or by actors that are only a few network steps away.

Mathematically, SNA calculated the position of a node (a policy actor or position) in the sociogram by the number of direct (node-to-node) and indirect (node-connected-via-other-node) steps between them in the network. Importantly for this analysis, some methods for laying out the sociogram (for example, ForceAtlas 2) also use a measure of repulsion. This places nodes that share no direct links far from each other in the sociogram.

Policy constellations as SNA modules

In Chapters 7 and 10, you will find sociograms that display the connections between coded policy actors and policy positions in various ways. You will see that actors and positions tend to cluster together. SNA can explore this clustering in detail by analysing the density of ties between the nodes, identifying groups that are known as modules in Gephi. Analysis of this modularity helps us identify the connected sets of actors and ideas that I call policy constellations. In effect, I carried out a less formal version of the graph analysis that Atari et al (2022) used to distinguish different clusters of moral foundations in responses to the Moral Foundations Questionnaire. Instead of using survey responses as data, I used my coding of the discourse I collated. Instead of using the Walktrap algorithm for community detection, I used the Gephi software to detect Louvain communities (Blondel et al, 2008) within the network of ties between policy actors and policy communities.

As a final step, I moved back from the SNA to link it to the analysis of ethnographic and discursive data. I superimposed the ethico-political bases that I found in these data (described in Chapter 6) on to the sociograms and policy constellations that I found in SNA, as presented in Chapters 7 and 10. This means that I can show how constellation members tend to share underlying ethico-political commitments as well as surface-level policy positions, again in line with the depth ontology of critical realism.

Conclusion: mixed methods for studying policy constellations

Different theoretical assumptions may have led me to a different set of tools to use in the analysis. More time, space and technical expertise might have allowed me to go deeper with, for example, discourse network analysis (Leifeld, 2017), qualitative comparative analysis (Ragin, 2008) or natural language processing (Khurana et al, 2023). I hope such efforts will follow this book.

Here, I have tried to present enough information about the mixed methods I used to study UK policy constellations so that readers can understand how I came up with the findings I present in later chapters. This combination of ethnography, elite interviewing, discourse analysis and SNA may also be useful in studying other places and policy cases.

These mixed methods enabled me to follow through on the promise to provide a critical realist approach that is distinct from the neo-pluralist policy theories that are commonly used in the field, with their emphases on individual policy entrepreneurs and their assumptions that social action is the sum total of individuals' actions (Kingdon, 2013; Jenkins-Smith et al, 2018). Due to this methodological individualism, neo-pluralist approaches fail to account for phenomena that emerge from collective action (Kirman, 1989). The policy constellations approach recognises the emergence of social action from collective processes, and that 'social structures, although the product of human individuals, have causal powers of their own, which cannot be reduced to the powers of those individuals' (Elder-Vass, 2007, p 27). Critical realists know that such underlying structures cannot be directly observed. Their presence must be inferred from the patterns of observable events and actions that they produce (Danermark et al, 2019).

For example, policy constellations are not created at the behest of any one organisation or individual. They emerge from the interactions between different people, organisations and their ideas. The next part of this book discusses the mechanisms of emergence of policy decisions through the actions of policy constellations.

PART II

Morality and Power in UK Drug Policy Constellations

6

Moralities in Action: The Ethico-Political Bases of UK Drug Policy

The central argument of this book is that policy is made through the interactions of people and organisations in policy constellations. These are loosely connected networks of people, brought together by shared normative preferences and material interests. They tend to want the same policies because they fulfil the same moral commitments and advance their social positions, often doing both simultaneously. The policy preferences that prevail and make it into government policy decisions are usually those that are held by the most powerful constellations.

In order to see whether and how this applies in UK drug policy making, it is necessary to identify the moral positions that are in play, to map the connections between policy actors and policy preferences, and to examine the forms of power that policy actors bring to these constellations. This will be done over the next three chapters in this second part of the book, which will show how it is possible to explain the outcomes of policy discussions.

The first of these three chapters uses ethnography and critical realist discourse analysis to analyse the moral positions that animate UK drug policy discussions. In my analysis, there are five common normative themes. I describe these positions as ethico-political bases because they mix moral commitments with political ideas to produce certain ways of thinking about the values that are most important to fulfil in drug policy.

Compassion is a common theme in policy discussions, even if it is expressed in different ways and towards different people. The other four bases for UK drug policy are commitments to traditionalism, paternalism, progressive social justice and liberty. These five ethico-political bases are shown schematically in Figure 6.1 and described later in this chapter. This diagram takes the form of a modified circumplex, with compassion at its centre, connected by clear lines with each of the other ethico-political bases. The bases that

Figure 6.1: The modified circumplex of ethico-political bases in UK drug policy

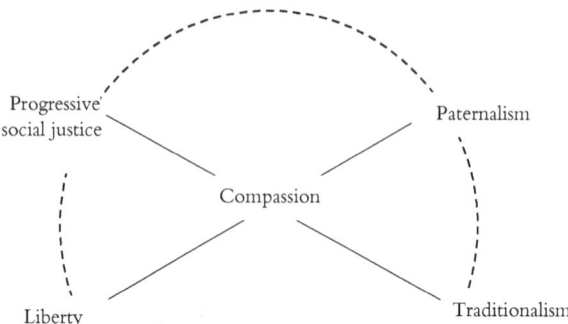

are diagonally opposite each other are morally incompatible. Those that are next to each other and connected by dashed lines can more easily be shared. The gap at the bottom between liberty and traditionalism is there because I observed little sharing of policy positions between policy actors who expressed these ethico-political bases.

Compassion: a shared, but differentiated value

Figure 6.1 presents compassion as a central value which is shared by all policy actors. Across the field, in a wide variety of speeches and documents, the idea that we should help other people who are in distress was very commonly expressed. Support for funding treatment of people who have drug problems, for example, was expressed across the policy field. This reflects what Haidt (2012) calls the moral foundation of care, while Schwartz (1992) calls it benevolence. I use the word compassion here because it expresses both the emotional nature of this concern for suffering (in Latin, *passio* means to suffer) and the way it is expressed between people (*com* is Latin for with). The word itself was used in documents as diverse as the Green Party (2019) election manifesto, which called for cannabis legalisation, and a report from the Centre for Social Justice (CSJ) on the 'case against legalising cannabis' (CSJ, 2018a). The CSJ called for a more compassionate approach to people caught in possession of drugs, but not for any change in the law.

This example shows that, in contrast to the views of some progressives, compassion is not restricted to any particular part of the drug policy field. Progressives may argue that traditionalists lack compassion because they want to punish people rather than help them. But traditionalists may argue in return that upholding prohibitionist laws is an act of compassion, in that it prevents people from suffering the harms of drug use.

What looks like hypocrisy to some people may just be a different interpretation of what it means to be compassionate for others. This is because compassion may be directed by different policy actors at different actions and target groups (Schneider and Ingram, 1993). An example is the lack of compassion that has previously been displayed towards working-class, unemployed people who die with heroin and other substances. This was visible in the lack of media attention to people who died with heroin compared to young people who die with new psychoactive substances (Stevens, 2017). I also saw it in the lack of attention or funding to prevent these deaths in the 2017 drug strategy (Stevens, 2019). This made claims to care for people's health while failing to act on these concerns look somewhat hypocritical. But it would be hard to sustain a claim – on the basis of the data I analysed – that there is a portion of the drug policy field which completely lacks compassion. Specifically, the UK government's allocation of £533 million for drug treatment in England over three years – with the specific intention to use it to prevent a thousand drug-related deaths – means that the drug policy field of 2021 is different from what it was in 2017, when the drug strategy came with no additional funding (HM Government, 2017, 2021).

There is, however, a greater willingness in some sectors of the drug policy field to combine compassion with toughness. In a parliamentary speech by the Labour MP Emma Hardy, she stated that we should 'never mistake friendliness and compassion for weakness' (Hansard, 2017a). Her colleague Fleur Anderson made a clear distinction in who is deserving of compassion. She focused it on the children who are exploited by drug dealers in 'county lines' supply operations (Hansard, 2021e). Her targeting of this group for compassion was in line with the widespread use of what Steve Rolles called the "imperilled child narrative", of which tropes appeared in several parts of the discourse. Protecting children from harm was often presented as a reason for changing drug policy. It was used to support calls for both increasing and reducing criminal sanctions for drug offences. This affective narrative was most effectively deployed in the campaign to legalise cannabis products for medical use (see Chapter 9).

Traditionalism: big and small C conservatism

In their study of moral foundations in the UK, Harper and Rhodes (2021, p 1324) link traditionalism to 'a broad suite of conservative-typical viewpoints', identifiable by – for example – people's respect for authority and the belief that one should conform to the traditions of society. In Schwartz's circumplex, conformity and tradition are the two values that are most closely linked (Schwartz and Boehnke, 2004). Haidt et al (2009) identified an 'ideological narrative' of 'social conservatism', in which people express more concern for ingroup loyalty, authority and purity than do people who are connected to the narrative of progressive liberalism or libertarianism.

They also show less concern for harm, except when it affects victims of crime. These concerns are compatible with MacCoun and Reuter's (2001, p 4) idea that one 'philosophical underpinning' for drug policy is 'legal moralism', or the belief that 'drug use is intrinsically immoral and must be banned for that reason'.

In my analysis, I spotted these tendencies alongside support for abstinence from drug use, stigmatisation of drug law offenders and punitive social control. This was occasionally presented in explicitly moralistic terms, as in Boris Johnson's (2021) description of 'vile' predatory drug pushers. It was also visible in calls for greater control of drug use and harsher sentences for drug offences, which came most often – but not exclusively – from Conservative Party politicians. So you might call this big C Conservatism. Harper and Rhodes (2021, p 1310) found traditionalism to be associated with 'older age, political conservatism, higher levels of insecurity with social change, and lower levels of concern about systemic inequalities'.

Many interviewees told me that the conservatism of UK drug policy is not just due to the dominance of the Conservative Party in recent elections. Several of them used the term "small C conservatism" to describe the beliefs of people across party divides. For example, Jack Straw, a former Labour Home Secretary, was described to me as "a classic natural small C conservative … personality-wise". Small C conservatism involves an aversion to radical change and risk-taking. It is not just a personality trait held by many powerful policy actors; it is also built into the systems of power that they operate. As an example, an anonymous interviewee described the Office for Health Improvement as a "rather timid organisation" which "sees campaigning for particular things as someone else's job".

In other interviews, people told me the rules of the institutional game that they had learnt to play. Ed Day, who was appointed England's national Drug Recovery Champion in 2019, told me about how this works. He said it had been "made clear" to him that certain topics should not be mentioned if he wanted to get things done. When I asked him if he had been explicitly warned off raising some issues, he told me that "it was no one ever said, 'don't mention that'. But it was politely put across that if you have access to the Minister and you want them to take what you're saying seriously, don't start with this". He mentioned two topics that it was made clear would be particularly unhelpful to bring up: cannabis legalisation, "or even decriminalisation"; and "drug consumption rooms" (AKA overdose prevention centres).

Traditionalist moral positions are also present in both moderate and radical parts of the political left. Mat Southwell told me about his younger days in the Militant Tendency (a left-wing group that gained some influence in the Labour Party in the 1980s). When he and his friends introduced motions on gay rights and drug policy reform, his Militant comrades were apparently horrified; "they completely freaked out", leading Southwell to leave the organisation. When Militant councillors ran Liverpool in the 1980s, they opposed the heroin prescribing practices of Dr John Marks; an example given by Sebastian Scheerer (1993, p 100) of the 'puritanical streak' in socialism.

Default paternalism: limiting freedom to protect from harm

The other main ethico-political base for the policy preferences that are most often institutionalised in British drug policy is paternalism. Paternalists 'assert that in the absence of intervention some people are unable to act in their own best interests. The state therefore has a duty to protect people from their own poor decision making' (Curchin, Weight and Ritter, 2022, p 412). This is a long-standing strain of thought in the promotion of public health, which has often involved the provision of both supportive services and state control to potentially unhealthy bodies. I used to use the historical example of quarantine to illustrate this point, little knowing that the COVID-19 pandemic would give us all direct experience of being controlled in pursuit of health protection.

This is not a position that is squarely present in moral foundations theory, in either its US or British forms. It lacks the spiritual content of Haidt et al's (2009) 'ideological underpinning' of the 'religious left'. It comes closer to MacCoun and Reuter's (2001) 'philosophical underpinning' of 'legal paternalism', in which legal barriers are set up to prevent people harming themselves, rather than because of a moral distaste for drug use.

The central texts of UK drug control are paternalist in nature. The international drug control system, as well as the Misuse of Drugs Act, attempts to limit the use of some substances to medical use alone. This is built on the assumption that the state – in the form of its appointed medical experts – knows best which drugs should and should not be consumed. Restrictions on liberty are justified on the basis that medical experts, and not individual citizens, know best how to limit the harms of drug use. Note how this is a discourse from which the pleasures of using drugs are absent. Official drug control provides exemptions only for medical benefit: the alleviation of pain and suffering. The use of these substances for fun or self-enhancement is placed out of this scope, on the opposite side of the ethico-political circumplex in Figure 6.1.

In the data, I observed a kind of default paternalism. Under conditions of uncertainty, default paternalism favours the controlling status quo over liberating reform. For example, we do not know for sure that enhanced harm reduction services that are new to the UK – such as drug checking and overdose prevention centres – would make a difference to drug-related harms at population level. The argument has been made against them on the basis that there is not sufficiently robust evidence. This argument was made by my interviewee Keith Humphreys in *The Lancet*, and by the drugs minister Kit Malthouse to the Scottish Affairs Committee (Scottish Affairs Committee, 2019; Humphreys et al, 2022). Privately, some public health officials told me they would like to see pilots of overdose prevention centres. Publicly, they avoid challenging the dominance of more traditionalist policies in order not to jeopardise the prospects of public health interventions being politically accepted and funded. This is a mechanism of default paternalism. When we do not know for sure that a more liberal policy will be effective, we stick to state control that limits freedoms. As Matthew Lesh told me, "You generally don't have to make the case to substantiate the status quo as hard as you need to make the case for something to be different. Particularly in drug policy reform, where there's a perception of risk."

This perception was certainly present in parliamentary debates. In one of them, the Scottish MP Anne McLaughlin gave a good example of what I mean by default paternalism: 'there is no conclusive evidence that cannabis does not exacerbate pre-existing mental health problems. Anyone with any experience of mental illness would never support anything that would exacerbate or cause psychotic episodes' (Hansard, 2015). She gave this uncertainty about the effects of cannabis as a reason for not supporting its legalisation. Unless we know for certain that reform would not cause harm, then we stick with the status quo. It is this idea that uncertainty inherently sustains caution and control that makes paternalism the default policy preference for people who share this ethico-political base. It is, incidentally, the same argument that was made against drug policy reform by the doyen of British addiction research, the late Professor Griffith Edwards, in his (2004) book on *Matters of Substance*.

Such paternalism is not solely pragmatic. It mixes normative with empirical questions in its call to both control and care for others. But people who hold paternalist policy positions tend not to see their preferences as having a particularly moral dimension. When I asked them about the role of morality in policy, they tended to focus their answer on actors from other policy constellations, particularly those who hold traditionalist views. The policy documents produced by public health professionals and researchers are heavily couched in the de-politicised, de-moralised language of evidence-based policy.

This mode of policy reasoning incorporates, within its utilitarian external shell, normative assumptions about what is worth pursuing and who is best placed to pursue it. There is less regard for traditional values of purity and abstinence but a consistent belief that a certain group of people with a certain mode of knowledge are best placed to decide what forms of drug use are to be accepted. Only forms of consumption that are consistent with the views of safe and responsible drug use that are held by medical and public health professionals are condoned. Letting people decide for themselves what drugs to consume is considered too risky. These preferences for safety, responsibility and the avoidance of risk are found in the more conservative quarter of the circumplex of basic values (Schwartz and Boehnke, 2004). In practice, default paternalism leads to policies that are often compatible with the repressive social control measures that are favoured by policy actors with more traditionalist values.

Progressive social justice: fairness as equality and the removal of disadvantage

Justice is sometimes used as a synonym for fairness. In the policy discourse I found a particular interpretation of fairness in the form of progressive social justice. This can be summarised as the idea that people should not be disadvantaged by who they are, where they come from or – in the case of drug policy – by what they choose to consume. This ethico-political base is closer to the idea of fairness as equality rather than proportionality (Atari et al, 2022). It echoes the 'ideological narrative' of 'secular liberalism', which Haidt et al (2009) also refer to as 'progressive liberalism'. The idea here is that protection from harm and the promotion of fairness (in the form of equality) are more important than ingroup loyalty, purity and respect for authority. This ethico-political base also reflects some aspects of MacCoun and Reuter's (2001) 'philosophical underpinning' of 'Millian liberalism'. The contemporary movement for progressive social justice has moved on from John Stuart Mill's version of liberalism and repudiates his support of the colonisation of the British empire. It does share the great utilitarian's belief that the state has a legitimate role in regulating behaviour when it harms others, but not in deciding what people can do with their own bodies.

Some aspects of social justice were found across the policy discourse. The discourse I analysed included factoids about the geographical concentration of drug-related deaths in the most socio-economically deprived areas. This included the UK's 2021 drug strategy (HM Government, 2021). The idea of fairness is also contained in the phrase 'levelling up', a slogan used by the Conservative Party in the run-up to the 2019 general election and since to signal its commitment to addressing deep, enduring regional inequalities. I observed, however, a particular and distinctive form of commitment to social justice that was highly sceptical that this could be achieved by a Conservative government which is reluctant to acknowledge structural inequalities of class, gender and race. Several of the people I interviewed used the term 'levelling up' ironically, expressing amused scorn for this slogan.

Mat Southwell expressed the ethico-political base of progressive social justice when he told me that some people are "fighting for marginalised people in society and trying to ensure that whatever model comes next is fairer in its design". He was echoing some of the people who used drugs that were interviewed by Rebecca Askew and who supported 'reform rooted in social welfare and human rights' (Askew and Bone, 2019, p 37). In Scotland, David Liddell told me that his work had always been about "the rights of marginalised people".

I call this *progressive* social justice in order to distinguish it from more traditionalist forms of social justice, such as that espoused by the conservative think tank, the CSJ (founded by Iain Duncan-Smith, a former leader of the Conservative Party). The defining feature of what I call progressive social justice is expressed by Amartya Sen in his book on *The Idea of Justice*: 'what moves us is ... that there are clearly remediable injustices around us that we want to eliminate' (Sen, 2009, p vii; cited by Atkinson, 2010, p 221). This is not just about reducing poverty, and so is a different vision of social justice than that proposed by the CSJ, which states that social justice is about addressing 'the root causes of poverty' (CSJ, 2023, np). These are listed as being family breakdown, educational failure, worklessness, addiction, debt and modern slavery. The CSJ's list does not include the deeper causes of poverty (such as class and global injustices) or refer to wider dimensions of inequality (such as racism and patriarchy). It is the focus on these deeper and broader structures of inequality that distinguishes progressive social justice both from traditionalist visions of social justice and from earlier left-wing movements that focused on a narrower range of inequalities. As seen in the name of the Labour Party, founded in 1900, this earlier focus primarily related to class.

People who gravitate towards the contemporary ethico-political base of progressive social justice tend to agree that punitive prohibition has failed and that it is inherently racist. They point to a long history of discrimination and ethnic disproportionality in the making and enforcing of drug laws. They also, although less frequently, point out the class inequalities in drug policing, such as the irony that Boris Johnson found his way to Downing Street despite his avowed illicit drug use while many Black and working-class young people face criminalisation for low-level drug possession. The most commonly coded policy belief among people who expressed this ethico-political base was support for the decriminalisation of drug possession. This was sometimes found in the same policy actors who wanted less use of stop-and-search by the police (Shiner et al, 2018), a position I also share (Akintoye et al, 2022; Douse et al, 2022). They and I argue not only that possession of all drugs should be decriminalised, but that criminal records for past offences should be expunged (Green Party of England, 2019; Akintoye et al, 2022; Garius and Ali, 2022). When supporting legalisation, they want this to be done in a way that benefits the communities who have suffered most from prohibition and criminalisation, recognising the historic wrongs that have been done by drug policy globally as well as in the UK (Daniels et al, 2021).

Social justice progressives are far less ambivalent than paternalist public health professionals when it come to their support for enhanced harm reduction services. They strongly support the provision of drug checking and overdose prevention centres, as well as the more established harm reduction services of opiate agonist therapy and needle and syringe programmes. They see harm reduction not just as a pragmatic means for limiting the damage of drug problems but as an expression of the human rights of people who use drugs.

This emphasis on the human rights of these people is another distinctive feature of this ethico-political base. It reflects a universalist concern for the human rights of all citizens, not just those who conform with authority and traditional standards of purity and sanctity. It is increasingly accompanied by the insistence that people who use drugs should be empowered to influence drug policies. There is ongoing discussion of whether drug policy researchers and campaigners should 'come out' about their own illicit drug use (Ross et al, 2020). And there are growing efforts to link drug policy to broader efforts to redress some of the wrongs done by colonisation (Daniels et al, 2021).

While paternalists can be accused of hiding their normative concerns within a carapace of utilitarian value-freedom, social justice progressives can be accused of oscillating between normative and empirical claims, and between Cairney's (2021) evidence-based and co-production stories, as it suits. In promoting harm reduction, for example, we are happy to use the language both of evidence-based policy ('the research shows it works') and of social justice (which demands that we respect the voices of people who use drugs, and not just the research literature). This is relatively unproblematic when the empirical evidence and the expressed desires of drug user organisations coincide, as in the case of the provision of needle and syringe programmes. These have a strong evidence base, as well as community support (Platt et al, 2018). It becomes more difficult when the views of members of disadvantaged communities are in conflict with each other, as they often are, or when peer-reviewed evidence and the ethics of equality, benevolence and universalism diverge.

Liberty: self-enhancement and making money

A senior fellow of the Adam Smith Institute summarised the ethico-political base of liberty as follows: 'We are moralists here in the sense that we think it moral for every adult to carve out their own life according to their own desires – that's the liberty and freedom thing' (Worstall, 2019). The liberty thing is a moral foundation that is found in both US and

British applications of moral foundations theory (Harper and Rhodes, 2021). In Schwartz's (1992) circumplex, this corresponds to the 'self-enhancement' values of self-direction and achievement. 'Libertarian' is one of both the 'ideological narratives' identified by Haidt et al (2009) and the 'philosophical underpinnings' listed by MacCoun and Reuter (2001). In the discourse I analysed, I found narrative tropes of individual freedom and bodily autonomy alongside support for legalisation of supply as well as decriminalisation of possession. Interestingly, there was a particular focus on the legalisation of psilocybin, the active ingredient in hallucinogenic 'magic' mushrooms, as well as cannabis.

A common position across all these groups is support for the legalisation of cannabis for recreational as well as medical use. According to a report published by Volteface, the

> goal is to limit young people's access to cannabis by undercutting black markets on price, choice and convenience, and to supply pure and dose-measured herbal cannabis, cannabis resin and edibles to adults for use in their homes. All products should be taxed. Taxation should be higher on higher-strength products, as in the alcohol model. (Power, 2017, p 13)

The stated aim here is to protect children from harm in the illicit cannabis market, again in line with the imperilled child narrative. It is interesting that this is the same narrative that was used in the successful campaign to legalise cannabis for recreational use in Canada, especially as some people close to these organisations in the UK have also spent time in Canada. This includes Blair Gibbs, former adviser to Boris Johnson and author of a favourable report on the Canadian model (Gibbs, Reed and Wride, 2021). It also includes Steve Moore, the founder of Volteface, who was an adviser to previous Conservative Prime Minister David Cameron.

Moore told me about the rush of money into the Canadian cannabis market that accompanied legalisation. In this corner of the drug policy field, equity is more likely to refer to investment than social justice. On both sides of the Atlantic, the argument that is made in public is often that there are large sums of money to be made for taxpayers rather than shareholders. I found several versions of the factoid that a legalised cannabis market in the UK would be worth £X billion. The estimated figure ranged between £2.5 and £6.8 (Starling, 2016; Pryor and McCulloch, 2019).

The imperilled child and economic narratives are the public faces of a deeper desire to free people from state control. In interviews with Chris Snowdon, Matthew Lesh and Daniel Pryor – who have all worked for one or both of the two main free market think tanks, the Institute of Economic Affairs (IEA), and the Adam Smith Institute (ASI) – they each expressed this basic commitment to individual freedom. Snowdon, in particular, expressed opposition to state control of the alcohol industry, including his deep scepticism of the policy of minimum unit pricing. Previously, Snowdon (2014) has acknowledged that the IEA has received 'small' donations from the alcohol industry. It is this kind of funding that has led Jim McCambridge, David Miller and others to worry about the economic influence of the alcohol industry on policy discussions (McCambridge et al, 2014; Miller et al, 2014, 2018). But I did not get the impression that Snowdon would need financial inducement to oppose state control. For him and other libertarians, this is a matter of what you believe in, not who is paying you.

There was a consistent divide between people who advocate drug law reform in the pursuit of progressive social justice and those who do so in pursuit of liberty. The former tended to mention the need for 'responsible' regulation of currently illicit drugs and avoided collaborating with private companies. The latter emphasised the need for commercial freedom in order to maximise revenues and tax incomes and to displace the illicit market. They had fewer qualms about being seen to collaborate with the cannabis and psilocybin industries. For policy actors and positions that share the libertarian ethico-political base, the preference for liberty applies to both people and commercial entities.

While libertarians and progressives may be divided on the form of legalisation they want, there is an interesting convergence in their support for harm reduction. Both Volteface and the ASI, for example, published reports supporting harm reduction in general and overdose prevention centres in particular (McCulloch, 2017; Bartle, 2019). This fits with what Matthew Lesh of the IEA called "practical liberalism". He described this as "a libertarian approach – or harm reduction approach – to things like alcohol and tobacco and drugs". Harm reduction is a morally flexible concept. It can express a libertarian concern for the freedom of people who use drugs, as well as the paternalist idea that people need protecting from themselves. The libertarians I interviewed preferred the former version of harm reduction.

Moral overlaps and mutual repulsion

We should not think of these ethico-political bases as sole operators. There are overlaps, and – importantly for the policy constellations approach – some sharp divides. As Miles and Vaisey (2015, p 259) put it, 'most moral constructs cover a broad conceptual space'. So we should not be surprised to find that the same policy space can include influences from more than one ethico-political base. Policy actors may also express values that reflect more than one ethico-political base. A particular policy position can also reflect multiple ethico-political bases. For example, support for recovery can reflect a traditionalist concern for the value of abstinence as well as a compassionate concern for people who have problems with drugs. Deirdre Boyd expressed both those values when I interviewed her. The provision of heroin-assisted treatment can express concern for the harms felt by people who are dependent on heroin, and respect for their freedom to use it. These two positions were both supported in a blog post by Tim Worstall of the ASI (Worstall, 2019). In promoting this overlap, Worstall was echoing the principles of the philosopher from whom his think tank was named. Adam Smith (1968 [1759]) combined support for free enterprise with concern for 'mutual sympathy' in his *Theory of Moral Sentiments*. The frequency of the overlap between ethico-political bases at the outside of Figure 6.1 with the central base of compassion is why the connections from the outside bases to compassion are represented as solid black lines.

Ethico-political bases that are next to each other at the perimeter of Figure 6.1 can also overlap. The compatibility of traditionalist social control with paternalist public health measures has often been noted, and not just by opponents of virus outbreak control measures (Lupton, 1995; Debbaut and Kammersgaard, 2022). This is a combined position that Askew and Bone (2019, p 38) – following MacCoun and Reuter (2001, p 63) – describe as hard paternalism. This provides no Millian exception to the moral duty not to take drugs. Paternalists can also overlap with social justice progressives when they demand that the state strictly regulate drug markets to prevent harms to the most vulnerable. This is referred to as 'soft paternalism' by Askew and Bone as well as MacCoun and Reuter because it does adopt the Millian idea that the limits of state control are at the boundaries of the citizen's body.

There are some ethico-political bases that are actively opposed to each other. This is seen in the opposition that Hunter (1992) observes between traditionalists and progressives on opposite sides of the 'culture wars'. Schwartz (1992) anticipated this clash by placing these values on opposite sides of his circumplex of basic values. The ethico-political bases of traditionalism and progressive social justice are diametrically opposed to each other on moral principles, not just on drug policy. Authority and sanctity are revered by traditionalists but tend to be downplayed, if not ridiculed, by progressives. Traditionalists' blaming of progressives for the social ills that cluster around drug use has been observed for decades (Young, 1971). Going back to Young's early days, progressives have in turn blamed traditionalists for the continuation of policies that they see as harmful and unjustified. It is hardly surprising that a certain amount of animosity has built up between the two groups. Dave Liddell, for example, discussed the traditionalist position that drug treatment should be conditional on the idea that people "give back". He viewed this as not just ineffective but morally "disgusting". He described his long career in the drug policy field as being based on valuing the needs of "marginalised people" and promoting their voices; in other words, progressive social justice.

Similarly, the control of other people that is assumed to be beneficial by paternalists is anathema to libertarians. I saw this in Chris Snowdon's antipathy towards public health professionals and agencies that seek to impose controls on other people and industries. Ethically motivated public health professionals and researchers now seek to minimise the influence of the emerging cannabis and psychedelics industries, as they have tried to do with the tobacco and alcohol industries. The lesson they learn from other legal markets is that the industry should be tightly controlled (Caulkins and Kilborn, 2019). So these public health professionals cannot find common cause with policy actors who promote the freedom of people and companies to choose how to use drugs for their own desires. Libertarians' distinctive views on the role of state intervention means they also disagree with both paternalists and progressives on the issue of taxation. Their general preference for lower taxes does not result from dispassionate analysis of fiscal policy but from an ethico-political preference for less state intervention in people's lives.

The pattern of attraction and repulsion is why these five ethico-political bases are placed as they are in Figure 6.1. Potentially complementary ethico-political bases are placed next to each other in the diagram. Those with which they most conflict are placed on the diagonally opposite side of the diagram, with no direct lines between them. Compassion is placed in the middle, as it is potentially compatible with all the others.

Conclusion: the ethico-political bases of UK drug policy

It may be possible to place ideas on drug policy on a one-dimensional spectrum, running from a least restrictive libertarian position through a moderately restrictive medical approach to a most restrictive criminal policy (Gerstein and Harwood, 1990). Here I provide a more nuanced and nationally specific account of the moralities that underlie UK drug policy, although I doubt that even my use of a diagram with two dimensions rather than one captures the full complexity of the UK drug policy field.

By combining insights from previous research on moral positions with data from this field, I have identified five distinctive but sometimes overlapping ethico-political bases. These bases are not universal or fixed. Different countries have different ethico-political bases, as we will see in Chapter 10 in the case of Scotland. I would expect different religious legacies and cultures (their different cultural structures) also to lead to differences between the UK and the US. I am not sure that purity is such a salient value in the UK as it has been found to be in the US (Koleva et al, 2012). Ethan Nadelmann, the former Director of the US Drug Policy Alliance, once told me that you cannot understand US drug policy without considering the distinctive religious beliefs that the Pilgrim Fathers – radically puritan English Protestants – brought to the continent they colonised.

These bases may also change over time. The relative salience of traditionalist, paternalist, progressive and libertarian values may wax and wane, and new values may emerge. The influence of social progressivism rose in the second half of the 20th century. Movements for women's liberation and racial justice gained influence while class politics and the union movement withered. External contexts will affect how people express their values. The increase in politicians' compassion directed towards people dying with drugs as their numbers have risen is a case in point. It will be examined in more detail in Chapters 10 and 11. Any future applications of the policy constellations approach will have to pay attention to specific geographic, political, socio-economic, cultural and temporal contexts.

To summarise the relationship between these ethico-political bases and previous efforts to understand the moralities that underlie policy positions, Table 6.1 compares these bases with both Haidt et al's 'ideological narratives'

Table 6.1: Comparison of how ethico-political bases relate to ideological narratives (Haidt et al, 2009) and philosophical underpinnings of drug policy (MacCoun and Reuter, 2001)

Ethic-political base	Ideological narrative	Philosophical underpinning of drug policy	Broad policy preference
Compassion	Not considered as a narrative, but protection from harm is highly valued within both the secular liberal and religious left narrative	Not directly considered by Reuter and MacCoun	Compassion can be claimed as a basis for a wide variety of policies
Traditionalism	Social conservatism	Legal moralism	Punitive prohibition and prevention of drug use
Paternalism	No direct parallel narrative, but reflected in the more secular elements of the religious left narrative	Legal paternalism	Mild prohibition, with support for non-controversial forms of harm reduction
Progressive social justice	Secular liberalism	Millian liberalism, with some reservations on Mill	Harm reduction and strictly regulated but legal drug markets
Liberty	Libertarian	Libertarian	Lightly regulated legal drug markets

and MacCoun and Reuter's 'philosophical underpinnings' of drug policy. I borrow the idea of adding a column for the broad policy preferences that are linked to these bases/narratives/underpinnings from Askew and Bone (2019). The table shows that there are some parallels between my findings and previous efforts to classify the underlying normative bases of policy positions. The purpose of identifying these ethico-political bases is to help us explain the outcome of drug policy discussions. The argument of the policy constellations approach is that it is such moralities that attract and repel policy actors towards and away from each other in supporting or opposing specific policy positions. To examine how this works, we can map the connections between these bases and the policy actors and positions which express them; in other words, the policy constellations of the drug policy field. This is done in the next chapter for the UK level of drug policy making.

7

Mapping UK Drug Policy Constellations

This chapter describes and analyses the social network of policy actors and policy positions, as presented in Figure 7.1. In Chapter 4, I explained that policy constellations are fluid sets of policy actors who come together in pursuing shared policy positions, based on common moral commitments and material interests. In Chapter 5, I described the methods of social network analysis that I used to map these connections between policy actors and policy positions. The resulting sociograms are presented in this chapter. They show the clusters in the overall network. Alongside detailed knowledge of the field, including data from policy documents and interviews, such clusters can be identified as the policy constellations which operate in the UK drug policy field.

Some policy constellations form around one ethico-political base in particular. They can collaborate with other constellations with compatible bases but act strongly against constellations with which their ethico-political bases are diametrically opposed. Some constellations are hybrids, bringing together people who may have some different policy preferences but who share enough – including ethico-political bases that are compatible with each other – to collaborate and agree with each other in supporting mutually acceptable policy positions. It is possible to identify even smaller, more tightly bound and connected sets of actors and positions that focus on a particular issue rather than a broader ethico-political base. These smaller constellations are usually found within other constellations but sometimes overlap them.

In UK drug policy, the two most powerful policy constellations are the public health and conservative constellations. These are at the top right and bottom right of Figure 7.1, respectively gravitating towards the ethico-political bases of paternalism and traditionalism. The first brings together medical professionals, academics, politicians and civil servants who base their policy preferences on the desire to prevent drug-related harms by regulating people's behaviours and treating their disorders. The second brings together politicians, ministerial special advisers, agencies of social control and other civil servants who base their preferences on a traditionalist desire to maintain social order, including the defence of traditional moral positions on what it is right to consume. The small C in the title of the conservative constellation is deliberate. Not all of these actors are in the Conservative Party, but they share a preference for the status quo, in line with Schwartz's (1992) basic value of conservation, as well as the British moral foundation of traditionalism (Harper and Rhodes, 2021).

Policy actors can belong to more than one constellation at once. These two constellations overlap in the hybrid, medico-penal constellation. This brings together agencies and individuals who share a concern for the ethico-political base of compassion but have differences in other emphases.

Their preference for traditionalism and paternalism prevents members of this hybrid constellation from endorsing policy positions which are seen as too radical and risky. These include policy proposals which challenge existing social hierarchies in pursuit of social justice or demand more individual and commercial freedom.

These other ethico-political bases are expressed in another cluster of policy actors and positions, which I call the drug policy reform constellation. This is at the left of Figure 7.1. These policy actors want change to current drug laws, including decriminalisation of possession and legalisation of supply. They also support innovative forms of harm reduction, including overdose prevention centres and drug checking services. Within this broad constellation, there are two smaller constellations that are divided by their diverging views on how drug policies should be reformed, as informed by their different ethico-political bases. At the top left of Figure 7.1, influenced by the ethico-political base of progressive social justice, is what I call the social justice constellation. At the bottom left, influenced by the ethico-political base of liberty, is the libertarian policy constellation. This ethico-political difference explains why collaboration between actors in these two wings of the drug policy reform movement is observed as uneasy, sporadic and largely uncoordinated.

Within these larger policy constellations, there are three particularly interesting smaller constellations. One is made up of people and organisations who advocate for recovery. Another is made up of people who hold particularly strongly traditionalist views on drug policy and so oppose both harm reduction measures and drug policy reform. The third micro-level policy constellation involves actors and policy positions that support drug policy reform in pursuit of racial justice. These are described in more detail in Online Appendix 7.1.

This chapter presents the main constellations in more detail, including tables which show a selection of the policy positions and policy actors (organisations and individuals) in these constellations. Note that rows on

Figure 7.1: Sociogram of policy actors (grey) and policy positions (black) in the UK drug policy field (with ethico-political bases in italics)

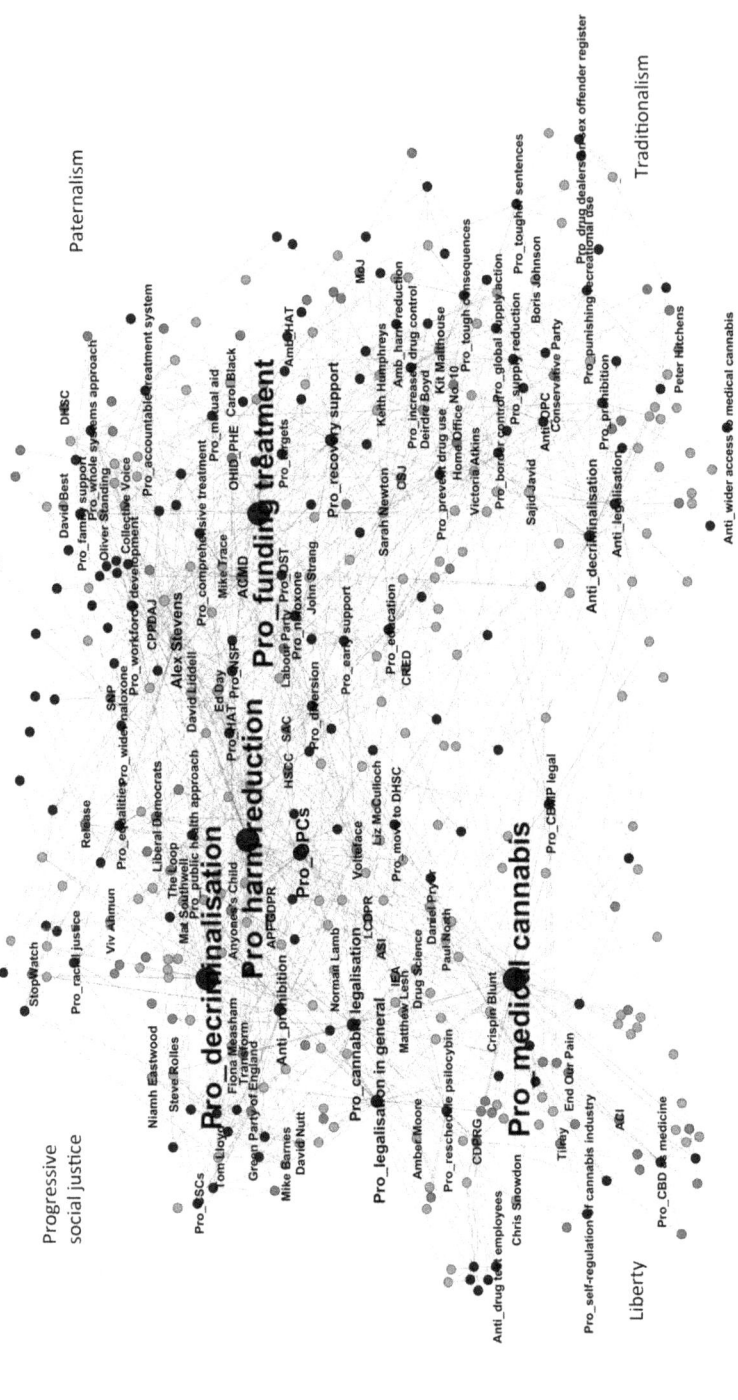

these tables do not link people and positions on these rows directly, but as members of the same constellation.[1] The chapter concludes with a schematic map, in Figure 7.2, of the overlapping and opposing policy constellations in the UK drug policy field.

Reading the map of policy constellations

Figure 7.1 shows the actors and policy positions that I found in the UK drug policy field. It also shows the ethico-political bases of UK drug policy making in relation to the positions and actors which are most influenced by them. Compassion is a shared ethico-political base which is not shown in the sociogram. I placed the four other ethico-political bases where I observed that the preponderance of policy positions was compatible with these bases. For example, supporting harsher punishment is typically associated with traditionalist values, while explicit support of creating greater social equality is a defining feature of progressive social justice. A taste for liberty goes with support for free markets like a horse and carriage. The paternalist positions showed care for people with drug problems but little support for their freedom to choose what to consume.

To make this sociogram, I used the ForceAtlas 2 layout in Gephi. Simply put, this places nodes of the network close together if they share several connections and far apart if they share no or few connections.[2] Policy actors (organisations and individuals) are represented as grey circles. Policy positions are represented as black circles. The size of the circles and their labels reflects the number of coded links between policy positions and the actors who supported them (their degree centrality). In order to make it more legible, the sociograms here exclude nodes which had less than two ties to other nodes. This means that it only shows 404 (80 per cent) of all the nodes, and 1,803 (95 per cent) of all the ties that are in the full analysis of UK-level policy actors. This does not affect the overall layout of the sociogram, which is calculated on the basis of the full UK dataset.

Indicative lists of some of the policy positions and policy actors (organisations and individuals) that I coded in the data can be found in the tables in the sections of this chapter that describe the policy constellations. These sections and tables describe nodes that were categorised into separate clusters ('modules') using the modularity statistic in Gephi. With the resolution parameter set at 1.5, this identified three modules in the data. The reason that there are three constellations despite their being four ethico-political bases is that there are relatively strong connections between the policy actors and positions that are informed by liberty and progressive social justice. Together, they form a broad constellation which supports drug policy reform.

A full list of the organisational policy actors and policy positions that were coded to each of these modules is given in Online Appendix 5.1.

Table 7.1: Selected members of the conservative policy constellation

Favours compassion and traditionalism		
Policy positions	**Policy actors**	
	Organisations	Individuals
Anti_decriminalisation	Centre for Social Justice	Boris Johnson MP
Anti_legalisation	Association of Police and Crime	Deirdre Boyd
Anti_overdose prevention centres	Commissioners	Dominic Raab MP
	Conservative Party	Fleur Anderson MP
Pro_border control	Commission on Race and Ethnic	Iain Duncan Smith MP
Pro_early support	Disparities	Keith Humphreys
Pro_education	Cannabis Skunk Sense	Kit Malthouse MP
Pro_prevent drug use	Department for Education	Peter Hitchens
Pro_prohibition	Home Office	Priti Patel MP
Pro_recovery support	Ministry of Justice	Sajid Javid MP
Pro_residential treatment	National Crime Agency	Theresa May MP
Pro_supply reduction	National Drug Prevention Alliance	Victoria Atkins MP
Pro_tough consequences for drug use	No. 10 Downing Street	
	National Police Chiefs Council	

This appendix also gives a full description of the organisational acronyms and expanded descriptions of the policy positions I coded. I used the module allocations to identify three main policy constellations. These are the conservative, public health and drug policy reform constellations that are shown in Figure 7.2. My identification of other, overlapping constellations is partly informed by looking for different numbers of modules by using different values of the resolution parameter[3] in Gephi, and partly by my qualitative observations of the field. My selection of positions to include in the indicative tables was informed by their ranking for closeness centrality, as well as my ethnographic observations. Closeness centrality is a measure of how well connected a node is to all other nodes in the network. I chose to include those that have these close connections in Tables 7.1, 7.2 and 7.3, showing members of each of the three main constellations.

There were some policy positions that are so commonly shared by policy actors that they add little information, because nearly all the policy actors expressed support for them. These included being in favour of drug treatment and of more research being carried out. These nodes were removed from the data before laying out the sociogram in order to show more clearly the distance between policy constellations. This frequent commonality supports the idea that both compassion and the pursuit of knowledge are common moral positions that are often shared by people who differ from each other on other ethico-political bases.

Placing the names of all the actors and positions on this sociogram would be overwhelming. I have selected some of them to indicate the types of

Table 7.2: Selected members of the public health policy constellation

Favours compassion and paternalism		
Policy positions	**Policy actors**	
	Organisations	Individuals
Anti_schedule 4 cannabis	Adfam	Alex Stevens
Pro_accountable treatment system	Advisory Council on the Misuse of Drugs	Dame Carol Black
		David Best
Pro comprehensive treatment	Association of Directors of Public Health	David Liddell
Pro_continuity of care		Diana Johnson MP
Pro_employment support	Change Grow Live	Ed Day
Pro_family support	Collective Voice	Lord Kamlesh Patel
Pro_funding treatment	Commons Health and Social Care Committee	Mike Trace
Pro_mutual aid		Oliver Standing
Pro_naloxone	Cross-Party Group on Drugs, Alcohol and Justice	Sir John Strang
Pro_needle exchange		
Pro_opioid substitution treatment	Department of Health and Social Care	
Pro_schedule 4 cannabis	Forward Trust	
Pro_targeted law enforcement	Joint Combating Drugs Unit	
Pro_workforce development	Multiple Sclerosis Society	
	National Addiction Centre	
	NHS addiction providers	
	Office for Health Improvement and Disparities	

actors and positions which are found in different areas and constellations in the sociogram. Again, this selection is informed by closeness centrality and my ethnography. I decided not to include full lists of individual policy actors in order to protect the anonymity of those who would not want to be named. The people named in Figure 7.1 and in Tables 7.1, 7.2 and 7.3 either gave me their consent to be named in this book or have put their names into the public domain by their public statements and media appearances on drug and other policies.

The analysis placed some positions which are directly opposed to each other in the same module, suggesting they are present in the same policy constellations. For example, the social network analysis (SNA) module that I am using as the basis for the public health policy constellation contains support of placing cannabis-based medicines in both schedule 2 and 4 of the Misuse of Drugs Regulations, in line with both the policy constellations approach and the advocacy coalition framework, that people who share underlying normative commitments can work together even if specific policy preferences may differ. This is because it is the underlying base, not the superficial policy, which motivates policy action. The health professionals and experts who believe in different ways of regulating cannabis as a medicine

Table 7.3: Selected members of the drug policy reform constellation

Favours compassion, progressive social justice and liberty		
Policy positions	**Policy actors**	
	Organisations	Individuals
Shared positions		
Anti_prohibition	APPG on Drug Policy Reform	David Nutt
Pro_cannabis legalisation	Commons Scottish Affairs	Harry Sumnall
Pro_decriminalisation	Committee	Mike Barnes
Pro_drug checking	Drug Science	Norman Lamb
Pro_harm reduction	Faculty of Public Health	MP
Pro_legalisation in general	Liberal Democrats	
Pro_medical cannabis	Scottish National Party	
Pro_overdose prevention centres	The Loop	
	Volteface	
Favour progressive social justice		
Amb_legalisation in general	Cranstoun	Fiona Measham
Pro_equalities	Green Party	Jeff Smith MP
Pro_home growing cannabis	Labour Campaign for Drug Policy	Mat Southwell
Pro_public health approach	Reform	Niamh
Pro_racial justice	Release	Eastwood
Pro_reform stop and search	StopWatch	Rebekah Delsol
Pro_strict controls on legal	Transform	Steve Rolles
cannabis sale		Viv Ahmun
Favour liberty		
Amb_decriminalisation	Adam Smith Institute	Amber Moore
Anti_home growing cannabis	Association for the Cannabinoid	Chris Snowdon
Pro_free markets	Industry	Crispin Blunt
Pro_reschedule psilocybin	Centre for Medical Cannabis	MP
Pro_self regulation of cannabis	Conservative Drug Policy Reform	Daniel Pryor
industry	Group	Matthew Lesh
	End Our Pain	Paul North
	HAVN Life	Steve Moore
	Institute of Economic Affairs	
	Tilray	

have more in common with each other than with both conservatives who believe that cannabis should not be used as a medicine and so should be in schedule 1 and with drug policy reformers who believe it should be legalised and so not covered by any schedule.

The conservative constellation

This constellation includes government departments and politicians who played important roles in recent policy making. They are linked to policy positions that include opposition to drug decriminalisation and legalisation. The policies they supported included drug education and prevention, using the criminal justice system to cut drug supply, and 'tougher consequences' for people who use illicit drugs. This constellation includes Boris Johnson, who was Prime Minster from 2019 to 2022, his drugs minister Kit Malthouse, Home Secretary Priti Patel and Secretary of Health and Social Care Sajid Javid.

Boris Johnson was a particularly interesting case. Despite having admitted to past use of cocaine and cannabis (Walker, 2021), he appeared very keen to ramp up punishment and deterrence regarding recreational drug use. During his premiership, there was much talk of drug problems being caused by middle-class drug users. There was also frequent media and political discourse on the problems caused by county lines drug supply, especially child exploitation. These two issues were often conflated, including in the parliamentary debates I analysed, as if middle-class cocaine use was a direct cause of county lines drug dealing. This was despite the fact that the official national assessment showed that county lines were largely supplying crack and heroin to dependent users in provincial towns, not to high-flying cocaine users in metropolitan cities (NCLCC, 2021). As Jack Spicer (2020) has argued, there is a danger that the blaming of county lines for violence and exploitation in the drug trade diverts attention from other causes of these harms.

The discursive tropes that linked the most harmful form of drug dealing to widespread demand for controlled drugs were used by several people to call for tougher law enforcement against drug offenders. These included Boris Johnson, Priti Patel, Kit Malthouse and several other MPs. Sajid Javid was linked to these policy actors by his signing up to the 2021 drug strategy document and being a joint author of its ministerial foreword. He has not often spoken publicly about drugs but was described by an interviewee as "quietly influential" on the 2021 drug strategy, a case to which we will return in Chapter 11.

This conservative policy constellation includes organisations that are charged with enforcing drug laws and cutting drug supply, such as the National Police Chiefs Council and the National Crime Agency. It also includes the Centre for Social Justice (CSJ) and some people who have worked both for this think tank and as special advisers to ministers in the Conservative government. The CSJ was mentioned by several interviewees when they discussed what one of them called the "lurch to recovery". They attributed the shift of drug policy priorities that occurred in 2010, when the Conservative Party entered power, to the beliefs of Iain Duncan Smith and others who circulated around the think tank he founded, including Deirdre Boyd. Duncan Smith was described by another, anonymous interviewee as "a huge driver of this agenda since before the 2010 election". He and various CSJ reports advocated the replacement of opioid substitution treatment with support for abstinence-based recovery services. That anonymous interviewee also described Dominic Raab (Minister of Justice under Boris Johnson and Rishi Sunak) as a supporter of the recovery agenda.

Being in favour of providing support to recovery appears in the same policy constellation as support for preventing drug use and punishing people who break drug laws. Each of these positions is compatible with traditionalist beliefs in abstinent purity, social conformity and respect for authority. They are in the sector of Schwartz's (1992) circumplex that favours conservation over innovation, as well as being compatible with Haidt et al's (2009) ideological narrative of social conservatism.

The public health constellation

At the top right of the sociogram are individuals, organisations and policy positions that support caring for people who use drugs but without giving them more freedom to use; in other words, a paternalist approach. This includes the Office for Health Improvement and Disparities (OHID, formerly known as Public Health England, or PHE). This is the body which funds drug treatment services in England. In the period analysed, OHID/PHE supported policy positions which are common among the policy actors that are clustered in this part of the network, which include that drug treatment funding should be increased, that there should be a comprehensive system of treatment, and that the drug treatment workforce should be developed.

Many of the policy actors allocated to this constellation, including Dame Carol Black, also supported the application of paternalism to treatment agencies as well as people who use drugs. The revival of central control of the drug treatment system was built on support for more transparency and accountability, and it included the establishment of the Joint Combating Drugs Unit, which plays the treatment coordination role that used to be filled by the National Treatment Agency until it was disbanded in 2013.

Not all the people who supported more funding for a comprehensive treatment system supported such centralism. Indeed, the government's position prior to 2021 was that local authorities were responsible for how they spent the public health grant in delivering drug treatment services. This changed after the Black review found major shortcomings in the treatment system. Nevertheless, Kit Malthouse was still proclaiming in December 2021 that it would be down to local agencies to decide how they spent the money (Hansard, 2021e). The experiences of treatment agencies, as far as I have been told, have been rather different, with some telling me that they do not feel free to spend the money according to their own professional judgement; they have to follow central guidance. Carol Black told me that firm central guidance was necessary to achieve her goal of creating a comprehensive treatment system. In her view, this would not happen if treatment agencies were left to their own devices.

This policy constellation also includes several drug treatment providers and their representative bodies, Collective Voice and the NHS Addiction Providers Alliance. It is unsurprising that these are the organisations who are most closely connected to the idea that more money should be spent on drug treatment services.

This is also the policy constellation into which my coding and the SNA placed me. I was rather surprised by this, as I spend more time working with drug policy reform organisations than with OHID. I have, however, worked for a long time with some of the treatment agencies listed in this policy constellation and recently started a research project on police drug diversion schemes in which OHID is a partner. I am also working on a research project on interventions for prison leavers for the Ministry of Justice. Many policy actors have connections that spread across policy constellations. I am one of them, and perhaps I am more of a paternalist than I previously thought. The caution and ambivalence I have sometimes expressed about the risks of drug legalisation may make me a suitable member of the more paternalist public health constellation.

The drug policy reform constellation

This constellation contains a range of policy actors and positions that link to the ideas that drug possession should be decriminalised, that drug supply should be legalised, that cannabis should be available for medical use, and that a wider range of harm reduction services – including overdose prevention centres and drug checking – should be provided. This constellation could also be called the drug policy reform movement, as long as it is recognised that 'social movements are not themselves formal organizations or political parties, but are looser networks of individuals and groups that may embrace a number of such organizations' (Scott and Marshall, 2009).

Like other social movements, and unlike coalitions in the advocacy coalition framework (Jenkins-Smith et al, 2018), this policy constellation is internally split on basic values, in this case between libertarians and social justice progressives. This makes it difficult to achieve coordination across the whole constellation. When I tweeted about this difficulty after presenting a preliminary version of Figure 7.1, Steve Rolles (2022) replied by saying 'I try to pragmatically straddle both worlds, but it's not easy!' He illustrated his tweet with a picture of a man suspending himself by doing the splits between two racing lorries. This was an apt visual metaphor for the attempt to create collaboration between policy actors that do not share the same ethico-political base and who have little in the way of mutual history or institutional framework to keep them together, even if they support some of the same policy positions.

The progressive social justice constellation

Policy actors that are allotted to this constellation include the two most prominent NGOs that advocate directly for drug policy reform: Release and Transform. I found references to the human rights of people who use drugs and other marginalised communities in documents published by both organisations. This constellation also includes the political parties that are most liberal on drug policy, including the Liberal Democrats and the Green Party. Senior staff of Release and Transform, Niamh Eastwood and Steve Rolles, collaborated with the Liberal Democrats in producing a report on how to legalise cannabis, along with the chair of the charity Drug Science, Professor David Nutt, former Chief Constables Tom Lloyd and Mike Barton, and Professor Fiona Measham, who runs a harm reduction charity called The Loop, which provides drug checking (Rolles et al, 2016).

When I interviewed Rolles, he said there was "cross-fertilisation" between his own organisation, Transform and others, including Release, the International Drug Policy Consortium and the Beckley Foundation. These organisations, he told me, "overlap". He even used the word "constellation" to describe them. Each of them specialises. Rolles mentioned that Transform focuses on drug regulation, while Release provides legal services. Both organisations also collaborate with individuals and organisations who campaign for racial justice. This includes Rebekah Delsol, one of the founders of StopWatch, which campaigns for change to the disproportionate policing of people who are racialised as Black. It also includes Viv Ahmun, who runs the Blacksox campaign for Black leadership in social justice issues and has been working with Transform.

The report on which Rolles and his co-authors worked was summarised on a Liberal Democrat campaign web page headed 'Let's legalise and regulate cannabis'.

> Both Labour and Conservative Governments over decades have been driven by fear rather than evidence. They have failed to tackle the social and medical problems that misuse of drugs can cause to individuals and their communities. Liberal Democrats would introduce limits on the potency levels and permit cannabis to be sold through licensed outlets to adults over the age of 18. (Liberal Democrats, n.d.)

The form of cannabis legalisation that is advocated in this snippet of the policy discourse reflects something interesting about the policy positions held by some members of the drug policy reform constellation. Those who are in favour of progressive social justice do not usually advocate a fully liberalised market in which self-regulating reigns. Rather, they are preparing for markets in which drugs are regulated in ways other than by prohibition.

Policy positions that were coded and then grouped by SNA into this area of the sociogram include that, once cannabis is legalised, there should be limits on potency, place and age of sale and purchase. They also included controls on marketing, advertising, packaging and price. Support for home cultivation and distribution through cannabis social clubs was also placed in this upper left part of the sociogram. There is a residual paternalism here. Vying with the belief that people should be free to consume what they want are the ideas that state regulation is necessary to reduce harms and that experts in the field are best placed to decide what those regulations should be.

Policy action in this corner of the sociogram is also motivated by the idea that drug policy should achieve social justice. My former employer Cranstoun is the only drug treatment provider to be allocated to the drug policy reform constellation (most of the others are to be found in the more paternalist public health constellation). It specifically brands itself as a social justice organisation. It is more radical in its support for enhanced harm reduction measures, including overdose prevention centres. It therefore aligns more closely with organisations like Release, whose staff see drug policy reform as a means of achieving social justice for disadvantaged groups, including people who use drugs, as well as people who are racialised as Black.

The libertarian constellation

In the bottom left of the sociogram in Figure 7.1, there are four distinct but compatible types of policy actor. There are bodies that have been set up to represent the interests of patients who want to be free to use cannabis for medical benefits, such as the United Patients Alliance and End Our Pain. There are two charities – the Beckley Foundation and Drug Science – that have supported research on the medical use of cannabis and psilocybin. There are think tanks that support greater liberalisation of drug markets, like the Institute of Economic Affairs (IEA), the Adam Smith Institute (ASI), the Centre for Medical Cannabis, and the Association for the Cannabis Industry. And there are companies that wish to produce and sell drugs that are currently controlled, including cannabinoids and psilocybin.

The oldest think tank in this space is the IEA, founded in 1955, which presents itself as 'the UK's original free-market think-tank' (IEA, 2022, np). When I interviewed its Head of Lifestyle Economics, Chris Snowdon, he told me about a range of policy positions which consistently expressed the belief that individuals and markets should be free to run themselves. The IEA is joined in its support for drug legalisation by its younger counterpart, the ASI. I was introduced to staff of both these think tanks and Volteface at an event hosted by the Conservative Party Drug Policy Reform Group, which also supports freer markets for cannabis and psilocybin.

In addition to support for the general freedom to benefit from drugs, support for the use of currently controlled drugs as medicines is a common aim for these policy actors, although there are differences between them in which drugs they are interested in, and even which parts of these drugs. Self-organisations of patients tend to demand the right to grow and use the whole cannabis plant. Industry bodies tend to be wary of home growing and more keen to free up markets for commercially produced plant extracts, such as delta-9 tetrahydrocannabinol (THC), cannabidiol (CBD) and psilocybin.

The occasional overlap of these liberty-loving policy actors with progressive support of enhanced harm reduction services was another interesting aspect of the analysis. Crispin Blunt, the MP who set up the Conservative Drug Policy Reform Group, told me he supported the provision of overdose prevention centres. Daniel Pryor of the ASI and Matthew Lesh of the IEA shared this position. The ASI published a report calling for such services to be opened (Bartle, 2019), as did Volteface (McCulloch, 2017). This suggests that even the more free market-oriented members of the drug policy reform constellation are not devoid of compassion for people at risk of dying with drugs. It is an expression of compassion that combines with an anti-authoritarian belief that people deserve this compassion even if they exert personal freedom in their choice of what to consume.

When Liz Truss became Prime Minister in September 2022, she took with her some of the ideas she shared with free market think tanks. She had previously contributed a clarion critique of 'the nanny state' to a collection of essays *On Social Freedom* (Lowe, 2019). Her libertarian thoughts were published by a short-lived think tank called FREER, which was hosted at the IEA.[4] The future Prime Minister wrote, 'neo-puritanism is in danger of holding us back. Instead of wagging a finger at people enjoying themselves and doing things differently, we should celebrate the potential of our freedom and individual choices'. It would have been very interesting to see where she might have taken drug policy, especially as she appointed Suella Braverman as Home Secretary. Truss' desire to celebrate people's individual choices would have clashed with Braverman's more traditionalist conservatism. Problems in managing both fiscal policy and the Conservative Party meant that Truss' time in Number 10 was cut short. The potential experiment in hybrid libertarian/traditionalist drug policy making never got off the ground, another example of how important developments in other policy fields are in causing stability and change in drug policy.

The hybrid medico-penal constellation

While the drug policy reform constellation is internally divided, there is interesting and influential collaboration between the conservative and public health constellations. This collaboration operates through what I call the hybrid medico-penal constellation. This continues the British tradition of combining medical and penal control of people who use drugs, which I described in Chapter 2, leaning heavily on Virginia Berridge's (2013) concept of the hybrid medico-penal framework.

The hybrid medico-penal constellation consists of some, but not all, of the actors and policy positions that form the public health and conservative policy constellations. More specifically, it contains those that fall in the overlap between traditionalist social control and paternalist health protection. The fundamental compatibility of these ethico-political bases was discussed in Chapter 6. It expresses itself in the endorsement of continuing criminalisation and support for cutting drug supply, for preventing drug use through education and early support, and for recovery services. These positions are endorsed by members of both the conservative and public health constellations. Their shared positions provide a basis for collaboration that enables policy actors to overcome less fundamental differences about the scale of punishment or types of treatment that are appropriate. In an interview, Steve Moore told me about the shared view "across Whitehall" (so including both the Home Office and the Department of Health) that the aim of government policy is generally "to reduce the consumption of temptation goods", like tobacco, alcohol and controlled drugs.

Institutional arrangements, as well as the overlapping ethico-political bases of the medico-penal constellation, support the ongoing collaboration between its two components. The long-institutionalised relationships of these policy actors structure the collaboration between them. The official home of the public health policy constellation is OHID, which is part of the Department of Health and Social Care. Health's long Whitehall dance with the Home Office over who will control drug policy has led to a position of stasis. The Home Office takes the lead but has to consult with public health officials and experts (for example, in the Advisory Council on the Misuse of Drugs) in the making of drug policy. Even if they did not want to, they would have to cooperate. There is no such institutional framework to counteract the forces of moral repulsion that hamper collaboration across the drug policy reform constellation.

The missing voice of people who use drugs

In analysing UK drug policy constellations, I looked hard for instances of influence by the people who are most directly affected: people who use drugs. These people have a rich variety of views and experiences to contribute to the debate (Askew, Griffiths and Bone, 2022). But this influence, if it even exists, was virtually invisible at UK level in the period I observed. It was more evident in Scotland, as will be discussed in Chapter 10. South of the border, we do see occasional glimpses of people who are in recovery from problematic drug use, as in Carol Black's consultations in the run-up to the 2021 drug strategy (see Chapter 11). But they tend to be people who represent a certain part of the drug policy circumplex.

An example is Mark Johnson, author of *Wasted* (Johnson, 2007) and founder of the charity User Voice (with which I am currently working on an evaluation of police drug diversion schemes). Johnson always presents a persuasive viewpoint when invited to give evidence to parliamentary and other committees. As in his book, he shows how it is possible for people to live through trauma, drug use, crime and imprisonment and to rebuild their lives through abstinence and recovery. Along with other advocates of recovery, he tends to focus on the benefits of mutual aid by peers and not on the role of opiate agonist therapy in keeping people alive until they can put drug use behind them. This experience is real, valid and informative, but it is only one aspect of the range of experiences and views of people who use drugs. I did not find representatives of other ways of living with drugs in influential parts of the UK drug policy field. Nobody who is avowedly prescribed an opioid maintenance prescription was, for example, referred to by my interviewees as an influential policy actor.

This is not because there is no one who can represent this viewpoint. When I interviewed the drug user activist Mat Southwell, he told me that the involvement of people who use drugs has made more of an impression at international than UK level. When I asked him what role people who use drugs should have in drug policy, he said:

> 'I think we should be very centrally involved. I think the sophistication of the debate is the UN – and the EU as well – to actually have a dialogue that includes those key populations affected by the HIV response and by drug policy, I think that's been a huge success. I think it's one of the reasons the UN's policies are starting to shift so dramatically. The fact that they embedded the responsibility to talk to the populations that are affected into their policies. It just had this incredible sensitising effect over time. When you have to work with the people that you're making policy for, you can't help but be influenced. ... This creates space for the hard, technical people to come in with the policies.'

He contrasted this to the UK, where "the drug user movement got taken down in the 1999 to 2004 period ... that had a really detrimental effect". He attributed some of the flaws in the current treatment system, as documented in the Black (2020b) report, to the absence of a strong representative voice for people who use drugs.

Conclusion: a map for explaining policy outcomes

To conclude this presentation of policy constellations in the UK drug policy field, Figure 7.2 presents a constellation map which is laid over the sociogram in Figure 7.1. This shows some of the policy constellations to be found there. The three main constellations are shaded in grey. As stated in Chapter 4, policy constellations can overlap and also operate at different levels, and so can be nested within each other. Here, the dotted lines are drawn around smaller constellations of actors. These smaller constellations were identified by a combination of SNA, using different parameters for the modularity statistic, and my observations of actors and ideas in the field. So in addition to the three main constellations, there are three smaller constellations whose labels are in italics in Figure 7.2.

The borders drawn in Figure 7.2 should not be seen as hard dividing lines. There are many ties between policy actors and positions that cross these borders. Constellations overlap because actors and positions can be connected to more than one of them. Interviewees pointed out that there is more overlap between competing groups in drug policy than is presented in media depictions of a highly polarised debate with just two camps. The need to look at constellations of attraction and repulsion – these 'networks of sympathies' – rather than simple dividing lines, is one of the reasons I developed the policy constellations approach. I argue that drawing the connections between policy actors and the positions they hold helps us understand how policy is made.

Figure 7.2: Sociogram of the UK drug policy field showing overlapping policy constellations

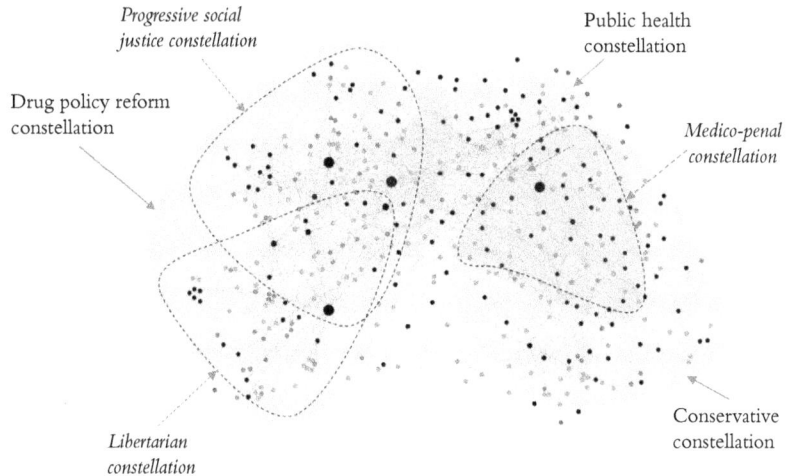

The general outline of the constellation map in Figure 7.2 mirrors the modified circumplex of ethico-political bases in Figure 6.1. The gap between the drug policy reform and conservative constellations is created by the incompatibility of traditionalism with progressive social justice and its difficult relationship with liberty. There are some nodes in the unshaded gap between these constellations, but the central node in this gap represents support for the partial legalisation of cannabis-based medical products that happened in 2018. As I will explain in Chapter 9, this was a forced compromise between traditionalists and libertarians, which is why I have placed it outside both the drug policy reform and conservative policy constellations.

My mapping of the UK drug policy field supports the idea that drug policy making is partly influenced by differences in people's ethico-political bases. Figures 7.1 and 7.2 show a coherent relationship between constellations of policy actors and their ethico-political bases. As expected in the policy constellations approach, policy actors tend to cluster together in constellations around policy ideas that share similar moralities. In order to use these constellations in explaining the outcomes of drug policy discussions, we also need to look at how power operates through them. I do this in Chapter 8.

8

Power in UK Drug Policy Constellations

The way that power operates in the drug policy field, as in others, is through networks (Heclo, 1978; Rhodes, 1990). I have called these networks constellations because they are imbued with the preferences and powers that their members bring. The socially structured positions of these policy actors combine with their culturally structured policy preferences to produce the outcomes of policy debates. This is not just the result of a cumulation of individual choices. It emerges from the collective combinations of people, policy positions and the forms of power they bring to the field.

So if we want to understand the outcomes of policy discussions, we need to understand the forms of power that policy constellations bring together. In this field, this is not usually done through coercive power. The government does not need to threaten its drug policy opponents with force to get its policies through, as it has with some previous policy problems. UK examples include the sovereignty of the Falklands and the closure of coal mines in the 1980s, when military or police force was used to win back territory or to limit the effects of industrial action (Reiner, 1985; Hastings and Jenkins, 2010). There are occasional instances where the government has used legal power, such as the 2017 legal case over the applicability of the Psychoactive Substances Act to nitrous oxide (Nutt, 2020). In this case, the Crown Prosecution Service used the Court of Appeal to overturn the advice of the Advisory Council on the Misuse of Drugs (ACMD) that the Act did not apply to laughing gas. This was an example of the relatively rare application of legal power. More commonly, the institutional power of policy actors close to government is enough to ensure that policy continues to meet their preferences without the need for military, paramilitary or legal action.

While such political power may be dominant in maintaining the overall shape of UK drug policy (for example, the ongoing existence of the Misuse of Drugs Act 1971 as the main legal framework), the precise shape of these policy decisions is affected by forms of social power. As discussed in Chapter 3, these include media, economic, epistemic and affective power. These forms of power are most effective when they are used simultaneously by policy actors who are skilled in what I call savvy social power.

This chapter will examine each of these forms of power in turn and will describe the mechanisms that are used to make them work. The chapter will explore two important and related aspects of the operation of institutional power through policy constellations. The first is how institutional power is reserved for insiders in the most influential policy constellations. The second is how institutional power flows through the politics of familiarity. The different distributions of political parties across the drug policy field are discussed in Online Appendix 8.1. This shows that both Labour and Conservative politicians can be found in multiple constellations. The left–right divide in party politics is not simply mirrored in the drug policy field.

This chapter examines some forms of social power that members of policy constellations bring to the policy-making process. I will use the concept of savvy social power to help explain how some policy actors have been able to achieve desired policy changes where others have failed.

Policy constellations and institutional power

Institutional power accrues to actors who occupy positions in official hierarchies that enable them to decide on other people's choices. These positions are not just set by official job titles and ranks. They are created by the network of connections that a policy actor has with other policy actors (individuals and organisations); in other words, their position in policy constellations. I have stated that it is members of the hybrid medico-penal constellation that enjoy the highest levels of institutional power. Here I explain how this power comes not only from their official positions but from the network of connections in policy constellations.

Insiders and outsiders in the institutional power game

A simplistic view of policy making would be that it is elected ministers alone who have the power to decide. When I put this view to the Scottish drugs minister, she laughed.

> 'I often hear people talking about ministers in power [ha ha]. And we do have power. It's the job of ministers to make decisions ... We will have more power and influence than many. But no minister operates in isolation within government. And actually part of my job is to embrace that. ... It is much more of a collective endeavour.' (Angela Constance)

To try and understand this collective endeavour, I asked all my interviewees to say which people and organisations tended to be most influential on drug policy decisions. There was a clear divide between the responses of policy actors who were inside or outside government circles in terms of who they saw as being influential. People who were close to the process, who worked for government agencies or departments, tended to mention other government departments or civil servants. For example, when discussing the 2021 UK drug strategy, two particular civil servants were mentioned as playing important roles; one from the Department of Health and Social Care and one from the Department for Work and Pensions. Neither of these individual policy actors was mentioned by any of the interviewees who were not themselves in a government role. They were clearly influential within the process but invisible to people outside it.

Interviewees who were employed outside government tended to name other non-governmental organisations as influential, in addition to institutions of government. These included the Home Office, Number 10, and Public Health England/Office for Health Improvement and Disparities. For Scotland, these included the Scottish government and "the Crown" (meaning the office of the Lord Advocate), as well as the UK Home Office. They were less likely to give the actual names of individuals other than high-profile politicians.

The exception to this trend came from people who are employed outside government but who have spent a lot of time working inside it, like Mike Trace, John Strang, Steve Moore and Carol Black. They were able to name particularly influential individuals within government. And these connections were reciprocated. Trace, Strang and Black were named by government-employed interviewees as being among the "go-to people when we want to get in contact with the field", along with representative organisations like the NHS Addiction Providers Alliance and Collective Voice (which represents large third-sector drug treatment providers).

Actors who spent time in government departments did not mention members of the drug policy reform constellation as having influential connections. The divide between people within and without government is permeable, but selectively so. The lack of reciprocation in the connections between people who are outside and inside the policy process reflects one of the ways networks can amplify rather than dissipate asymmetries in power (Faul, 2016). This is reinforced by the power of personal connections.

The politics of familiarity

Throughout my research for this book, I came across repeated examples of how important personal familiarity is in building the connections through which policy is made. I started my interviews by asking people a gentle question about how they got into working on drug policy. This produced accounts of the building of personal connections which often spanned long careers. Carol Black reported positive personal relationships with senior ministers going back to Alan Johnson, who was Secretary of State for Health and then Home Secretary under the New Labour government of the 2000s. She was selected by Sajid Javid (when he was Conservative Home Secretary) to review drugs policy after she had done a similar review of employment policy for David Cameron when he was Prime Minister. This request, she told me, came "through DWP [Department of Work and Pensions], through Iain Duncan Smith [the DWP's then Secretary of State]". It followed her work on two previous DWP reports during her time as its National Director for Health and Work. She also had good working relations with Priti Patel and Matt Hancock during their time as Home Secretary and Secretary of State for Health and Social Care. Dame Carol was evidently a well-known and trusted figure in Whitehall.

These processes of familiarity work across policy constellations but were most influential on policy when they brought people into the medico-penal constellation. Steve Moore was able to discuss his ideas on cannabis legalisation with Home Secretary Amber Rudd. "Personal connections matter", he told me, "you can't really move anything forward without that". The medical professionals I interviewed also knew each other of old. John Strang and Ed Day, in particular, described repeatedly serving on government advisory panels. Kit Malthouse, drugs minister at the time of the 2021 drug strategy, was a long-time ally and adjutant to the then Prime Minister, having worked with Boris Johnson during his time as Mayor of London. This relationship eased the path for Malthouse from local government to being the minister responsible for UK drug policy.

I also asked my interviewees how networks of policy actors form. Their answers fitted with my previous observation that people come together through informal social networks of mutual affection, trust and esteem (Stevens, 2021). Sociability is a key element of this process. One interviewee told me about how "the Westminster bubble" works, with a particular focus on how people become insiders with Conservative ministers.

> 'Basically, it's just drinks, drinks, drinks ... It's constant nonsense events that they might go to and do more drinks and do more networking. But they build up a phone book of super influential contacts and people that will have worked in government. And then they fill positions ... People go in there, get the experience to get the contact books, and then they get jobs.'

There are obvious advantages to this way of working. Operating through networks of personal contacts is easier and less bureaucratic than having to advertise posts in accordance with equal opportunities policies. That makes these processes quicker and less costly than they might otherwise be. It also makes things more pleasant for the people involved, who form relations of mutual trust and affection. Through these relations, we gain confidence that the work will be done in a way that we are happy with. There are also opportunities for the sharing of mutually beneficial information and favours. This kind of familiarity helped me in my work, including the writing of this book. I was able to do favours for people, like helping with draft texts or making personal introductions, that meant I could ask for reciprocal favours in return. This is one of the ways that the politics of familiarity reinforce the material interests of some policy actors, by sharing opportunities that are often hoarded within closed social networks (Tilly, 2003).

There are also obvious downsides to sharing out institutional power through the cultivation of personal relationships. One is the ongoing exclusion of new voices from drug policy debates. If these discussions are confined to a relatively closed circle of "the same old faces", then it is less likely that new ideas will be generated and discussed. Chris Snowdon described how "you speak to the usual suspects, and they give you the usual lines". This chimes with previous researchers' warnings of the stultifying, narrowing effect of excluding alternative viewpoints (Oliver and Faul, 2018). It also has the effect of entrenching the inequalities that equal opportunities policies were invented to address. Familiarity often forms along axes of class, gender and race. Unequal access to the forms of social capital – education, shared experiences, familiar accents and common tastes – that build familiarity and esteem continues to reproduce political and economic inequality (Bourdieu, 1984; Savage et al, 2013; Tyler, 2020).

The politics of familiarity rests on and reproduces the underlying social and cultural structures that produce such inequalities. Social positions – like class, race and gender – influence who gets accepted into these 'networks of sympathies'. Acceptance reinforces the ability to influence which ideas and people will be included in the most powerful constellations. So these institutional processes reproduce the social and cultural structures of the drug policy field.

Forms of social power in drug policy constellations

Primed as I was by theoretical ideas on social power, I also observed other ways that actors worked in concert with others to achieve desired policy outcomes. This includes use of the media, money, knowledge and emotions. The most influential policy actors were able to combine these forms of power in deploying what I call savvy social power.

Media power: the unequal ability to set the agenda

The media of newspapers, radio, television and online communication transmit information about drugs to the public. They also influence drug policy outcomes by creating particular perceptions of what the public knows and wants through different framings of policy problems and solutions (Manning, 2016; Sumnall et al, 2023). I discuss the peculiar role of political polling in this process in Online Appendix 8.2. Media articles, as well as political polls, play a role in constructing perceptions of what Kingdon (2013, p 162) calls the 'national mood'. Media selection and processing of information support modes of thinking about policies that reproduce existing asymmetries in power (Thompson, 1990; Habermas, 2006; Stanley, 2015).

The social structures of class and media ownership affect who can best use these forms of social power. The personal connections that policy actors have created with journalists, from school ties onwards, are affected by our class positions. Journalism is one of the least equal careers in terms of the social background of its practitioners. A report for the National Council for the Training of Journalists found that '80 per cent of journalists had a parent in one of the three highest occupational groups, compared to 42 per cent of all UK workers' (Spilsbury, 2022, p 7). This means that the social connections that lead to media influence are also unequally distributed.

The lopsidedness of the journalistic profession is compounded by the concentration of media ownership (Chomsky and Herman, 1988). The owners of newspapers, broadcasters and websites influence policy indirectly through the choices they make about whom to employ as editors and content creators. These are the people who then decide which policy actors and positions will be broadcast. For example, the relatively small constellation of strongly traditionalist prohibitionists may be, in the words of Steve Rolles, a "fading force". But it is still present in the media. The avowedly puritan journalist Peter Hitchens is still invited to give his view that illicit drug use is morally wrong and inherently dangerous. And it is noticeable that these invitations now seem to come more frequently from particular outlets, like GB News and the *Mail on Sunday*. Both outlets are owned by wealthy individuals who support a range of socially conservative positions.

The *Daily Mail* (owned largely by Viscount Rothermere) and the *Daily Telegraph* (owned jointly by the Barclay brothers until Sir David Barclay's death in 2021) were mentioned by several interviewees as the most influential newspapers in the drug policy debate. *The Times* and *The Guardian* were also mentioned as being particularly useful for influencing policy actors rather than the general public. When the government wanted to steer the media's reception of the 2021 drug strategy, it did so by pre-releasing some of the more punitive elements of the strategy to *The Times'* sister paper in the Murdoch stable, *The Sun*, under the hyperbolically tough headline, 'DRUG

CRACKDOWN. Boris unleashes all-out war on drugs to clean up Britain's crime-plagued streets' (Wooding, 2021). It was this toughness that other newspapers and TV stations picked up on in reporting the strategy, rather than the new spending for drug treatment that is discussed in Chapter 11. Despite the decline in circulation of the printed press as readers turn to the web, these newspapers still retain influence on the agenda and so on the content and outcomes of policy debates.

Economic power: money talks

Organisations that hope to influence policy need money to fund their efforts. Steve Moore, former adviser to David Cameron, told me that "money means endurance. What money does is pay people to stick at it". The source of these funds is a controversial issue. There are accusations – from all three sides of the debate between conservatives, reformers and public health professionals – of inappropriate influence from wealthy donors. The focus of attack from conservatives is George Soros, the financier and philanthropist whose money funds the Open Society Foundation (OSF). Several of the organisations in the progressive part of the drug policy reform constellation have received funding from OSF.[1] Public health actors tended to think it problematic that much of the funding for the legalisation of cannabis and psilocybin has come from companies that hope to profit from these markets becoming legal.

One such company was Tenacious Labs. Its director was quoted by Sky News as saying that there are three routes to influencing policy. The first is campaigning to build 'popular acclaim' for a cause. The second is traditional lobbying by using personal connections with policy makers. The third is to fund a parliamentary group (Rayner, 2023). Tenacious Labs provided the secretariat of the All-Party Parliamentary Group on cannabidiol. This group has close links with the Conservative Drug Policy Reform Group (CDPRG). Both groups are chaired by the same MP, Crispin Blunt. It was at a meeting of CDPRG that I met an executive of Tenacious Labs. He told me that his favoured model for regulating cannabis was provided by the current regulation of alcohol, as this is the closest to self-regulation by the industry.

Money creates the ability to employ skilled consultants and to host events at which "drinks, drinks, drinks" are provided to ease the creation of influential connections. This can lead to a state of what Steve Rolles called "corporate capture", where the companies that profit from a product win control of its regulation. Rolles had observed this in some places in North America where cannabis has been legalised. Some public health professionals are concerned that this is already the case with the UK food and alcohol industry (Miller and Harkins, 2010).

When I discussed these issues with Chris Snowdon, he – unsurprisingly – expressed a different opinion. His employer, the Institute of Economic

Affairs (IEA), is often accused of being in the pay of corporate interests. The IEA has been criticised for taking money from the tobacco and food companies (Gornall, 2019) and has repeatedly resisted greater government control of these industries. Many of the tweets that emanate from the IEA get the dismissive reply 'Who funds you?'. The IEA usually declines to respond. When I asked Snowdon that question, he said the IEA is funded by "voluntary donations". I asked him specifically about funding of drug policy reports by George Soros and by cannabis companies. He said, "I don't personally worry about them very much because I really think that you can judge an argument on its own merits". When I asked him about what funding model he would prefer, he said, "I think a large number of smaller donations is better … If you're 90 per cent funded by a particular individual or corporation then I suppose that there's this risk that, at the very least, you might bite your tongue when you could say something else". In another interview (not with Steve Rolles), I was told that Transform had lost the support of a wealthy donor, partly because he saw Transform as being "a bit too left wing" and "anti free market". Perhaps if Transform had bitten its collective tongue on what that interviewee described as "these wider social justice issues", it might have retained this funding.

The risk of leaving advocacy to private funding is that people and positions that are not popular will continue to be unrepresented in the drug policy debate. As we will see in Chapter 10, the deliberate funding of advocacy groups of people with direct experience of drug problems has had an influence on Scottish policy on drug-related deaths that we have not seen in England. For now, we can conclude this brief discussion of economic power by noting that money can enable different constellations of policy actors to have more influence than they would have without these financial resources.

Epistemic power: the uses of 'evidence-based policy'

A remarkable feature of the drug policy discourses was the ubiquity of calls for 'evidence-based policy'. These claims can be seen as policy actors' attempts to claim epistemic power, or the ability to work with others to dominate what is known. The claims came from every shade of the political spectrum and from members of every policy constellation. Evidence was called on in support of diametrically opposed ideas and policies: that cannabis is more or less dangerous than alcohol; that punishing people for drug possession does or does not deter them from use; that overdose prevention centres would be a risk or a boon to public health; and so on.

In one debate, the government minister Nick Hurd remarked on these competing evidential narratives. The debate was on the change that was made to the legal classification of third-generation synthetic cannabinoid receptor agonists, which I have discussed elsewhere as an example of the corporate power of the British pharmaceutical industry (Stevens, 2021). The minister was assailed by opponents citing evidence and claiming that the government was 'immune to the mayhem that their general policy on drugs is currently generating' (Peter Wishart MP). In response, Hurd said, 'speakers today have presented one side of the debate, but those on the other side believe with equal passion that the evidence tells a different story' (Hansard, 2019a).

The drug policy constellation that favours tough control of drugs is not – as its opponents sometimes claim – an evidence-free zone. Neil McKeganey, formerly a professor at Glasgow University, has provided academic arguments against harm reduction (McKeganey, 2010), as well as frequently being quoted in the Scottish media. South of the border, Dr Marta Di Forti of King's College London has been a speaker at one or more of the events of Craig McKinlay's All-Party Parliamentary Group, which opposed cannabis liberalisation. She is regularly quoted in media articles that oppose such law reform. Steve Moore told me that her co-author, Professor Sir Robin Murray, was the most commonly cited academic by commentators who opposed Moore's efforts to legalise cannabis products for medical use. In a different corner of the drug policy debate, the CDPRG also called on experts in support of its favoured positions. It stated that 'the Royal College of Physicians, the Faculty of Public Health, the Royal Society for Public Health and The British Medical Journal (BMJ) have all called for an end to criminal sanctions against people who take drugs' (Moore, 2019, p 15).

With Chris Snowdon, I discussed this use of "evidence as ammunition". After I put this phrase to him, he said:

> 'I think generally speaking a lot of evidence and indeed arguments, documents, publications that we produce or anybody else produces; I think they're primarily designed to give ammunition to people who already agree with you. ... I wouldn't be doing what I'm doing if I didn't think you could change people's mind with good arguments and good evidence. But I think the reality of it – certainly from our perspective as a Westminster think tank – is that you've got a parliamentary debate coming up tomorrow. We're going to be discussing cannabis legalisation. We know who's going to speak out in support of that. Can we give them a bit of ammunition to make their case?'

This offers a nice insight into how policy constellations operate. Actors working in the same policy space keep abreast of each other's actions and opportunities. This enables them to provide mutual support on the basis of shared beliefs and goals, without a need for direct coordination. The mutual attraction of shared beliefs and the joint knowledge of the rules of the game enable this everyday type of concerted action. This is the game that policy actors play in attempting to win epistemic power by institutionalising their knowledge as the dominant knowledge.

As the saying goes, evidence is often used in policy debates like a drunk uses a lamppost: more for support than illumination.[2] I discussed this phenomenon in my (2007) article on 'the survival of the ideas that fit'. It was also observed in David Brewster's study of cannabis policy making, in which he quotes a senior Home Office civil servant. 'Sometimes, dare I say, you might have to marshal the evidence in such a way that it supports the decision ... rather than find the evidence which demonstrated what the most sensible way forward would be' (Brewster, 2023, p 91).

But still, the lamppost does light the way home. Snowdon and others were able to give examples of how long-term use of evidence in policy debates had shifted the terms of these debates and so the range of imaginable, feasible policy solutions. Evidence is sometimes used to block policy proposals which would, according to the most rigorous research we have available, be actively harmful. An example comes from the successful actions of public health professionals to block conservative policy actors from imposing limits on the length of time that patients could be prescribed opioid substitution therapy (OST). The government asked the ACMD to look at this during the coalition government of 2010–2015, when the "lurch to recovery" was in full swing. In their much-delayed ministerial response to the ACMD, Steve Brine MP wrote, '[t]he ACMD has produced unequivocal advice, in line with the strong international evidence base, against time-limiting OST, which the Government accepts in full' (Brine and Newton, 2017, p 1).

Two years later, I drafted the ACMD's (2019) recommendation on reducing the number of people with drug problems who are released from prison on a Friday. This was because the sub-committee I formed to write this report was repeatedly told by practitioners in the field, and by the charity NACRO (2018), about the problems people face if they are released so late in the working week. They may have multiple appointments to attend to arrange housing and probation contact, as well as picking up a methadone prescription. If they cannot get to these appointments and then these agencies close for the weekend, they may be cut off from support; sometimes with fatal consequences.[3] This recommendation was not initially accepted. So I was pleasantly surprised by the later decision to follow the ACMD's advice on this issue (MoJ, 2022). When I asked a civil servant who was close to this decision why it had been taken, they told me that there had been no particular clamour for it but that "the evidence was there".

Despite the apparently direct use of evidence in these instances, I am still not sure that they count as examples of 'evidence-based policy'. For example, the ACMD's recommendation on reducing Friday prison releases was not based on a hierarchy of evidence or a randomised trial showing that it would work. Rather, it was based on our compassionate concern to reduce the excessive number of people who die shortly after leaving prison (Farrell and Marsden, 2008). In announcing its decision to reduce Friday releases, the Ministry of Justice emphasised that this was intended to 'cut crime and make streets safer' (MoJ, 2022). Our use of evidence is filtered through our ethico-political bases.

In my interview with Angela Constance, the Scottish drugs minister, the first answer she gave to my question on what influences policy was on the importance of using the evidence. But that was not the only influence she mentioned. "We need to have the courage to talk about what the evidence tells us, ... but we need to combine that with lived experience". Indeed, she brought her own lived experience as a social worker in Scottish prisons. "I know from my background that if we are needlessly criminalising people then that will not work for them or the country". She saw a "tension between policy makers, academics and people with lived experience". These groups bring different forms of knowledge to the contest for epistemic power.

Affective power: personal stories "cut through"

My interviewees contrasted the use of scientific evidence to political manoeuvring. They also distinguished it from the use of personal stories which trigger emotional responses. I was told that you need such stories if you want to "cut through" in the crowded world of policy narratives. This fits with developing knowledge from the quantitative study of narratives that they need emotional content and the dramatisation of moral conflicts if they want to attract attention (Hopp et al, 2020a).

Keith Humphreys gave me his perceptions of the power of affective stories to change minds on moralised topics.

> 'If you measured British attitudes about people with HIV five minutes before Princess Diana hugs that patient and five minutes after they would have been wildly different. Or Australian attitudes towards people who use drugs five minutes before the Prime Minister bursts out crying because his daughter is addicted to heroin. ... You can do all this for rational planning, and then something like that happens and then people flip.'

In the data I collected, I saw many examples of affective pleas. These were sections of texts where policy actors presented a story about human suffering that was clearly designed to elicit an emotional response leading to policy change. These came from all sides of the drug policy debate. They often involved the imperilled child narrative, arguing that urgent action was needed to protect innocent children from harm. For example, Conservative MP Nickie Aikin asked the drugs minister Kit Malthouse, '[d]oes he agree that we must treat the drug barons involved in county lines as predators who are using and grooming children?' (Hansard, 2021e). The idea that harsher law enforcement was needed to protect children and young people was a common trope expressed by people in the conservative policy constellation. They did not often name individual children, although the sad story of Leah Betts – a teenager who died after using MDMA in 1995 – continued to loom large in the public imagination (Black and Pettifor, 2017).

Leah Betts' parents campaigned for tougher law enforcement after her death. They were successful in deterring at least one journalist from using MDMA (Barnett, 2017). Meanwhile, people in the drug policy reform constellations named a number of children who suffered from what their parents saw as overly restrictive and harmful drug policies. These included, as we will see in Chapter 9, young boys who were suffering severe conditions that were relieved only by cannabis-based medicines. They also included other teenagers who had died with MDMA, including Martha Fernback. The families of older people who had died with heroin also joined campaigns for more liberal drug laws. This included the historian Pat Hudson, whose son Kevin Lane died in a public toilet in Carmarthen in 2017. I have experienced the emotional power of these stories and been moved to tears. Interviewees told me of several politicians who had been similarly moved.

The emotional heft of these moving stories can be translated into affective power. An advocate of cannabis legalisation made the case for using affective pleas in policy making. In a report that was published jointly by Volteface and the Adam Smith Institute, he wrote, 'convincing personal stories must play a great part in demonstrating that the cannabis issue also has a human aspect if progress is to be made' (Starling, 2016, p 7). I heard and read similar advice being given to people who were interested in decriminalising drug possession, legalising the use of psilocybin for medical purposes and banning various substances. Such affective pleas were, for example, common in presenting the need for the Psychoactive Substances Act 2016 to protect young people (Stevens, 2017).

There may be limits to what can be achieved through the power of personal stories, especially in the absence of data to back them up. Ed Day made this point about the interplay of epistemic and affective power from his perspective as Drug Recovery Champion.

> 'The two things that cut through at the policy making level are having data … particularly if it's value-for-money-type data – and then sometimes personal stories. On a one-to-one basis, personal stories win out. But once you get into that policy making group and then the committee, the personal stories tend to be forgotten and slightly pushed to one side and it's all about the data and the facts, and if they're not there then therefore it doesn't happen. That's my observation of it.'

Affective and epistemic power play different roles for different people at different points in the policy process. People with direct experience in the field can work with other policy actors to use affecting personal stories to get an issue on the agenda and to push for particular policies. Affective pleas may be more persuasive than dry statistics and wordy reports in changing politicians' minds. But once the issue enters the world of "groups and committees", the epistemic power of the usual experts is reasserted. The selection of these experts – and their selection of what facts to produce and prioritise – take over. A vivid example of the ebb and flow of affective, epistemic and institutional power through policy constellations is presented in Chapter 9 in relation to policy on medical cannabis.

Savvy social power

The cases I examined also include fascinating examples of what I call savvy social power. These were provided – in different forms – by Steve Moore, in the case of medical cannabis legalisation, and Professor Dame Carol Black in the case of the 2021 drug strategy. They were able to combine their highly developed understandings of how the policy process works with finely tuned political skills and extensive contacts across policy constellations. They used them to achieve their desired policy outcomes.

Several interviewees mentioned that Professor Black was highly skilled in presenting issues to ministers diplomatically and persuasively. When I interviewed her, she told me that one of the reasons she had been selected to lead the review on drugs was that "I think they saw me as someone who'd never been anybody to criticise them outright in public". She stressed the words "in public". There seems to be a tactical, selective quiescence that is adopted by people who gain access to the inner circles of drug policy making. They select the subjects they choose to speak about and keep quiet about others. There are issues they feel they can make progress on. Raising them will not discredit them in the eyes of more powerful actors. And they select the times and places in which they will be critical of government. Dame Carol told me, "I think I have said pretty tough things to ministers. I've always done it totally privately and I've always asked the civil servants to go out of the room ... I see no point in embarrassing [ministers] and once a civil servant's in the room, it's documented". This accorded with the views of other influential interviewees, including that of a senior civil servant, that "we should never embarrass them in public".

In Steve Moore's case, savvy social power took a rather different form. He used the experience and contacts he gained as adviser to David Cameron to develop a sophisticated, strategic approach to the campaign for the legalisation of cannabis for medical purposes. Instead of following a quiescent, self-censoring approach to building mutually beneficial relationships, he used the politics of familiarity, generous funding from a privately wealthy backer and strongly affective pleas to force ministers into a position where they could not but change policy in his desired direction. The ability to do this successfully relied on the connections and forms of power that Moore had gathered through his engagement in policy constellations over many years.

Savvy social power may be akin to what other authors have called policy entrepreneurship (Kingdon, 2013). The term entrepreneur suggests a heroic individual taking risks to build a profitable business. I would like to emphasise two things. One is that actors with savvy social power are not motivated, as far as I can see, by personal profit. Rather, they use their skills in fulfilling the ethico-political commitments that had shaped their careers. The second is that savvy social power is not just an individual property. It emerges from the social networks of connections – the constellations of preferences, positions, people and powers – in which policy actors embed themselves.

Conclusion: powers and structures

In this chapter, I have shown how policy actors use institutional and social power to work in concert toward shared goals. The connections through which these forms of power operate are not just networks of people. The people who work together in policy constellations bring with them their moral assumptions, their policy preferences and the various forms of power that they hold. To understand these processes, we must step down from the level of individual action and motivations. Powers and preferences emerge through processes of collective action, which themselves are driven by the underlying mechanisms that create social and cultural structures. The power that policy actors can bring to policy constellations depends on the social positions that they hold, which provide constraints and opportunities to influence policy. The weight that they can bring to policy debates through their various forms of power depends on the underlying social structures through which these powers are distributed, just as the preferences they hold are culturally structured.

To explain policy making, we need to pay attention to the influence of these underlying social and cultural structures on individual and collective actions in particular policy cases. The next part of this book does this for three different areas of the policy field: the legalisation of medical cannabis, the differing responses to drug-related deaths in England and Scotland, and the UK's new drug strategy of 2021.

PART III

Cases in Drug Policy Making in the UK

9

The Limited Legalisation of Medical Cannabis

Recent debates over medical cannabis offer fascinating examples of the interplay of various forms of power and morality with different policy constellations. The bare facts of the case are that cannabis-based medical products were moved from schedule 1 to schedule 2 of the Misuse of Drugs Regulations in November 2018. Schedule 1 is the place for drugs which have no medical purpose. By moving these products to schedule 2, the government enabled some forms of cannabis to be provided legally as medicine. These bare facts overlay a much more complex and interesting story, a tale that involves the use of different epistemic understandings of what cannabis does and some striking examples of the use of economic, affective, media and savvy social power to change policy. It also shows the ongoing capacity of the most influential policy constellations to use their institutional power to limit the scale of change.

The change in policy was triggered by media "uproar" over the cases of two boys – Billy Caldwell and Alfie Dingley – who suffer from rare, treatment-resistant forms of epilepsy. Mark Monaghan and colleagues have called this a case of a manufactured scandal (Monaghan, Wincup and Hamilton, 2020). I see it as also being an example of political cornering: the skilful manoeuvring of politicians by other policy actors into a position where they have little choice but to make the desired decision. In this case, the think tank Volteface and its founder Steve Moore were key policy actors, along with Charlotte Caldwell, Billy's mother. They were able to use affective power, together with their social connections, financial backing and media power, to change policy. Their ability to do so depended on previous exercises of epistemic power to undermine the case for continued prohibition.

In the aftermath of the 2018 legalisation, the Home Office – in concert with official bodies like the Advisory Council on the Misuse of Drugs (ACMD) and the National Institute for Health and Care Excellence – used its institutional power to limit access to cannabis-based medical products. This successful rearguard action is described in the final section of this chapter.

The chapter starts by looking at the policy constellations involved. It then examines the contest for the epistemic power to establish whether cannabis has a legitimate role as medicine. The role of economic, affective and media power in the manufactured scandal, and how politicians were cornered in June 2018, will then be explained. These processes were carried out by individual policy actors. Their ability to do so was influenced, enabled and constrained by their socially structured positions and powers, and by the cultural structures within which they operated, including libertarian, paternalist and traditionalist views on cannabis.

Policy constellations around medical cannabis

The policy actors involved in the campaign to legalise cannabis for medical use come largely from the drug policy reform constellation. Actors from both the progressive social justice and libertarian wings of this constellation expressed compassion for the suffering of people who use cannabis for medical purposes. Among progressives, there is concern about the unfairness of punishing people for using and growing a plant that relieves this pain. For libertarians, there is a desire to enable both patients and private companies to benefit from cannabis. Their position is that people should be free to choose their own medication (Flanigan, 2012). This runs counter to the paternalist idea that government-appointed expertise is needed to limit the risks of the inappropriate use of under-tested products, as well as the traditionalist idea that cannabis has no place in the official pharmacopoeia.

Nevertheless, the legalisation of cannabis-based medical products could not have occurred without the consent of actors in the medico-penal constellation, which brings institutionally powerful traditionalists and paternalists together. The politicians who had the power to change the law were Conservative ministers, primarily in the Home Office. Their policy positions place them in the conservative constellation. The institutional preference of the Home Office has always been to favour tighter control, a position that goes back to the days of Sir Malcolm Delevingne (Berridge, 2013). In any move to legalise a drug for medical use, the Home Office could not act without consulting members of the public health constellation. When it is considering changing the legal status of a drug, it has a legal duty to consult the ACMD, many members of which come from medical professions. And it would also need the political cover of the medical stamp of approval for any such decision.

In the run-up to the debates of 2018, the positions of these policy constellations were well known. There were long-standing campaigns by people who use cannabis for medical purposes and their allies in the drug policy reform movement. These had met with a flat refusal from the Home Office to contemplate change. For example, the MPs Paul Flynn, Tonia Antoniazzi (both Labour) and Layla Moran (Liberal Democrat) joined a demonstration in Westminster by the United Patients Alliance (UPA) in October 2017 (Cowburn, 2017). This coincided with the first parliamentary reading of Flynn's private members' bill on Legalisation of Cannabis (Medical Purposes). This bill was supported by a cross-party coalition[1] of MPs, including Caroline Lucas (Green), Jeff Smith (Labour), Ronnie Cowan (Scottish National Party [SNP]), Crispin Blunt (Conservative) and Alistair Carmichael (Scottish Liberal Democrat). At the demonstration, Flynn accused the government of 'political cowardice' and of running drug policy as an 'evidence-free zone'. One of the members of UPA, a young man suffering from Crohn's disease, was quoted as saying that '[c]annabis helps me to have a much better quality of life than I get on the medications my doctor can prescribe me ... The UK Government needs to act on the evidence which shows that cannabis has medicinal value and change the law immediately' (quoted by Cowburn, 2017, np).

This demonstration came a year after the publication of the report by the All-Party Parliamentary Group on Drug Policy Reform (APPGDPR, 2016) on *Access to Medicinal Cannabis* and two years after the debate which was triggered by the petition of 220,000 people calling for cannabis legalisation (Hansard, 2015). The Home Office was not moved to change policy by this traditional political campaigning of demonstrations, petitions, reports and private members' bills. Its response to the petition was similar to several other statements it made in the period 2015 to 2018: 'Substantial scientific evidence shows cannabis is a harmful drug that can damage human health. There are no plans to legalise cannabis as it would not address the harm to individuals and communities' (Home Office, as quoted by Ferguson and Grant, 2015, np).

The competition for epistemic power on cannabis

As this statement from the Home Office shows, and contrary to Flynn's claim, cannabis policy is not an 'evidence-free zone'. The discussions I observed were rather saturated with claims and counter-claims that drew on scientific evidence. These disputed the role of cannabis in the treatment of medical conditions and the dangers it poses to adolescent mental health. Members of conflicting policy constellations competed for epistemic power, the ability to establish their version of knowledge as the legitimate basis for policy action.

One of the reasons for the longevity of this debate is the complexity of the topic. Cannabis is a very complicated plant, containing a large number of potentially active phytocannabinoids (ACMD, 2016c). The most well known is delta-9- tetrahydrocannabinol (THC). This is described as the one that gets you high. The next most famous is cannabidiol (CBD). This is thought to moderate some of the effects of THC (Niesink and van Laar, 2013; ACMD, 2021). It may have its own effects on mental health and emotional state. At least some users find that CBD reduces anxiety (Crippa et al, 2011).

Incidentally, this means that CBD meets the absurdly broad definition of a psychoactive substance that is used in the Psychoactive Substances Act 2016. The Home Office has never clarified this, nor has it taken steps to enforce the Act against the booming trade in CBD products. The ACMD (2021, p 8) has reported that the psychoactive effects 'may only occur at doses of CBD higher than those available from consumer CBD products'. This has not prevented companies with names like TRIP advertising CBD for its psychoactive properties, including as a remedy for 'hangxiety' (Palmer, 2022, np).

There are complicated scientific arguments about the status of cannabis as a medicine. The APPGDPR (2016) report stated that there was 'good evidence' that cannabis is helpful in treating 'chronic pain, including neuropathic pain; spasticity; nausea and vomiting, particularly in the context of chemotherapy; and in the management of anxiety'. It added that there was 'moderate evidence for the use of cannabis in sleep disorders; appetite stimulation in the context of chemotherapy; fibromyalgia; PTSD; and for some symptoms of Parkinson's disease' (APPGDPR, 2016, p vi). These lists were written by Professor Mike Barnes and Dr Jennifer Barnes, who acted as scientific advisers to the APPGDPR. It is interesting, given how medical cannabis was eventually legalised, that the lists did not include treatment-resistant forms of childhood epilepsy.

The policy constellations that opposed liberalisation of cannabis had research champions of their own. They used their evidence to make the counter-argument that cannabis is too dangerous to be used as a medicine. They drew on research from Professor Sir Robin Murray and Dr Marta di Forti of King's College London, among others. These researchers have repeatedly warned about the correlation between use of cannabis – especially in its more potent form of 'skunk' – and mental health problems among young people (for example, Di Forti et al, 2015, 2019; Murray et al, 2016). So prominent has their work been that one campaigner for legalisation accused Murray and di Forti of building up 'a family business in skunk scaremongering' (Reynolds, 2015, np).[2]

On the other side of the scientific argument are researchers including Professor David Nutt of Imperial College London, who works with Professor Barnes in the Medical Cannabis Working Group of Drug Science, the charity that Nutt set up after he was sacked from the ACMD (Nutt, 2021). Nutt has suggested that the causal impact of cannabis on mental health has been exaggerated. The ACMD also made this point while Nutt was a member (ACMD, 2008). In turn, Nutt has been accused of overstating the benefits and understating the risks of cannabis by a fellow psychiatrist (Hoeh, 2022).

These disagreements were mirrored in patient experience reported to the House of Commons by Anne McLaughlin MP:

> A very close associate of mine has bipolar. She was a regular user of cannabis. She asked two different psychiatrists, 'Did that make it worse?', and one said yes and the other said no. She asked them whether it caused her bipolar, and one said, 'Possibly', and the other said, 'You possibly started to use it to cope with the effects of an undiagnosed condition.' That is the problem. (Hansard, 2015)

In one of the last ministerial stands against the legalisation of cannabis for medical use, the policing minister Nick Hurd quoted the ACMD's finding that cannabis can 'unquestionably cause harm to individuals and society' (Hansard, 2018b). This was an instance of selective quotation. The quote is accurate. It appears in both the ACMD's first (2002) report on the classification of cannabis and the letter by the ACMD's then chairman, Professor Sir Michael Rawlinson, that covered the Council's (2008) follow-up report. But in that letter, the quote comes directly after Sir Michael's recommendation against tighter control on cannabis, on the grounds that it 'more closely equates with other Class C substances than with those currently classified as Class B'. Sir Michael also noted that '[c]riminal justice measures – irrespective of classification – will have only a limited effect on usage' (ACMD, 2008, p 1), a point that Mr Hurd chose not to relate to Parliament.

There has been much use of competing academic and advisory accounts of the evidence base to argue for particular positions on medical cannabis. These arguments have not been resolved scientifically and were not decisive on the policy outcome in 2018. It would, however, have been much harder to legalise some cannabis products for medical use if there had not been some scientific evidence that cannabis has medical benefits. As noted in Chapter 4, evidence is neither necessary nor sufficient for policy change. This requires the combined deployment of other forms of power.

Economic, affective and media power in changing policy: the art of political cornering

In their interesting study of how cannabis was legalised for medical purposes, Mark Monaghan, Emma Wincup and Ian Hamilton (2020, p 1931) combine the concept of punctuated equilibrium in policy processes (Baumgartner and Jones, 2009) with scandal theory (Butler and Drakeford, 2005) to argue that, '[t]he case of medicinal cannabis suggests that policy reform can occur when a scandal is successfully manufactured'. Monaghan and colleagues show how we need to go beyond the general concept provided by Baumgartner and Jones to discover the specific contexts and modes of action that cause punctuations in policy equilibria. They show how the numerous press reports of the cases of Billy Caldwell and Alfie Dingley preceded the 2018 policy change on medical cannabis. These two boys, aged 12 and six at the time, were suffering multiple seizures that were only reduced by cannabis-based medicines. Monaghan, Wincup and Hamilton note the role of a number of policy actors in fuelling reporting of their plight, including Volteface, End Our Pain and UPA. Their article proves the point of Butler and Drakeford (2005, p 238) that '[i]f scandals are constructed, then, they are manufactured with a purpose'. In this case, the purpose was to achieve legalisation of medical cannabis. For some, including the actors around Volteface, the aim was a legal market for both medical and recreational cannabis (Starling, 2016; Power, 2017). The manufacturers of the 2018 scandal were successful in legalising cannabis for medical but not recreational use.

Scandals do not always lead to policy change. In that sense, scandal theory – like Kingdon's (2013) concept of policy windows – needs additional explanation of how a particular opportunity led to a specific policy outcome. In my analysis, I was able to go even deeper into the mechanisms of how this scandal was created, for what purpose, and how it led to policy change. I did this by interviewing people who were involved in creating and reacting to it. I can add my auto-ethnographic observation of being directly – if peripherally – involved in that reaction as a member of the ACMD.

An outside observer of this successful political operation, Steve Rolles, commented on it admiringly. He described the situation going into 2018 as being a "disjuncture" between a growing number of patients and clinicians who saw benefits in using cannabis medicinally and "a legal and medicines regulatory system that wouldn't allow it because the products didn't meet the criteria to be allowed for prescription and there were legal issues around scheduling". In 2018, he saw "a tabloid uproar around these kids who are having hundreds of seizures a day but being denied their medicine which would reduce their seizures to zero". He described these issues as "very dramatic and very emotive". And he told me that Volteface was "very clever in exploiting that to cross the finish line"; to get beyond the "disjuncture" that had been created by years of research and campaigning.

Paul North, the current director of Volteface, told me how they did it. He said, "the best option you've got to create policy, particularly in the current Johnson government, is to pull the levers which politicians can do little about". He said that policy did not change because the evidence for medical cannabis was mounting, or because government ministers wanted it to change. Rather,

> 'the way in which the levers were pulled was by putting politicians in a situation where they had to engage in it. They had to have a stance and

they also had to engage with the outcry of the public over something which is clearly upsetting. People don't like seeing kids in pain. If you know this medicine stops this person having a fit, should we do it? Yeah, especially if it's a kid. So I think [it's about] putting politicians in an environment where they can't move politically, so that they are now in a position where they have nowhere else to go.'

This manoeuvring of politicians into a position where they "have nowhere else to go" is what I mean by political cornering. In this case, it involved highly skilled, politically savvy, analytically informed political action by a micro-level constellation of actors, in which two key players were Steve Moore and Charlotte Caldwell.

In another instance of the politics of familiarity, Steve Moore told me that he got into working in drug policy "inadvertently" through his relationship with Paul Birch and his brother. Moore had known them for "20 odd years". The Birch brothers built their economic power by developing and selling the social network website Bebo to AOL in 2008 for a reported US$850 million (about £450 million at the time). Paul Birch used some of the money to fund Transform, End Our Pain and then Volteface, the think tank that Moore started up in 2015. Moore had other powerful connections. He helped David Cameron launch the 'Big Society' policy concept (Moore, 2016) and came into Downing Street with Cameron when he became Prime Minister in 2010. These connections were to prove very useful in the campaign to legalise medical cannabis. But "in the absence of Paul's money", Moore said, "I don't think anything much would have happened".

When Moore started work with Birch on cannabis policy, he "wasn't particularly conversant in the issue at all". He soon realised that there was "a lot of more grassrootsy kind of campaigns, but there were none that has any funding and none of them were particularly sophisticated in terms of how they operated". So, "I kind of just used the tools of my trade". These tools included polling and focus groups. His research told him that cannabis "was quite a confounding issue … what you have is a lot of people saying it helps my grandfather with his arthritis and then you've got other people saying it's driven my nephew mad". Moore also found that the issue had low "salience", with "no one feeling this is a massive issue that needed to be addressed".

In describing how Volteface went about changing this, Moore gave me an insight into how a savvy policy operation of this type works. He described the grassroots organisations as "little more than Facebook groups" who "didn't have any political strategy, or any data, or a theory of change". Of Transform, he said, "they didn't really know anybody … they were operating more at a theoretical level". The distance between Volteface and other campaigners for reform was also maintained by forces of ethico-political repulsion. Steve Moore had connections to the Conservative Party, while the campaign for legalisation had traditionally been led by people connected to other parties, including the Labour MP Paul Flynn. Volteface and its funder were motivated by a libertarian desire to see a freer market for cannabis, as well as compassion for people who suffered from not being able to use it medically. Other campaigners in the field mixed such compassion with a stronger commitment to progressive social justice. This helps explain why Volteface worked apart from the existing campaigners rather than seeking to work in allyship with them.

As Moore explained, a politically savvy operation needs connections and a strategic plan, as well as money. Moore planned "a lightning strike", not the more traditional, "plodding" approach of existing campaigns. The Home Office, he said, are expert in "dragging things out". "With the Home Office, you just need to blow the doors off".

Moore was inspired by the work of the late Steve Fox and the success of his argument that cannabis is safer than alcohol in enabling legalisation of cannabis for recreational use in several US states (Fox et al, 2013). But Moore realised that the cultural context of the UK was "completely different". So a different argument would be needed. In the polls and focus groups, he saw an opportunity to win salience and sympathy for policy reform. "It felt to me", he told me, "that the medical cannabis issue was the one that could be where you could shift the dial somewhat. The data suggested that there was significant levels of support for it". There was also "a kind of playbook" developed in Germany, Australia and some states of the US "which was mainly focused in on childhood epilepsy".

In "off the record meetings" with ministers and senior officials, Moore "got a sense" that change could happen "with the right campaign and the right campaigner". He also had several conversations with his contacts within the system of medicines regulation. By 2018, he was confident that if the government were put under enough pressure, they would refer the issue to the Chief Medical Officer and she would recommend that patients be allowed to use medical cannabis.

When Charlotte Caldwell called Moore in 2018, he knew what he wanted to do. Until this, he did not have the "right candidate" to "execute the plan". Caldwell was already a seasoned campaigner, raising large amounts of money to fund her son's treatment. She had been able to get a prescription for cannabis oil from a doctor in Northern Ireland, but the police put a stop to it, which is when she called Moore. He knew that he could get the right candidate a prescription for medical cannabis from a trial that was running in Canada. And he knew that, if that person flew back to the UK with that cannabis, it would be confiscated. This would be a newsworthy story that would put pressure on the government. This was the plan he executed with Charlotte and Billy Caldwell.

The journalist Ian Birrell accompanied the Caldwells as they flew back to the UK. On Sunday 10 June 2018, Birrell published an article in the *Mail on Sunday*. Its headline was a direct challenge to the government: 'Leave us alone or ARREST ME'. Birrell wrote, '[t]he desperate mother of a boy suffering from severe epilepsy plans to fly back to Britain tomorrow with a consignment of medical cannabis obtained in Canada and declare it to customs officials' (Birrell, 2018, np). On the Monday, the cannabis was duly confiscated at Heathrow airport. Caldwell was not arrested. She held a press conference that afternoon and demanded that Billy be allowed his prescription, with several MPs and experts offering support in multiple media outlets. While the press conference was happening, Moore had been called into the Home Office where, on his account, ministers "didn't have a clue" how to respond. Later that day, the Home Office issued a statement that Nick Hurd would meet Charlotte Caldwell. It reminded readers that 'Border Force has a duty to stop banned substances from entering the UK' (Busby, 2018, np).

On the Wednesday, Caldwell told viewers of ITV's *This Morning* that Billy's seizures had come back and that the policing minister had 'actually signed my son's death warrant. Nick Hurd needs to give him back his medication and at least have the decency to say to me "right Charlotte, we will work with you"' (BBC News, 2018, np). The issue was reaching what Moore called the "crescendo moment". On the Friday night, amid mounting "panic" at the Home Office, the Home Secretary ordered that the medicine be returned to the Caldwells. They received it on the Saturday. This was, according to the Home Office, under an 'exceptional licence' for a 'short-term emergency' (Marsh and Badshah, 2018, np).

Throughout this week, Moore maintained "clear communication channels" with his contacts "around the Home Secretary". These included somebody who had previously worked on the Volteface focus groups. Officials and ministers may have preferred that the Caldwells returned to Northern Ireland and move out of the media spotlight, but Charlotte tenaciously refused to stay quiet.

Moore told me that the issue was discussed in cabinet on the following Monday, with Prime Minister Theresa May being "quite furious" about it (she had not, according to Moore, been involved in the decision to provide the emergency licence). But Home Secretary Sajid Javid wanted the issue dealt with quickly, and there "was enough support around the cabinet table", including from Michael Gove, then Secretary of State for the Environment. So Javid went to the House of Commons the next day and announced that there would be reviews by the Chief Medical Officer and the ACMD (Hansard, 2018a). The fact that he tabled this as a statement on 'cannabis-based medicines' indicated that he had already conceded that such products did have medicinal use and so were not compatible with being in schedule 1. Steve Moore's pre-planned "lightning strike" had succeeded, thanks to

Charlotte Caldwell's affectively triggering the power of the media to force ministers into a corner, from which their only way out was to legalise cannabis products for medical use.

This was a politically savvy operation by two skilled campaigners, but its success relied on the constellations of actors and ideas in which they circulated. Years of more "plodding" campaigning by groups like End Our Pain, UPA, Transform, Release and the APPGDPR had weakened support for strict prohibition of cannabis. The affective pleas of Alfie Dingley and Billy Caldwell's mothers – as supported respectively by End Our Pain and Volteface – found an echo in Parliament. In the debates I coded (for example, Hansard, 2018b, 2018a), MPs often made their own affective pleas on behalf of people who were suffering from the absence of legal medical cannabis. Paul Flynn accused Nick Hurd of having a 'heart of stone' for refusing these pleas. Others also spoke of the need for 'compassion' (Hansard, 2018b). No MP, except Hurd himself, spoke in favour of continuing the absolute ban on medical cannabis. Such pleas were combined with two other modes of argument. These were references to the evidence on the effectiveness of cannabis as a medicine and to other countries that had already legalised it for medical use.

The people I interviewed who were directly involved in this act of political cornering, Paul North and Steve Moore, focused on this as the immediate, proximal cause of the 2018 legalisation of medical cannabis. People who were not directly involved placed this in the context of the longer movement for reform. Steve Rolles acknowledged that his organisation, Transform, had played little role in the events of 2018. But with nearly 25 years of experience in the field, he could see how it fitted into the older campaign; "years of work by politicians like Paul Flynn, other advocacy groups and cannabis groups and medical organisations and patient advocates and so on who kind of got it, who helped move public opinion to a point where it was possible". Years of building the epistemic and affective case for policy reform had cut away at the legitimacy of continued prohibition.

When this long-standing policy position was put to the test in June 2018, it crumbled, like the communist governments of central and eastern Europe in the autumn of 1989, stripped of internal authority and lacking forceful external backing. In 1989, the dictators of East Germany, Czechoslovakia and Hungary looked east for Russian support, which was no longer there. When Conservative politicians looked for support to hold the line on medical cannabis from their traditional supporters in the right-wing press, it had disappeared. Even the ministers whose job it was to hold this line did not really believe in it. In 2021, Nick Hurd said that 'it was quite clear to me and I think Saj[id Javid] – I can't speak for him – that we were in the wrong place on the law. The law needed to change and we were having to manage a very emotional, very difficult confrontational situation' (Hurd, quoted in IfG, 2021, p 11). Nobody likes to be put in a corner.

The affective and epistemic power of campaigners had already undermined the political legitimacy of withholding cannabis-based medicines. Parliamentary opinion as well as the media-mediated 'national mood' had swung behind the compassionate case for reform. There was no longer any powerful media or political players who were backing up the argument that the suffering of these two young boys was necessary to prevent greater harms. This particular brick in the prohibitionist wall had to fall. But there is always a sting in the tail, as was proved with subsequent decisions on medical cannabis.

Institutional power in the rearguard action against expanding medical cannabis

Nick Hurd also told the Institute for Government that 'the system did eventually respond' to the events of summer 2018 (Hurd quoted in IfG, 2021, p 11). Media interest in the cases of Billy Caldwell and Alfie Dingley died down as their immediate needs were met. There was some coverage in the run-up to legalisation on 1 November 2018 but relatively little thereafter (Monaghan, Wincup and Hamilton, 2020). Meanwhile, the cogs of institutional action ground into gear. The ACMD was asked to give a more considered opinion on scheduling. The National Institute for Health and Care Excellence (NICE) was commissioned to review the evidence on cannabis-based medical products.

This is where my peripheral part in this story comes in. As a member of the ACMD, I took part in its consideration of the scheduling of these products. The initial report that Javid requested stated that '[o]nce the definition of a Cannabis-derived medicinal product has been developed, the ACMD advises that only products meeting this definition be moved into Schedule 2 of the Misuse of Drugs Regulations pending our further advice' (ACMD, 2018b, p 2). This was not based on full discussion between members of the Council. There was no time for that in the schedule set by the Home Secretary. Instead, a poll was circulated to us by email so that we could indicate agreement or disagreement with the proposed recommendation. I disagreed, on the basis that the harms of cannabis were not sufficient for it to be placed alongside potentially lethal opioid medicines in schedule 2. I argued, by email, that it should be in schedule 4(ii). I later published this argument in the *British Medical Journal* (Stevens, 2018).

By the rules of schedule 2, people need a prescription to possess or import cannabis-based medicines and face getting a criminal record for doing so without prescription. If cannabis were in schedule 4(ii), these activities would not be punished. People could import and possess cannabis-based medicines for their own personal use without a prescription, as users of anabolic steroids currently do. Mine was a very marginal position among ACMD members. My colleagues did not want to take the risk of enabling wider, unprescribed access to these products. They were later supported by 166 specialists in the treatment of pain who wrote to *The Times*. They stated that cannabis 'will provide little or no long-term benefit in improving pain and may be associated with significant long-term adverse cognitive and mental-health detriment' (Munglani, 2018).

At the next in-person ACMD meeting, I asked why cannabis-based medicines should be in schedule 2 rather than 4. I did not get a clear answer. The question was deflected to the representative of the Home Office, which always sends a civil servant to ACMD meetings. This civil servant did not give me a reason for the choice of schedule 2. They assured me that this choice would be reviewed. I was not invited into subsequent ACMD discussions on this topic. The ACMD's follow-up on its initial scheduling advice did not recommend moving cannabis-based medical products further down the scheduling ladder (ACMD, 2018a). In Steve Moore's terms, I was operating at too theoretical, too distant and too poorly connected a level to have a direct influence on this decision.

Just before the legalisation of cannabis-based medical products in November 2018, prior to the NICE review, the NHS website warned patients that 'very few people in England are likely to get a prescription for medical cannabis' (NHS, 2018). NHS agencies rely on NICE to decide which medicines will be available for NHS prescriptions. In England, NHS-prescribed medicines are free for children, people aged over 60 and expectant and recent mothers, and at limited cost for the rest of the population. Everywhere else in the UK, NHS prescriptions are free to everyone. Outside the NHS, a regular supply of medical cannabis can be very expensive and unaffordable for many people. So there was much interest in what NICE would recommend and much disappointment among cannabis patients and businesses when the guidance was published (Foster, 2019; NICE, 2019b). By the standards it uses, the NICE committee judged that there was limited evidence that cannabis-based medicines were effective or, crucially, cost-effective. The NICE committee recognised, for example, that Sativex® (the brand name for nabiximols, which is an equal mix of THC and CBD) could effectively relieve spasticity associated with multiple sclerosis. However, the costs would have to reduce from £375 to £188 per pack in order to meet the cost:benefit threshold that NICE uses to decide which drugs the NHS should provide (NICE, 2019a). The list of conditions for which cannabis-based medicines are appropriate was, according to NICE, much narrower than the list the Professor and Dr Barnes had given to the APPGDPR, and the evidence was weaker than they had suggested (APPGDPR, 2016).

Under further pressure from his mother, the NHS agreed to provide a prescription for Billy Caldwell in September 2019. This was still denied to other children in similar predicaments, including three-year-old Charlie Hughes. In July 2019, a judge granted Charlie's parents permission to bring a judicial review against NICE over their refusal to endorse NHS prescription of the medicine that Charlie needed. This was settled out of court in March 2021 (BBC News, 2021a). NICE issued a clarification to its guidance. This stated that their original guidance 'should not ... be interpreted by healthcare professionals as meaning that they are prevented from considering the use of unlicensed cannabis-based medicinal products where that is clinically appropriate in an individual case' (NICE, 2021, np). Despite this clarification, no NHS body has agreed to fund a prescription for Charlie Hughes at the time of writing this book. The number of people who have been prescribed unlicensed cannabis medicines by private doctors has risen to over 40,000 per year. But the number receiving such prescriptions on the NHS is less than five per year (Lord Kamall, 2022), with some reports that the total number of people who have received such a prescription is only three (Stevens, 2022).

In other parts of Whitehall, institutional inertia was also kicking back in. In response to various calls for more research on the medical use of cannabis, including from the ACMD, the National Institute for Health Research (NIHR) set up a programme to fund such studies (NIHR, 2018). But when I searched the NIHR's awards and outputs directory in January 2023, there were no projects listed that were studying medical cannabis. Steve Moore told me none had been funded. Two upcoming trials were mentioned in Ben Stevens' (2022) piece as being funded by NIHR, but they have not yet seen the light of day.

Backbench MPs raised the issue of limited access to medical cannabis in three debates in spring 2019 and the autumn of 2021. They failed to persuade Home Office ministers either to introduce new legislation or to use the new drug strategy to expand this access (Hansard, 2019b, 2021d, 2021b). I was told that Matt Hancock showed some interest in increasing access to medical cannabis when he was Health Secretary, having been moved by personal stories of patients. In March 2020, he made it easier for those with a prescription to import their medicine (HM Government, 2020). But then came the COVID-19 pandemic, which consumed all his political attention. Since Hancock resigned over a classic example of a British political scandal – combining sex and hypocrisy – his successors (including Sajid Javid) have shown little interest in medical cannabis.

In December 2021, Jeff Smith led the second reading of his Medical Cannabis (Access) Bill (Hansard, 2021c). In this debate, there were now people prepared to question whether it was wise to expand access to medicines that had not yet been through the usual process of testing. Conservative MP Katherine Fletcher called on the combined epistemic weight of the 'British Paediatric Neurology Association, the General Medical Council, the National Institute for Health and Care Excellence and the Royal College of Physicians'. All had issued guidance expressing caution on prescribing medical cannabis. Fletcher quoted NICE's statement that 'there is no recommendation against the use of cannabis-based medical products', but 'it still does not address the issue of a positive evidence base for the safety and effectiveness of these drugs' (Hansard, 2021c).

Here we see the limits to the savvy use of media and affective power. As Ed Day told me, once the emotional case has been made, the process moves on to the evidential and bureaucratic arguments that take place within Whitehall. Javid's way out of the policy corner that Steve Moore had placed him in left room for the reinstatement of the institutional power to control who gets access to which drugs. In concert with the Chief Medical Officer and the ACMD, the Home Office created a system that satisfied mediated calls for two young boys to be allowed their prescriptions but has not provided this relief to more than a handful of patients through the NHS.

Members of other policy constellations, like Mike Barnes, David Nutt and their collaborators in Drug Science's Project Twenty21, have provided some assistance to other patients by negotiating subsidised access to private prescriptions. This is a system that, again, perpetuates inequalities in legal access to controlled drugs. It still provides an opportunity for policy actors with an economic interest in expanding the cannabis market, like the companies that are working with Project Twenty21, to use their economic power to build their epistemic case. Results from the project are, according to Drug Science (2023), encouraging. But they are not of the sort that is likely to persuade NICE, which tends to prioritise randomised trials rather than observational studies of the type that Project Twenty21 is running.

Since 2018, the economic power that was placed behind the campaign for medical cannabis legalisation has receded. Paul Birch has withdrawn from the field. The interest in investing in the UK cannabis market, which Steve Moore described as an overspill from the North American cannabis investment "bubble", has fallen away as that bubble burst. Many cannabis investors have had their fingers burned.

Policy arguments are rarely finally resolved. For now, the medico-penal constellation has reasserted its power to control decisions on medical cannabis. At the end of my interview with Steve Moore, I put it to him that the current situation is what you would end up with if the government just wanted to solve the problem of Alfie and Billy but go no further. He smiled ruefully and said, "exactly".

Conclusion: savvy social power and political cornering in the legalisation of medical cannabis

In 2015, medical cannabis was a relatively marginal issue supported by members of the least powerful policy constellation. Organisations like Release saw it as an issue of justice for people who used cannabis to treat their own ailments. Libertarians saw it as a matter of principle; that people should be free to decide on their own medication. Between 2015 and 2021, the epistemic power of medical cannabis researchers was combined with the economic, affective and media power of people who wanted to both expand the market for cannabis-based products and enable access to them in order to relieve suffering. In June 2018, the "plodding" work of traditional campaigners was topped off with a "lightning strike" of savvy social power by Volteface, Steve Moore and Charlotte Caldwell, backed by money from Paul Birch. They skilfully placed political decision-makers in a corner where they had only one way out. This was the proximal cause of the legalisation of cannabis-based medical products in November 2018, but it was made possible by years of work by other actors in other constellations of people, ideas and powers.

By 2021, the idea of using medical cannabis had numerous supporters across policy constellations. It had become compatible with the general support for compassion and advancing knowledge. There is still institutionalised resistance to the idea that patients themselves are best placed to decide what substances to take as medicine. The fear of the mental health problems that may be caused by cannabis infuses conservative positions on its use as a medicine. Paternalists and traditionalists have combined to prevent any further slippage of the drug policy ratchet.

The balance of powers between these positions currently holds medical cannabis in an iniquitous limbo. People with money can get medical cannabis products if they need them, but the state will not generally provide these medicines to those who cannot afford a private prescription.

The most visible actors in these debates are the individuals involved, such as Paul Flynn, Steve Moore, Charlotte Caldwell and Sajid Javid. Less visible are the established institutions that were called into advise, such as the ACMD and NICE. But behind all these actions, at a deeper level of social reality, lie the cultural and social structures that enable and constrain the preferences and powers of these actors. The collective emergence of moral preferences for liberty or control, combined with the social distribution of economic and institutional power, heavily influenced the outcomes of these debates. As Steve Moore told me, the policy cornering operation that he ran in 2018 depended on the financial backing he received from private sources. This acceleration of policy change was then braked by the socially structured ability of conservative politicians and paternalist public health professionals. They used their institutional power to retain the key principle on which they both depend for the preservation of their professional positions: that government-appointed experts know best which products should be available and who should be allowed to use them. Affective and economic power can only take a campaign for policy change so far in the face of deeply embedded structures of inertia in British drug policy making.

This has primarily been an English, Welsh and Irish story. The since-deceased Paul Flynn represented Newport in the Welsh county of Monmouth. Steve Moore and Charlotte Caldwell are from Northern Ireland. Dave Liddell told me that the "public health emergency" of drug-related deaths "crowded out" all other drug policy issues in Scotland. It is the varying responses to this emergency in England and Scotland that are explained in Chapter 10.

10

Responses to the Drug Deaths Crisis: Explaining Differences at UK and Scottish Levels

Ever since the end of the heroin drought of 2010–2012 and the simultaneous onset of fiscal austerity, drug-related deaths have been rising across the UK. This also coincided with a new emphasis on abstinence instead of harm reduction in drug treatment policies in both England and Scotland. Despite many recommendations to use evidence-informed interventions to reduce these deaths, it took until 2018 for the Scottish government to take action. The UK government was even slower to respond. It largely ignored these deaths in its 2017 drug strategy (HM Government, 2017), although they were a focus of the 2021 version (HM Government, 2021).

This chapter and the next will explore the policy constellations which surround the same issues in these two different polities: the UK level centred around Westminster and the Scottish level at Edinburgh. In both countries, there are long-standing debates between supporters of harm reduction and abstinence-based services. Both governments have faced calls to do more and have resisted doing so until recently. We will explore the different ethico-political bases of these two different national debates. This will help explain the different responses to the drug-related death crisis north and south of the Anglo-Scottish border. This explanation will rely not just on looking at the preferences of policy actors and political parties. It will incorporate the deeper cultural structures – the ethico-political bases of drug policy making – which are different in England and Scotland.

I have written elsewhere about the reasons and mechanisms for the inaction on drug-related deaths in England (Stevens, 2019). Chapter 11 examines more recent developments at UK level. So I will concentrate more in this chapter on Scottish policy constellations. Comparing these two nations shows how we can use the concepts of the policy constellations approach to explain different processes and outcomes in different settings.

In Scotland, we have the case of how a minimal and belated response to rising deaths was transformed into a substantial increase in funded and rhetorical support for saving lives. I identify two main opposing constellations in the Scottish drug policy field: a dominant reformist constellation and a challenging abstentionist constellation. Both these constellations developed a narrative that the high level of deaths were nationally 'shameful', a narrative that tapped into both the shared compassion of policy actors and the particular desire of nationalist politicians to prove that Scotland could handle its own problems. This doubly affective narrative was given additional power by national campaigns (including from one of the main Scottish newspapers) and the epistemic consensus that something had to be done. The opening – by Peter Krykant – of an unsanctioned overdose prevention centre (OPC) in Glasgow in 2020 provided a focus of these affective and epistemic concerns. By 2021, the Scottish government had devoted a much larger sum of money to drug treatment and declared a 'national mission' to reduce drug-related deaths.

The UK's drug-related death crisis: not enough or the wrong kind of treatment

In Chapter 2, I included some of the figures that show the scale of the UK's drug-related death crisis. Figure 2.1 showed that the number of deaths in Britain that were officially recorded as drug-related rose by 87 per cent between 2012 and 2019, and by 181 per cent between 1996 and 2019, with a small reduction recorded in 2020 (when the COVID-19 pandemic affected both deaths and their recording). It is this dramatic increase that led researchers and public health professionals to declare a crisis of drug-related deaths on both sides of the Anglo-Scottish border (Kimber et al, 2019; Nicholls et al, 2019; Rae et al, 2022).

The sharp rise in deaths provided plenty of grounds for blame. Many of us pointed the finger at governments who were cutting funding for drug treatment. Policy actors who agreed on this also disagreed with each other about what should be done with the money that remained. People in the public health constellation and the progressive wing of the drug policy reform constellations saw enrolling more people in opioid substitution therapy (OST), and for longer, as essential. We blamed the failure to do this for the rise in deaths. In our support, we cited epidemiological studies, like Pierce et al's (2015) estimate of OST saving hundreds of lives. We also pointed to the evidence that people who got into treatment were often in it for too short a period to benefit from a reduction in the risk of dying (Hickman et al, 2018). Systematic reviews of high-quality research suggest that OST reduces deaths (Sordo et al, 2017; Santo et al, 2021), but there is an elevated risk of dying within the first few weeks of starting and ending

OST. So if many people are cycling through short periods of treatment, there is a much smaller effect on population levels of death than if a large proportion of people who use heroin were stably maintained on methadone or buprenorphine.

The complexity of this argument did not impress people who held different views on OST. Those who preferred abstinence-based treatments blamed OST for the rise in deaths. This was an extension of the criticisms of OST that preceded the turn to recovery in the Scottish and UK drug strategies of 2008 and 2010 (Scottish Government, 2008; Lloyd, 2009; HM Government, 2010; MacGregor, 2017). At that time, it was not deaths that were causing such concern. They had been relatively stable for a few years in both countries. It was more the stubbornly high rates of relapse and the small proportions of people in drug treatment who achieved their desired goals of abstinence and recovery (Ashton, 2008; Easton, 2008). An interviewee told me "there were certain elements of the government at that point really pushing the system [towards recovery]. There was a lot of talk of people being parked on methadone and a lot of very negative, pejorative talk about what treatment services have gone before".

I spoke to Deirdre Boyd about this. She had been influential in the late 2000s in advising Iain Duncan Smith on his support for shifting funding from OST to abstinence-based recovery services. When I interviewed her, she had recently met with the Deputy Prime Minister, Dominic Raab, to discuss these issues. In our discussions of the drug-related death crisis, she emphasised the reduced number of beds available for residential rehabilitation. Only one per cent of people in treatment, she told me, are in such services. Her argument was echoed north of the Anglo-Scottish border by Annemarie Ward, the founder of FAVOR UK. Ward had a high profile in media discussions of drug policy. She was named as influential by several other people I spoke to in Scotland. She drew on her own experience of recovery to make the case for abstinence-based treatment. She also published a blog on the research evidence for residential rehabilitation, challenging 'the claims that there is no evidence base for it or 12 steps'[1] (Ward, 2020, np).

The blog contained interesting and useful references, including official guidance and systematic reviews that suggest that residential rehabilitation and 12-step mutual aid are more effective than other forms of treatment in helping people to achieve abstinence. The problem here is that the studies that Ward included in her blog do not show that these services are effective in reducing deaths. In her interview with me, Catriona Matheson referred to evidence suggesting that people in abstinence-based treatment have a high risk of dying. This echoed an Australian study showing that residential detoxification and rehabilitation services were the forms of treatment with the highest death rates (Lloyd et al, 2017), as well as a Norwegian study that showed high rates of death on leaving drug-free treatment (Ravndal and Amundsen, 2010). Pierce et al (2015, p 5) also supported the finding that '"drug-free" treatment is associated with a higher all-cause mortality risk'. It should be noted that even higher rates of death have been observed among similar people who are not in any treatment at all (Walley et al, 2020). Most recently, a Scottish study of 46,453 people who received any OST between 2011 and 2020 found that rates of drug-related death were more than three times higher for those off OST than those who were on it (McAuley et al, 2023).

Many people who have been through residential rehabilitation and the 12 steps want other people to have access to forms of treatment that they found to be life-saving. The 12th step encourages them to 'carry the message' (Wilson, 1939), to find meaning in helping other addicts to follow their path. There is a clash here, not just between ethico-political views on the good life but also between different forms of knowledge. On one side we hear about vivid, deeply felt experiences of the pains of addiction and the fulfilment of recovery. On the other, we find the more dispassionate calculations of survival curves and adjusted hazard ratios. These are the stock in trade of people who make their living by studying death. To adapt Habermas' (1986, p 241) turn of phrase, in the clash of such irreconcilable forms of knowledge, 'the strongest interest will happen to be the one actually implemented'.

Reactions to rising deaths

In neither England nor Scotland was there a swift reaction to the rise in drug-related deaths. When I interviewed Professor Catriona Matheson, who had recently resigned as chair of the Scottish Drug Deaths Taskforce, she told me that she and colleagues like Dr Roy Robertson were already concerned about the rise in deaths in Scotland by 2015. This was about the same time that Annette Dale-Perera and I discussed our concerns and suggested to fellow members of the Advisory Council on the Misuse of Drugs (ACMD) that we write a report on the issue. It took years, and different paths through different policy constellations, until substantial action would be taken at either Scottish or UK level.

Indifference to deaths in England

At UK and English level, there was very little reaction in the 2017 drug strategy to our work for the ACMD (2016e) on how to reduce deaths. Our main recommendation was that investment in OST be, at least, maintained. This did not happen. Funding for drug treatment was cut (Black, 2020a). The ACMD also recommended improved recording and investigation of drug-related deaths, provision of assertive outreach services, central funding of heroin-assisted treatment, reduction of the socio-economic drivers of problematic drug use, and consideration of the establishment of OPCs in areas with high concentrations of injecting drug use. Ironically, the last of these was the only recommendation that was actually followed. The government did consider opening OPCs but decided against it (Atkins, 2018). None of the other recommendations were actually implemented, even though the government formally accepted them in its response to the ACMD (Brine and Newton, 2017).

In the article I wrote about this non-reaction to rising deaths in the 2017 UK drug strategy, I focused on two explanations (Stevens, 2019). One was that the people who were dying were not the type of people who elicit sympathy from conservative politicians and voters. They were largely middle-aged working-class men living in deindustrialised towns and cities, far away from the centres of power and wealth in London and the south-east of England. In Schneider and Ingram's (1993) terms, they were 'deviants'. In Butler's (2016) terms, their deaths were not 'grievable'. In the terms of the policy constellations approach, these deaths were not salient to members of the most powerful policy constellations, and so little action was taken to prevent them.

The other explanation I gave in that article was that members of the conservative policy constellation performed a 'moral sidestep' when confronted with evidence about these deaths. They were challenged with empirical argument about the numbers and causes involved, and with evidence on the best way to reduce them. Instead of meeting these challenges head on with empirical evidence of their own, traditionist policy actors who did not want to change course presented this as a moral conflict between irresponsible liberals and righteous defenders of abstinent purity. As an example of the moral sidestep, I quoted Prime Minister Theresa May's response to the challenge by the Scottish National Party (SNP)'s Ronnie Cowan on why she would not support OPS:

> I have a different opinion to some Members of this House. Some are very liberal in their approach to the way that drugs should be treated. I am very clear that we should recognise the damage that drugs do to people's lives. Our aim should be to ensure that people come off drugs, do not go on drugs in the first place and keep clear of drugs. That is what we should focus on. (Hansard, 2017b)

Theresa May was pushed out of office in 2019. Her successor, Boris Johnson, introduced a new drugs strategy in December 2021. As I will show in the Chapter 11, this included some new funding for the reduction of drug-related deaths but not support for OPCs. Within the more traditionalist wing of the medico-penal constellation, the moral objection to the provision of some harm reduction services remains.

Policy constellations in Scotland

To understand the different paths taken in the response to drug-related deaths in England and Scotland, we need to understand the differences in the presence of policy constellations in Scotland compared to the UK policy level that I described in Chapters 6, 7 and 8.

Before looking at Scottish drug policy constellations, let's briefly examine the contexts within which they operate. Important contexts include the size of the nation and its constitutional status. Having a smaller population and polity means that the policy constellations are more tightly networked in Scotland than at UK level. There was less of the distance between governmental insiders and outsiders that I observed at UK level. The politics of familiarity operate on a different scale in Scotland, with more opportunities for personal connections across policy constellations. In recent years, the Scottish government has also developed a distinctive approach to policy making which combines the two narratives of following evidence and co-production (Cairney, 2017, 2021).

Constitutionally, Scotland has its own legal system, but the Misuse of Drugs Act is 'reserved'. This means that it is the UK rather than the Scottish Parliament which has the power to change the drug law of Scotland. This is a major bone of contention in Scottish drug policy debates. When challenged on the rising death toll, nationalist supporters of Scottish independence tended to put at least some of the blame on the UK government for failure to reform drug policy. Unionists saw this as an excuse for the SNP's own failure to tackle rising deaths.

Another crucial feature of the Scottish context is its distinct ethical and political inheritance. The vote share of the Conservative and Unionist Party in Scotland was smaller than Labour's in every post-war election until 2015, by which time Labour had been usurped by the SNP as Scotland's largest political force. The SNP continued the more statist approach that was a distinctive feature of the Scottish labour movement. Before the Second World War, '[t]he social gospel of the Scottish churches, which concentrated on the need to abolish or legislate away material impediments to man reaching God, was mirrored in the desire of the Labour leaders to improve the material and moral standards of the Scottish working class' (Knox, 1988, p 627). Knox documented how the Scottish churches, which had in the nineteenth century seen poverty as the result of the moral failure and intemperance of the poor, came to modify their position towards social rather than individual reform, a position known as 'ethical socialism'.

Figure 10.1 shows a sociogram of policy actors and policy positions in the Scottish drug policy field between 2015 and 2021. It is constructed in the same way as Figure 7.1 in Chapter 7. The difference is that it includes

Figure 10.1: Sociogram of the Scottish drug policy field (with relevant ethico-political bases in italics)

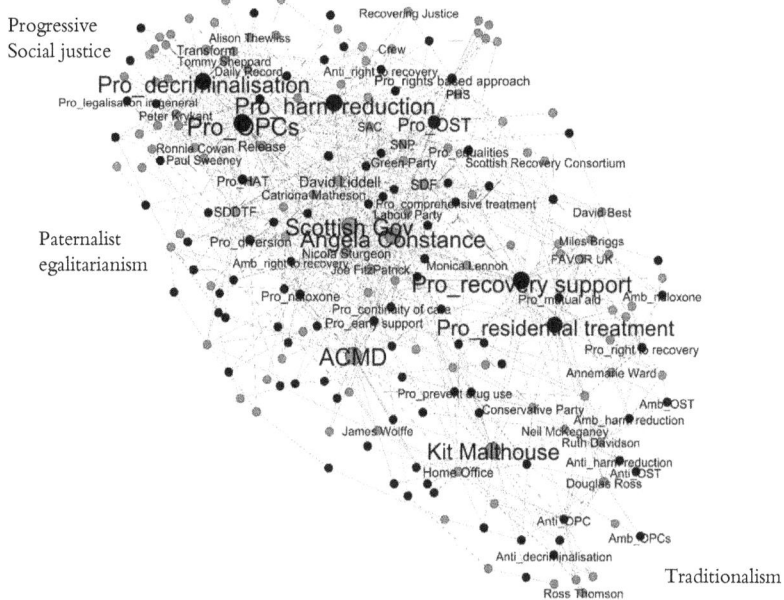

only those individuals and organisations that I coded as being actors in the Scottish drug policy field. This includes Members of the Scottish Parliament, some Scottish MPs and others employed in England whom I observed to be active in Scottish events and debates. It also includes some organisations that are based in England (for example, Transform and Release) who also work with partners in Scotland. And it includes the UK drugs minister Kit Malthouse. He occasionally travelled to discuss drug policy in Scotland and also played a role in blocking Scottish agencies' wishes to open an officially sanctioned OPC. The UK Home Office is an actor in Scottish drug policy, but the UK Department of Health and Social Care is not. This is because drug law is reserved to Westminster, whereas health policy is devolved to Edinburgh.

The sociogram again excludes nodes that had less than two ties to other nodes in order to create a clearer view of the policy field. So it contains 208 (75 per cent) of the nodes and 765 (93 per cent) of the ties between them in the Scottish dataset. This filtering was done after the sociogram was laid out.

I again used the Gephi modularity statistic to identify closely connected 'Louvain communities' (Blondel et al, 2008) in the social network of policy actors and positions. For the analysis of Scottish policy constellations, it seemed most practically adequate to split the field into two main

Figure 10.2: Sociogram of the Scottish drug policy field showing policy constellations

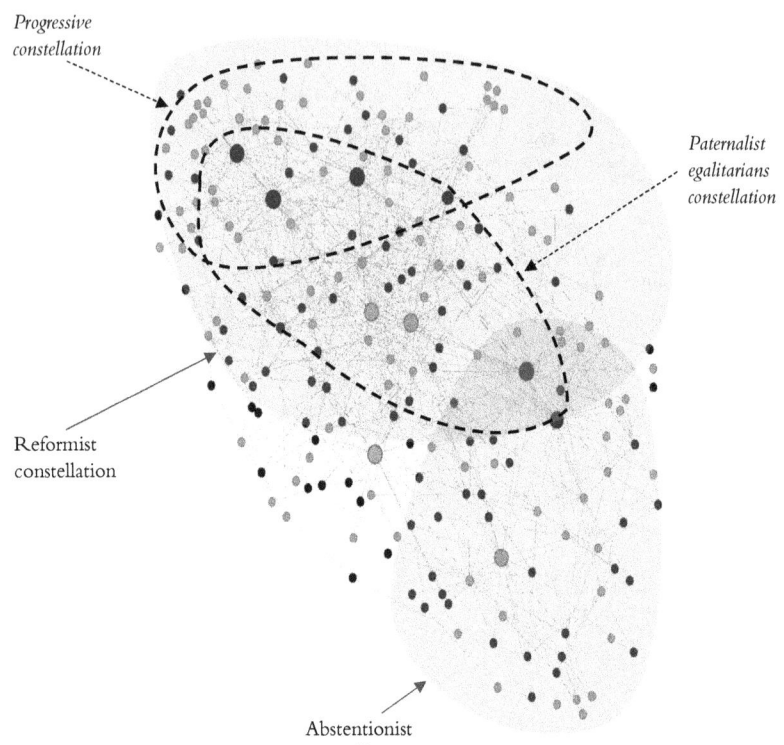

constellations – abstentionist and reformist – as shown in Figure 10.2. Some of the central policy actors (organisations and individuals) and policy positions of these constellations are shown in Tables 10.1 and 10.2. A fuller list of organisations and positions, with their module allocation, is given in Online Appendix 5.1. Interestingly, this two-constellation model may make the Scottish drug policy field more similar to the Swiss than its UK-level counterpart. In his analysis of Swiss drug policy, Kübler (2001) also found two competing 'coalitions' focused on abstention and reform.

By comparing the sociograms of the Scottish drug policy field to those for the UK level, we can see some interesting differences. One is that there is a smaller, less concentrated constellation of support for traditionalist policy positions. This comes together around a narrower range of policy positions than I found in the conservative corner of the UK drug policy field. Outwith the Conservative Party, I did not find much support in Scotland for tougher sentencing and shaming of drug-related offenders. But there is a common preference in the bottom right-hand corner of the Scottish sociograms for

Table 10.1: Selected members of the reformist policy constellation

Policy positions	Policy actors	
	Organisations	Individuals
Amb_right to recovery	Daily Record	Aileen Campbell MSP
Anti_right to recovery	Scottish Green Party	Alison Thewliss MP
Pro_continuity of care	Labour Party	Anas Sarwan MSP
Pro_decriminalisation	Public Health Scotland	Becky Wood
Pro_diversion	Release	Catriona Matheson
Pro_equalities	Scottish Affairs Committee	Fiona McQueen
Pro_harm reduction	Scottish Drug Deaths Taskforce	Joe FitzPatrick MSP
Pro_MAT	Scottish Drugs Forum	Nicola Sturgeon MSP
Pro_naloxone	Scottish Families Affected by Alcohol and Drugs	Paul Sweeney MP/MSP
Pro_NSP		Peter Krykant
Pro_OPCs	Scottish government	Ronnie Cowan MP
Pro_OST	Scottish National Party	Lord Stuart McDonald
Pro_public health approach	Scottish Recovery Consortium	
Pro_rights based approach	Transform	

policies that promote abstinence from illicit drugs. This is why I call this the abstentionist constellation.

Traditionalist policy actors are thinner on the ground in Scotland. This is partly due to the relatively smaller electoral support for the Conservative Party in Scotland. But it is also due to the greater role of a different ethico-political base, which is support for equality. This type of fairness was often present in the Scottish policy discourse and not just in the form of equality of opportunity, as promoted by the Scottish Conservatives' (2021) election manifesto. The election manifestos of the four other main parties in Scotland promote fairness as equality of outcome. Labour and the Liberal Democrats explicitly promised to pursue 'social justice'. The Green manifesto was peppered with references to fairness and equality. And in her foreword to the SNP manifesto, the First Minster presented her vision of a Scotland 'with kindness, compassion, fairness, equality and enterprise at its heart' (Sturgeon, in SNP, 2021, p 3).

I am tempted to conclude that Scottish politics continues to be influenced by the ideals of ethical socialism. Not all of these parties would see themselves as being socialist, but they all supported the principles of equality that were enshrined in the UK-wide Equalities Act 2010 (one of the final acts of the New Labour administration). The Scottish Government (2018a) introduced the Fairer Scotland Duty, committing public bodies to achieving 'equality of outcome' in 'material conditions', a quintessentially socialist, universalist aim.

The inclusion of enterprise in Sturgeon's (2021) vision reminds us that Adam Smith – the great advocate of both free trade and 'mutual

Table 10.2: Selected members of the abstentionist policy constellation

Policy positions	Policy actors	
	Organisations	Individuals
Anti_decriminalisation	Church of Scotland	Annemarie Ward
Anti_legalisation	Conservative Party	Annie Wells MSP
Anti_OPC	Corra	Douglas Ross MSP
Pro_buvidal	Cyrenians	Kit Malthouse MP
Pro_CBMP (cannabis-based medical products) legal	FAVOR UK	Miles Briggs MSP
	Free Church of Scotland	Monica Lennon MSP
Pro_mutual aid	Home Office	Natalie Logan MacLean
Pro_prevent drug use	Methodist Church of Scotland	Neil McKeganey
Pro_recovery support		Peter Wishart
Pro_residential treatment	Phoenix Futures	Baroness Ruth Davidson
Pro_right to recovery	Recovery Enterprises Scotland	
Pro_supply reduction	River Garden	

sympathy' – was a Scot. But free market liberalism now has a much lesser presence in the Scottish than UK drug policy field. There are, for example, only two right-wing think tanks in Scotland: Reform Scotland and Bright Blue Scotland (Mykkänen and Freshwater, 2021). Of the two, Bright Blue presents itself as more 'liberal'. Neither has produced reports on drug policy, although one staffer of Bright Blue Scotland did write an article in *The Scotsman* newspaper advocating the opening of OPCs and the decriminalisation – not legalisation – of drugs (Silke, 2021). Silke argued for a 'public health approach', not a libertarian approach. In my discourse analysis, I did not observe much influence of the ethico-political base of liberty in the Scottish drug policy field.

Paternalism was present in the Scottish drug policy field, but with a strong overlap with egalitarianism. The idea that the state owes it to citizens to redress social inequalities is much more firmly embedded in the Scottish than the English polity. The duty of the state to control private activities that threaten public health is also more influential in Scotland than at UK level. This may be a reason why the minimum unit pricing of alcohol – that policy so detested by Chris Snowdon and the Institute of Economic Affairs – has been adopted in Scotland but not in England.

In analysing drug policy discourses, I came across fascinating echoes of these different moral visions for Scotland. On one side, inheriting religious belief in temperance and redemption, were policy actors who advocated abstinence-based residential rehabilitation as the cure to Scotland's drug-related ills. On the other side is a policy constellation that also expresses compassion for the suffering of working-class people who use drugs, but it does so through the practices of harm reduction to protect public health. All my Scottish interviewees and many items of Scottish discourse referred to this divide. It was also found in Atkinson et al's (2019) analysis of newspaper articles on the proposal to open an OPC in Glasgow. Using Bacchi's (2009) 'what's the problem represented to be?' framework, they found discourses that diverged between supporters of public health and proponents of abstinent recovery. The public health position tends to be the one with the highest level of institutional power in Scottish drug policy, although there is also support here for services which aim at recovery from problematic drug use (as shown in the shaded overlap in Figure 10.2). Nicholls et al (2022) found 'widespread support' for OPCs in their interviews with government and third-sector staff in Scotland, as had also been found among Scottish people who inject drugs (Trayner et al, 2020). Opposition to OPCs tended to come from Conservative politicians and advocates of abstinence-based treatment. The forces of ethico-political repulsion have maintained a divide between these two parts of the Scottish drug policy field: the reform and abstentionist constellations.

I also observed this ethico-political divide in the debate around the proposed 'right to recovery'. The need for this was identified in a report by FAVOR UK (2021, p 6) on residential rehabilitation. 'Despite there being general duties ... placed upon Local Authorities to provide services to those seeking help with drug/alcohol issues, there is no statutory right that can be challenged if someone doesn't get a particular type of service'. Douglas Ross, leader of the Scottish Conservative Party, launched a consultation on the Right to Addiction Recovery (Scotland) Bill in October 2021. He accused the existing treatment system of being 'fixated' on providing methadone, an approach which had 'failed for years' (Ross, 2021, p 3).

Responses to the proposed right to recovery fell broadly into the same two opposing camps as shown in the shaded constellations in Figure 10.2. Some providers of abstinence-based residential rehabilitation services were strongly in favour, as were the Church of Scotland, the Methodist Church and the Free Church of Scotland. There was also support from politicians (mainly Conservative, but also from Labour). The response from advocates of harm reduction and public sector treatment professionals was more reserved. They saw the need to improve access to treatment but were sceptical that creating a specific right was the way to do it. So they ended up opposing the proposed bill in a joint statement from the Scottish Drugs Forum (SDF), the Scottish Recovery Consortium, Crew, Families Campaign for Change, HIV Scotland, Recovering Justice and Release (SDF, 2022). Opponents of the specific right to recovery tended to support a broader rights-based approach to social and health policy in general, as shown near the top left of the Scottish sociogram.

The Scottish government was in the uncomfortable position of straddling this divide (similar to Steve Rolles' precarious attempts to straddle the divide between social justice and free market libertarianism in the UK-level policy field). Senior members of the SNP refused to commit themselves either way. Nicola Sturgeon said she was 'open-minded' about the right to recovery (Webster, 2021, np). Angela Constance told me that before deciding on the bill, which had not yet been formally presented to Parliament, "I would need to see it". This could be seen as a sagacious reserving of judgement until the details are known or as a tactical avoidance of taking a position that would disappoint at least one of the two sides in the debate. Perhaps it was both these things.

The ties between these policy actors and their positions suggest an interesting relationship between policy constellations and the distinct ethico-political bases that animate drug policy discussions in Scotland. Policies motivated by compassion can again be found across the policy field, so this does not appear in Figure 10.1 as a distinct ethico-political base. The centre of the social network of policy actors and positions is taken up by a closely networked constellation that shares a commitment to paternalist egalitarianism. It combines the universalist belief that outcomes, not just opportunities, should be equal and the paternalist belief that the state has both a right and a duty to intervene in the lives of citizens to promote the common good. The actors who share these beliefs are grouped in a paternalist egalitarian constellation within the broader reformist constellation in Figure 10.2. It overlaps with another constellation within the reformist constellation. This is made up of actors and policy positions that reflect a belief in more radical forms of progressive social justice, especially support for decriminalisation of possession and the establishment of OPCs to protect people from dying, even if they continue to use heroin and other illicit drugs. The progressive belief in legalisation is outside the overlap between egalitarian paternalists and progressives, as it was expressed only by members of the latter constellation.

The egalitarian part of the reformist constellation includes all the main Scottish political parties except the Conservatives. This is because of their broadly shared positions on drug policy, including support for diverting drug possession offenders from prosecution and for the provision of harm reduction services, as well as support for recovery. This constellation contains the Scottish government and senior ministers, as well as "nationally commissioned organisations" like the SDF, the Scottish Recovery Consortium and Scottish Families Affected by Alcohol and Drugs. This is not because they always agree with each other or coordinate their actions. Rather, it is because they gravitate towards each other, acting loosely in concert towards the achievement of similar goals.

It is a more granular analysis (with a lower value for the modularity parameter in Gephi) which identified the separation between the egalitarian paternalist and the more progressive parts of the reformist constellation. This latter included Peter Krykant, the activist who set up the unsanctioned OPC in Glasgow in 2020/21, as well as other actors who supported legalisation, including Transform and Ronnie Cowan MP. There are discussions across these parts of the reformist constellation. Krykant was invited into direct discussions with both First Minister Nicola Sturgeon and drugs minister Angela Constance, again showing the more tightly networked nature of the Scottish drug policy field.

Policy constellations and the response to drug-related deaths in Scotland

There was a 22 per cent cut in annual funding for Scottish drug and alcohol services (from £69.2 to £53.8 million) in the year between 2015/16 and 2016/17, even as deaths rose (Audit Scotland, 2019). In the period 2015–2018, pressure mounted on the Scottish government. This came from various members of both the dominant reformist and challenging abstentionist drug policy constellations.

In July 2017, the then public health minister promised a 'refresh' of the drug strategy. It was initially intended to include a 'seek, keep and treat' framework (Campbell, 2017). This would have meant providing assertive outreach (as recommended by the ACMD, 2016e) to get more people into treatment and retain them there. The idea came partly in response to the accusation – from the SDF and others – that part of the reason for the higher death rate in Scotland than England was the smaller proportion of people who were in drug treatment. However, the strategy document that Joe FitzPatrick launched in November 2018 (Scottish Government, 2018b) did not include the 'seek, keep and treat' framework. Dave Liddell told me that this was for two reasons. One was that "the recovery community put the boot into the keep part". Keeping people on methadone would conflict with their desire to support abstinence.

The other reason that treatment could not be provided to more people for longer was lack of funding. Only £20 million per year of additional funding was provided to achieve the strategy's aims. This was seen as inadequate by many in the field. Some, including some of my interviewees, accused SNP ministers of trying to please all parts of the drug policy field, "to dampen down controversy", rather than focusing limited resources on the most effective policies.

There was, however, little in the 2017 strategy to please conservative traditionalists. No denouncement of the evil of vile drugs. No promises to 'crack down' on 'drug barons'. And when prison was mentioned, it was in the hope of reducing its use, not imposing harsher sentences. Similarly, there was little to encourage libertarians. There was no promise to decriminalise possession, let alone legalise sale. The use of cannabis or psilocybin for medical purposes was not even mentioned.

Despite the strategic refresh, drug-related deaths continued to rise in Scotland. In July 2019, recorded annual deaths exceeded the symbolic threshold of a thousand (PHS, 2019). The *Daily Record* launched a campaign on drug policy, having earlier published a call from Dave Liddell to decriminalise drug possession (McGivern, 2019). The *Record* is one of Scotland's mass circulation newspapers, traditionally supporting Labour against both the Conservatives and the SNP. It now argued for both decriminalisation and the opening of OPCs in an editorial announcing its campaign. 'People are dying. We have to help them by treating drugs as a health issue and not turning users into criminals' (Daily Record, 2019, np).

Drug-related deaths came increasingly to be seen across the political spectrum as a national 'shame'. The numbers were presented as shameful by both the green socialist writer and rapper Darren 'Loki' McGarvey and the former leader of the Scottish Conservative Party, Baroness Ruth Davidson (McGarvey, 2019; Davidson, 2021).

Policy actors often made comparisons to other countries. The shaming factoid that Scotland has the highest drug-related death rate in Europe was commonly used.[2] Dramatic comparisons were also made to other disasters. Baroness Davidson (2021) gave a sensational list of things that had killed fewer people than the Scottish drug deaths crisis. The list included: Hurricane Katrina; the sinking of the Titanic; the attacks on both Pearl Harbor and the World Trade Center; the bombings on London transport in July 2007 and of the Manchester Arena in May 2017; the downing of flight PA103 at Lockerbie; the Dunblane mass shootings; the Blantyre mining disaster of 1877; and – delving even further back in British history – the charge of the Light Brigade at the battle of Balaklava. It was as if the mere deaths of over a thousand fellow citizens per year were not enough to stir up action. An affective effort had to be made to translate this fact into a national scandal. Other than a suffering child, what could be more affective than presenting drug policy as not only ineffective but also shameful? It was this shame, I was told by Dave Liddell and others, that led to a change in policy, and then minister, by the SNP.

In July 2019, the Scottish government set up the Scottish Drug Deaths Taskforce (SDDTF). Its role was 'to examine the evidence and make recommendations to help save and improve the lives of people who use drugs' (Scottish Government, 2022c, np). Its membership was deliberately inclusive, with representatives of families and people with direct experience of drug problems, as well as academics. The mixture of different forms of knowledge that they brought to these discussions was sometimes a bit awkward. I was told of disputes between knowledge that was based on peer-reviewed research written by qualified experts, and the different knowledge that comes from 'lived experience'. The reports that the Taskforce produced tended to present the same kind of harm reduction advice that the ACMD had produced in 2016. The Taskforce also looked directly at the possibility of decriminalisation, which the ACMD had not. For the ACMD to have done so would have broken the implicit rule of not frightening the political horses in Westminster. My view is that this was why another ACMD (2016b) report, which explicitly recommended decriminalisation, was not published but rather marked confidential, even though a previous report had found little evidence that criminalisation worked and had openly recommended diversion 'away from a criminal path to a psychosocial/treatment path' (ACMD, 2016a, p 10). In a different ethico-political climate, the Scottish Taskforce was freer to recommend decriminalisation, which it eventually did (SDDTF, 2021b).

By then, the SNP party conference had unanimously passed a motion supporting the decriminalisation of drug possession (BBC News, 2019). In the same month, the Scottish Affairs Committee of the UK House of Commons published the report of its inquiry into *Problem Drug Use in Scotland*, which also recommended decriminalisation. Many of the policy actors who are in the sociogram in Figure 10.1 appeared as witnesses before the committee. I spoke in a session alongside senior police officers. All expressed reservations about a criminal justice approach to drugs. As I told the committee, it was remarkable to hear senior police officers resile from the idea that prohibition and criminalisation are necessary to reduce drug-related harms. Assistant Chief Constable Steve Johnson of Police Scotland told the committee that criminalisation is 'deleterious [... in] pushing people into a place where there is more harm' (Scottish Affairs Committee, 2019, p 39). He supported the Scottish government's move to a 'public health approach'.

The committee's report supported such an approach. It also supported decriminalisation and the establishment of overdose prevention centres. It heard evidence from both the UK drugs minister Kit Malthouse and the Scottish Lord Advocate James Wolffe that this would be unlawful under the Misuse of Drugs Act. This is legally questionable (Fortson, 2017). But it persuaded the committee to recommend that the UK government change the law, not that Scottish agencies go ahead and open OPCs without a surer legal basis (Scottish Affairs Committee, 2019, p 38).

This questionable legal advice did not deter Peter Krykant from opening the first publicly advertised OPC in a converted vehicle in September 2019. His was a deliberate attempt to shame the Scottish government into action, as well as to directly save lives. Krykant had moved from the abstentionist position that he had adopted in the early years of his own recovery from problematic drug use towards support of harm reduction and legalisation of drug supply. He managed to run the service without being prosecuted, although he was once arrested for allegedly obstructing a police search (the charge was dropped). The service ran on donations and the unpaid work of volunteers, including the Labour politician Paul Sweeney. This was not sustainable. The service closed in May 2020. While it was open, it reversed nine overdoses among eight people (Shorter et al, 2022). The fact that it was able to run without being closed down by the police led many to question the reason that ministers gave for not opening an officially sanctioned OPC. The SNP blamed the UK government for not changing the law, demanding devolution of drug laws, in line with their overarching ambition for Scottish independence.

Media coverage of Krykant's unsanctioned OPC added to the clamour for more to be done. The drug policy debate in Scotland came to a head when the drug-related death figures for 2019 were published in December 2020. When the shocking numbers of deaths were announced, Darren McGarvey (2020) accused the minister Joe FitzPatrick of being 'incapable of leading us anywhere but the mortuary'. In Parliament, Liddell recalled, FitzPatrick cut a forlorn and isolated figure. He 'agreed to leave' his post (BBC News, 2020). He was replaced by Angela Constance, whose remit was narrowed to just focus on drugs. This was a turning point towards a more substantial approach which aligned the SNP's policy on drugs more closely with its broader ambitions to transform Scotland.

During 2020, the Drug Deaths Taskforce had been working on gathering the evidence and consulting widely on appropriate responses. It prioritised six areas for 'immediate action'. They were '1. Targeted distribution of naloxone 2. Implement immediate response pathway for non-fatal overdose 3. Optimise the use of Medication-Assisted Treatment 4. Target the people most at risk 5. Optimise Public Health Surveillance 6. Ensure equivalence of support for people in the Criminal Justice System' (SDDTF, 2020, p 4). Note that these priorities do not include residential rehabilitation or other abstinence-based services. One of the first substantive reports to be published by the Taskforce was its work on *Drug Law Reform* (SDDTF, 2021b).

Decriminalisation was becoming a mainstream position in the Scottish policy debate. Even the Moderator of the Church of Scotland came out in favour of it as a means of reducing deaths (although he made clear he was speaking in a personal capacity and not for the Church) (BBC News, 2021b). Decriminalisation had not been included in the SNP's manifesto for the UK general election in December 2019, but it was in the manifesto for the Scottish Parliament election in May 2021 (SNP, 2021). At this election, opposition parties denounced drug deaths as 'a shameful sign of the SNP's failed drugs policy' (Scottish Conservatives and Unionists, 2021, p 36). This did not prevent the SNP again being the largest party in the Scottish Parliament, although its share of the vote fell and it needed a power-sharing agreement with the Scottish Greens to form a government.

Meanwhile, the cries of 'shame' continued. People from both reformist and abstinence-focused constellations saw action on deaths as being too limited and too slow. The campaign for change from the media and civil society grew. In January 2021, Nicola Sturgeon responded by announcing that an additional £50 million would be spent annually on drug treatment (Sturgeon, 2021). This would add up to £250 million over the five years of the Parliament, of which £100 million would be spent on residential rehabilitation. Catriona Matheson told me she could hardly believe her ears when she was told this shortly before Sturgeon's announcement. It was the allocation of a substantial sum of money to residential rehabilitation that shocked her most. This had not been recommended by her Taskforce. She did not see this as an "evidence-based" decision. There were, she thought, "glaring gaps" in the statement, for example around young people and prevention. Her expressing her reservations was not warmly welcomed by the new drugs minister, Angela Constance. This was a "bad start" to the working relationship between Matheson and Constance. The Taskforce was more focused on harm reduction. Matheson saw this as justified by the evidence. In her view, money was being "sprayed around everywhere to try and keep people happy". The "Twitterati" and the recovery advocates were "appeased" by spending money on residential rehabilitation. Dave Liddell also told me that the money for residential rehabilitation was an effort to satisfy vocal policy advocates, like FAVOR UK, rather than being based on evidence. For Matheson, the "final straw" came when Constance told the Taskforce to finish its work early, by July 2022. Matheson resigned from the Taskforce in December 2021.

When I interviewed her, the minister herself had a very different view of these events. She was candid about the problems she faced and her party's partial responsibility for them. She restated that drug law is reserved to the UK government, but she acknowledged that the criminal justice and health systems are the responsibility of the Scottish government. "We have to be frank", she said, "that we've not done as well with the powers we have as we should have ... the fact that we don't have enough people in treatment is on us". The extra money announced by Sturgeon was to be part of the solution to this. Constance justified the spending on residential rehabilitation, which so troubled Professor Matheson, on the basis that it was an "acknowledgement that it is an expensive form of treatment" and so cannot be left to local funding.

This is the same argument that the ACMD and I made for funding of heroin-assisted treatment (ACMD, 2016e). In Scotland, this argument was heeded in 2019 when a specialist heroin-assisted treatment clinic was opened in Glasgow (Glasgow City Council, 2019). The epistemic power of public health experts was more impactful in an ethico-political context that was more conducive to the establishment of harm reduction services. Neither the ACMD nor the Scottish Drugs Death Taskforce recommended dedicated funding for residential rehabilitation. But the affective power of personal testimonies combined with the epistemic power of lived experience of recovery advocates in Scotland was sufficient to force the government to allocate a specific budget to this form of treatment.

The weight that the abstinence-favouring policy constellation could bring to the Scottish policy debate was not enough to sway the public health establishment. Before she left, Matheson's Taskforce published the *Medication Assisted Treatment (MAT) Standards* (SDDTF, 2021a). The most commonly mentioned medications in the report were methadone, buprenorphine (both used as substitutes for heroin), and naloxone (the antidote to opiate overdose). There is no mention of medicines that are used to support abstinence, such as naltrexone (NICE, 2007). Abstinence is mentioned in the document, but only to say that it should be offered as a choice alongside MAT. The standards were produced by a sub-group of the Taskforce which included clinicians from several disciplines. They were presented as being both 'evidence-based' and 'developed through extensive consultation with multiagency partners that deliver care, and, with the individuals, families and communities with experience of problematic drug use' (SDDTF, 2021a, p 6). This attempt to straddle Cairney's (2021) two narratives of 'evidence-based policy making' and 'co-production' was only directed towards the policy preferences of the reformist constellation. The Taskforce did not publish guidance on abstinence-based or residential treatment.

The debate between abstinence and harm reduction in general, and on the right to recovery in particular, continues. This debate is rehearsed across the UK. It has been particularly sharp in Scotland, perhaps because of the scale of deaths, the salience given to them by media and campaigning organisations, and their inherently affective nature. The outcomes of these debates at the UK and Scottish levels have been rather different. Scotland moved sooner than the UK government, and at greater relative scale, to invest in both abstinence-based and harm reduction services. The annual spending for drug treatment that Scotland announced in January 2021 was much bigger, per head of population, than the spending announced by the UK government for England in December of that year. And, as we will see in the next chapter, the investment in England was secured through a different combination of constellations, narratives, ethico-political influences and forms of power.

Conclusion: explaining policy responses to drug-related deaths

By the end of my data period in December 2021, the UK and Scottish responses to drug-related deaths had some similar features. Both the UK and Scottish governments had found money to spend on drug treatment and supported the provision of comprehensive treatment services. The mix of services, and the paths of their development, were different in these two polities. To explain this, we need to pay attention to their different contexts, policy constellations, ethico-political bases and forms of power. My argument here is that the differences between the two nations emerge partly from their different cultural structures and particularly from the greater salience of ethical socialism and the relatively lesser force of traditionalism on drug policy in Scotland.

In Scotland, policy constellations operate in a distinct context of national size, constitution and cultural inheritance. Their combined uses of epistemic and affective power have produced a specifically Scottish policy mix. There is now official commitment to a rights-based approach and a 'national mission' to reduce drug-related deaths (Sturgeon, 2021). This reflects the normative commitment to achieve social justice through what I observed as paternalist egalitarianism. There is now a raft of initiatives that codify the desire to promote equality, human rights and public health in a way that incorporates both scientific and experiential knowledge. These include the Fairer Scotland Duty and the National Collaboration, chaired by Professor Alan Millar, which 'will develop and implement a human rights-based approach to ensure that the voices and rights of people with lived and living experience are at the centre of policy and decision making' (Scottish Government, 2022b, np). Specifically for drug policy, there is the ambition to ensure that services meet the standards for medication-assisted treatment and the multiple recommendations of the Scottish Drug Deaths Taskforce's final report (SDDTF, 2021a, 2022). This goes alongside the Scottish government's ambition to complete the post-war vision of state support 'from the cradle to the grave'[3] by creating a National Care Service alongside the NHS to provide socialised social as well as health care (Scottish Government, 2022a).

For criminal justice policy in Scotland, Fotopoulou and Aston (2023, p 151) have expressed their concern that 'whilst the language of the policy context signals a progressive approach, there is a gap between policy and practice'. They share this concern with many of the people I spoke to about Scottish drug policy. Indeed, it was also shared by the Scottish drugs minister. She told me, "where the Scottish government's been on a bit of a journey is that we have some excellent laws and we have some wonderful, visionary, progressive policy. But actually, it needs to be delivered on the ground".

In Scotland, the combined powers of the reformist and abstinence-focused policy constellations worked to persuade senior ministers within the governing party that substantial response to drug-related deaths should be a key part of its policy agenda. There was a kind of imminent critique of the SNP; shaming senior politicians by pointing to the gap between the party's ambitions to transform Scotland to create justice and rights for all and the rising tide of deaths in the poorest communities. Constance finished our interview by telling me that getting this right was an important test for the SNP. "Unless we start getting it right for the most stigmatised and marginalised folk in society, we don't get it right for anybody". The most powerful members of the dominant drug policy constellation internalised the most affectively powerful challenge of their rivals for power. In doing so, they changed both written policies and spending plans to create a more substantial, if belated, response to drug-related deaths.

In England, where there is a different balance between drug policy constellations, we need a different explanation for why the UK government changed tack on drug treatment spending between its drug strategies of 2017 and 2021. This explanation is provided in Chapter 11.

11

The UK's Ten-Year Drug Strategy

For decades now, the UK government has laid out its plans for drug policy in the form of official drug strategy documents. The first of these was published in March 1985 under the title *Tackling Drug Misuse* (Home Office, 1985). It presented a range of policies that were to reappear in various guises in subsequent documents. Its proposed solutions to 'drug misuse' included working with international partners to cut supply, enforcing domestic drug legislation, and programmes to prevent the use of controlled drugs and to treat people who develop problems with them. The latest drug strategy was published in December 2021, entitled *From Harm to Hope: A 10-Year Drugs Plan to Cut Crime and Save Lives* (HM Government, 2021). These strategies are the results of complex processes of interaction and debate which take place largely within the machinery of government. They are influenced by the generative mechanisms of policy making, including its underlying social and cultural structures. These create the preferences of particular policy actors and enable or constrain them in putting these preferences into policy by putting them in advantaged or disadvantaged positions in the policy making process. This means that drug strategies are excellent cases for developing our understanding of how drug policy making works.

The 2021 strategy provides a particularly interesting case because it was so surprising. Much of it was reminiscent of previous documents. It was presented, like several of its predecessors, as a new approach which would at last reduce the harms of drugs. This was to be achieved by a combination of supply reduction, law enforcement, prevention and treatment. So far, so familiar. The surprising element was that this strategy, for the first time in over a decade, came with substantial funding attached. The first drug strategy of the most recent Conservative era, published in 2010, made big promises but was doomed to failure by the lack of funding to back these pledges up (Stevens, 2011b). The 2017 strategy added no new funding, instead continuing the cuts of the austerity programme that began under David Cameron's Chancellor, George Osborne (HM Government, 2017; Stevens,

2019). The 2021 strategy, by contrast, came with a promise of £533 million to spend on drug treatment in England over the next three years.

The first half of this chapter presents a discourse analysis of the drug strategy. It will discuss the drug strategy as a self-contradictory discourse. It shows some of the conflicting ethico-political positions that were written into the drug strategy document. These show the struggle between traditionalist and paternalist policy actors to maintain control over the policy agenda, a struggle which produced new money to spend on drug treatment. Online Appendix 11.1 provides a critical account of the strategy as a statement of fact (or of factoids).

The second half of this chapter will provide an explanatory critique of how this rather surprising document came to be. It will use analysis of the various policy constellations involved to show how power and morality played out in the deciding of what the drug strategy would contain. This included the deployment of various forms of power in the "policy zoo" that surrounded the drug strategy. The story of one particularly influential policy actor – Professor Dame Carol Black – will be told. I will argue that her work is best understood as a particularly skilful exercise in savvy social power. The chapter concludes with a summary of how the strategy was influenced by the contest between the two dominant ethico-political bases of British drug policy and what this tells us about how policy is made.

The drug strategy as a moral discourse

The 2021 drug strategy covers a wide range of topics, including prevention, supply reduction, demand reduction and harm reduction. One of the people who wrote it told me that it was the product of many minds. Multiple people and government departments contributed ideas and text. It is not surprising that it is uneven in tone. But the most fascinating aspect of it, from a critical realist point of view, is the oscillation it displays between the various normative positions that it expresses. Underlying them all is an inconsistent hopping between – on the one hand – the commitment to traditionalist values of protecting the innocent and punishing the wrongdoers and – on the other – a mixture of a paternalist, technocratic commitment to evidence-based policy and the translation into a policy of compassion for people who have deep and complex needs. The ethos of liberty is notably absent, although there are some nods to social justice. This comes in the Conservative form of 'levelling up', rather than the progressive form of righting intersectional inequalities.

Moral posturing

Some idea of the relative priority given to each of these ethico-political bases can be gathered from a crude count of the number of times the document uses various words. 'Crime' appeared 96 times, excluding its presence in the header of every page which trumpeted the strategy's ambition 'to cut crime and save lives'. Outside the header, 'lives' appeared a relatively infrequent 28 times. By contrast, 'recovery' is mentioned 87 times, including in a section to itself. Harm reduction is mentioned explicitly only five times, and three of those are in the sections contributed by the devolved governments of Wales and Northern Ireland. This is fewer than the 13 mentions of 'levelling up'. The minimal inclusion of narratives of regional and economic fairness is also reflected in five mentions for 'disadvantage' and three for 'deprivation'.[1]

These figures give a rough, indicative picture of the priorities proposed by the strategy and of the dominance of the crime control narrative. A closer reading displays more details of the narratives that are constructed in the document from its beginning. The Prime Minister's foreword provides some fascinating examples. Boris Johnson previously told *GQ Magazine* that cocaine had had no effect on him but that cannabis was 'jolly nice'. But he also said that he had 'become very illiberal about it. I don't want my kids to take drugs' (Morgan, 2019). Johnson has seven acknowledged children (Stewart, 2021). It is possible that they or some other close relative has taken drugs and have come to some harm. This has happened with other politicians who have supported drug treatment and harm reduction, such as the former New South Wales Premier Bob Carr and Australian Prime Minister Bob Hawke. Both had close family members with a drug problem and subsequently softened their policies on illicit drug use (Zampini, 2018). Whatever his personal motivations, Johnson presented a distinctive approach in the 2021 drug strategy and was reported to be the most powerful influence in ensuring that it included money for drug treatment.

In his foreword to the strategy, we can see how Mr Johnson attempts to present the problem of drugs in a particular way, leading naturally to his preferred responses. His foreword taps into pre-existing narratives and moral positions. It silences and blocks others. Perhaps the most interesting aspect of this short item of discourse is the way that it leads all these narratives back to a profoundly conservative, traditionalist moral position: that we need to protect the purity of society from the evil of drugs.

The foreword includes a clear but selective statement of what the drug problem is. 'The financial cost of drug misuse is', we are told, 'absolutely staggering'. But the problem is not just economic. It is both 'incalculable' and 'measured not in pounds lost but in lives shattered'. We read of 'innocent families' whose lives are 'blighted' by 'vile' gangsters who drag 'vulnerable victims' into a life of crime. The primary narrative used to frame the problem – here as throughout the strategy – is the link from drugs to crime. This is embedded in the cited £20 billion estimate of the cost of the drug problem, which, as discussed in Online Appendix 11.1, is largely derived from a questionable estimate of the scale of drug-related crime. It is also repeated throughout the foreword, which presents a familiar tale of 'addicts' preying on their neighbours. They and 'the criminals who supply them' play the role of what Nils Christie (1986a, 1986b) called suitable enemies, directly opposed to the ideal victims of 'innocent families', the 'vulnerable' and 'small business owners'. It would not suit this narrative to mention the fact that losses from drug-related shoplifting fall largely on the major corporations who control the majority of the high street retail trade. Ideal victims are, after all, both powerless and individual. Major corporations that have powers of their own could not serve such a useful role in the social construction of the drugs–crime narrative (Ingram et al, 2007).

This narrative does not just focus on utilitarian costs to families, communities and small businesses. It links this directly to a deeper moral purpose, which is to protect innocence from evil. The justification given for the promise of new penalties for recreational drug use is that they are needed '[b]cause drugs cause crime and crime ruins innocent lives'. It is not apparently enough to present crime as a harm in itself. The purity of society that is represented by innocence must be stressed in order to prove the urgency and rectitude of punishment. In their addition to the Prime Minister's foreword, his Home Secretary, Health Secretary and minister for policing back up his crusade for purity by promising to be 'relentless in our tenacity, to utilise every tool at our disposal to drive drugs out from our cities, towns, and villages'. The aim is clearly a drug-free Britain.

This is a profoundly traditionalist narrative. The foreword is flecked with pseudo-evidentiary statements. But its motivating force comes from the explicit linkage of such factoids to the traditional moral foundation of purity/sanctity. It appeals to the idea that we could live unblighted lives in crime-free communities where everyone agrees that drug use is 'not acceptable', if only we would join the Prime Minister in his ten-year campaign. It skips back a generation in the discussion of drug policy moralities. In Chapter 3, I mentioned Ritter's (2022) observation that drug policy debates have tended to move away from discussing drug use as sinful towards framing it as harmful. In Johnson's foreword, he attempts to re-establish the harmfulness of drug use as inherently evil.

New money to save lives

The 2021 strategy marks a turning point in the funding of drug treatment services in England. The previous plea that I drafted for the ACMD (2016e) for spending on opioid agonist therapy to save lives had come to nought (or less than nought, in the form of substantial cuts to spending). In the government's response to this ACMD report, ministers stated that the government was 'determined to drive improvements for citizens who use services at the same time as delivering better value for the taxpayer' (Brine and Newton, 2017, appendix B, p 2). 'Value for the taxpayer' here acts as a euphemism for ongoing austerity. In very strong contrast, the 2021 strategy promised £533 million in new money to spend on drug treatment and recovery services in England over three years.

With this money came a new framework for transparency and accountability in spending. This was mentioned as necessary by several people in the paternalist, medical wing of the medico-penal constellation in interviews and policy documents. This is another reminder, alongside the revival of the drugs–crime narrative, of the time between 2000 and 2013 when the National Treatment Agency (NTA) ran a highly managerial system in which local Drug Action Teams had to report on progress against centrally set targets. The coalition government of 2010 had a stronger commitment to localism. When the NTA was dissolved in 2013, the central targets went with it. The ACMD reported in 2017 that the lack of transparency and accountability was harming the commissioning of services. It recommended 'more transparency and clear financial reporting' (ACMD Recovery Committee, 2017, p 5). At the time, the government disagreed and rejected the ACMD's recommendation. It stated instead that local authorities should 'assure themselves' of the safety and effectiveness of the services they commission (DHSC, 2018, p 6). The issue did not go away and was raised again in the Black report, which called for fundamental change in the management of the drug treatment system (Black, 2021). These recommendations, like several others put forward by Dame Carol, made their way into the subsequent drug strategy. Nevertheless, Dame Carol told me of her worries that the treatment system may not be able to turn the new money into visible progress in time to save the system from new cuts in 2025.

So the drug strategy is indeed a fascinating piece of policy discourse. It contains multiple examples of the narratives, tropes and factoids that peppered British drug policy debates in the 2010s. It revives the moralistic, traditionalist repudiation of drugs use while also resurrecting the narrative that drug policy can reduce crime and deaths by investing in drug treatment, a narrative which reinforces the idea that drug policy is done to protect the community and people who use drugs from their inherent pathology and criminality. This is a narrative that combines the traditionalist and paternalist tropes that are conveyed by the two wings of the medico-penal constellation. It therefore continues to silence the progressive and libertarian ideas that drug use can be pleasurable, beneficial and profitable. The drug strategy thereby reflects the ethico-political positions of the mixed group of people who wrote it, with their occasionally contradictory – but often overlapping – concerns for both traditionalism and paternalism.

Explaining the development of the drug strategy: the role of policy constellations

Morality operates through policy constellations in which policy outcomes emerge from the collective processes of argument and agreement. To explain these outcomes more fully, we need to go beyond the schematic description of policy constellations and get into the detail of how the drug strategy was made, who was involved, and how they worked in concert to produce desired policy outcomes.

It takes a zoo, and zoos have hierarchies

I interviewed several people who were directly involved in the writing of the 2021 drug strategy. They all confirmed that it was the product of multiple authors. One of them compared these authors to a "zoo", brought together quickly from various departments to write the document fast. A zoo is not chaotic, even though it might sometimes be messy. There is order. In this case, the director of the process was Kit Malthouse, the junior Home Office minister for policing and drugs. He oversaw the document's drafting, although he was not as closely involved as some of my interviewees. One of them told me, "he did not read 70 drafts, like I did", but he kept a close eye on the development of the strategy. When I asked interviewees whether junior health ministers, like Jo Churchill, had impact on the drug strategy, I was told, "she would have been aware of it happening, but I'm not aware that she had any particular influence on it". The established institutional arrangements within Whitehall, with the Home Office in the lead on drug policy, prevailed.

The relationship between actors in this policy zoo was hierarchical. Some of them had different forms and levels of power. For example, I was told about a "back-and-forth" argument about "prevention and messaging". This interviewee attempted to use the epistemic power of their knowledge of prevention campaigns: "from my view, the science shows that a lot of these things don't work". They described how there was no direct way of telling the ultimate decision maker about this evidence, so the information is always filtered.

> 'I'm not important enough to get a meeting with the Prime Minister, so I'm always going to have to go through somebody and explain to them, "Look you have to tell the Prime Minister that this actually scientifically is not true" … But then that person, that's the boss you know. I don't get to be in that meeting.'

Looking at some parts of the strategy document, this interviewee's efforts were effective in that the section on prevention does not advocate mass media campaigns. But the messiness of the process is exposed by the presence – in the section on 'reducing the demand for drugs' and in the press announcement – of promises to use the strategy to send messages that will deter people from using drugs. This is an outcome of the institutional power of Number 10 and the Home Office to impose a 'tough' narrative over the evidence-informed objections of experts in the field. Institutional power trumps epistemic power, at least in the short term.

This was confirmed by another interviewee who told me that the drug strategy document was a mixture of ideas that came – on the one hand – from civil servants reviewing the evidence and the stakeholders consulted for the Black review and – on the other – "political whims". The interviewee added, "If you're in the team, you can see which bits [of the drug strategy] explicitly refer to the streams of work which came out of the Black review … and the bits which are not based on any already tried approach that works". Examples given of these unevidenced ideas included the proposed 'tough consequences' for "middle class drug users or recreational drug users … sort of naming and shaming people, doing high-profile things. … You and I already know these kind of things don't work". The interviewee said they could see why politicians might want these policies on the grounds of being "fair, that we're not just picking on working-class, poor people all the time". But they also reported that these proposals "definitely didn't get any backing in terms of stakeholders". These proposals made it into the drug strategy despite repeated attempts by officials to "steer" ministers and their special advisers towards something that was more "evidence-based" and less "scatty".

When I asked interviewees where these unevidenced proposals came from, the usual answer was that they were inserted into the process by "Number 10". It proved frustratingly difficult to pin down what this actually means. Few interviewees were willing or able to name individuals who worked at Number 10 Downing Street who actually proposed these ideas. The address is used as shorthand for people who work on the authority of the Prime Minister, but it is hard to tell if these ideas came from Boris Johnson himself. One interviewee confessed that they could not remember the names of the "various SpAds" (special advisers) who have "come and gone" through Number 10 but did report that they (the advisers) "had a handle on it [the drug strategy]". The interviewee said, "you're never quite sure where they're coming from in terms of what's their motivation".

Interviewees did describe how the process of getting these unevidenced proposals into the strategy worked. They told me that SpAds "pick up on" the ideas that their ministers want in the policy, in this case Boris Johnson's reported wish to "make an example of some high-profile people sniffing cocaine at dinner parties".

'It's the SpAds that will then turn that into a concrete proposal. They'll come to a task force group and get kicked around. ... You could continue presenting the evidence in simpler and simpler formats, but it doesn't necessarily put them off the more headline-grabbing, tough type of thing that makes them feel like they're doing something a bit more popular with voters.'

This still leaves unresolved the question of where these proposals originally came from. A clue is provided by the fact that some of these proposals had previously appeared in reports published by the think tank the Centre for Social Justice (CSJ) at the time that Rory Geoghegan was its Head of Criminal Justice (CSJ, 2018a, 2018b). He then served as the Prime Minister's Special Adviser on Justice and Home Affairs between November 2020 and September 2022. In that role, he would have had direct input into the drug strategy from Number 10. As it happens, I worked briefly with Geoghegan while I was seconded into the civil service in 2009 (Stevens, 2011c). He was notably more traditionalist in his views on crime and punishment than other colleagues. Direct importation of morally aligned people and policies from think tanks into government is one of the ways that policy constellations influence policy.

Dame Carol Black: broker, entrepreneur or savvy power player

Examination of the key role played by Professor Dame Carol Black in the development of the drug strategy throws a particular light on drug policy making. It also enables us to develop ideas inherited from previous policy theories, including on policy brokerage and entrepreneurship.

Professor Black is a distinguished clinician and medical researcher. She was born to a working-class family but was marked out early for leadership. She was head girl at her grammar school and president of the Students' Union at Bristol University. She came late to the study of medicine but made substantial advances in knowledge and treatment of scleroderma, a chronic connective tissue disease that used to be untreatable and often fatal. She rose to become President of the Royal College of Medicine, among a plethora of other prestigious positions. She was chosen by Prime Minister David Cameron to lead *An independent review into the impact on employment outcomes of drug or alcohol addiction, and obesity* (Black, 2016). Given that Cameron had made it clear that he wanted the review to recommend that receipt of welfare benefits by people who use drugs should become conditional on being in drug treatment, many of us in the field were pleased that Professor Black did not recommend such a stringent measure. So we were rather surprised when Sajid Javid, then Home Secretary, selected her to lead another review in 2019. This Black review was published in two parts (Black, 2020b, 2021).

The first part provided many of the factoids that were cited in the drug strategy. The second part included many of its policy proposals, including substantial investment in drug treatment.

The interesting policy question is why Carol Black's work got made into policy when so many other reports had been left unimplemented. Several interviewees told me that Professor Black herself was key to this. One told me, "I think what was key about Carol's review is *she's* quite influential. Politicians listen to her. She has the ear of people who she can influence". I have italicised 'she' here, because it is not the review that is being presented as influential but Professor Black herself. It may have helped that by the time of the second Black report in 2021, Sajid Javid – who had commissioned her review as Home Secretary – then received her second report after becoming Secretary of State for Health. The institutional support he provided may have been important, but interviewees repeatedly told me that it was Professor Black's qualities, skills and connections that made the difference.

Is this a case of brokerage or entrepreneurship? For Sabatier and Jenkins-Smith (1993), a policy broker is someone who can bring together different people and information in ways that enable policy learning and change. For Kingdon (2013), a policy entrepreneur is an advocate who invests their own resources in achieving a preferred policy goal. I asked Dame Carol directly if she saw herself as performing either of these roles. She replied:

> 'I would say I'm somewhere in the middle. I have worked for two years to bring people and departments together. I would never claim that it's the best way to do this. I mean, compared with people who've been in the field for years and who know addiction. If there was anything entrepreneurial about it and people have thought of this before, I was desperate to see a whole system brought together. I would still say unless we get a whole system we will have failed. I wanted – and again I don't think that you'd call this entrepreneurial – I want people who've been addicted and who've now come through it and want to be part of the system to be much more part of the recovery process. So if there were things I wanted, to push them to make this a chronic condition. ... I'll keep bugging them to do that. I'm passionately interested in making this better.'

This is a fascinating account of what drug policy making involves. Dame Carol clearly played a key role in bringing people and ideas together. But it seems rather odd that this was still necessary. Every British drug strategy has promised cross-departmental coordination. Keith Hellawell and Mike Trace ran the anti-drug coordination unit back in the late 1990s and earned the sobriquets of Drug Czar and Deputy Drug Czar. But they lost these roles when the unit was disbanded in 2001. As Home Secretary, Amber

Rudd (2017, np) promised to 'personally chair' a drug strategy board with senior representation from all relevant departments 'to ensure everyone is accountable'. But Rudd resigned in 2018 and the board rarely met. The fact that Dame Carol still saw such a need to "bring departments and people" together in 2021 says something about the usual absence of cooperation.

Despite Dame Carol's role in convening various policy actors and positions, I am not persuaded that her work is fully described by either brokerage or entrepreneurship. She was certainly well connected. According to one interviewee, "she had Matt Hancock on speed dial".[2] Priti Patel was reported to be a big admirer. Having quick access to the Secretary of State for Health, the Home Secretary and other ministers was obviously a boon in getting her own policy preferences into the drug strategy. And she certainly had a strong preference for a whole-system approach that would support recovery. But I did not observe her taking the risks that would be associated with entrepreneurship. Rather the reverse. Her strategy was to work persistently behind the scenes in ways that made people feel they were safe and supported.

Neither do I see much evidence here of the kind of transactional policy making described by Rhodes (1990). One interviewee described the repeated discussions in the run-up to the strategy announcement as "horse-trading". When I asked the person who used this phrase whether there was actual bargaining in the form of transactions, they replied with an example that was more of an argument about the best use of public money. There was "a lot of toing and froing and competition" about which proposals would be included in the strategy, what wording would be used, and how much money the Treasury would allocate. But there does not seem to have been much in the way of transactions where Professor Black or others had to give up power or resource to get the policy they wanted. Rather, Black's success in completing the 2016 review of addiction and employment seems to have increased her institutional power to get her 2021 report implemented. The building of various forms of power are mutually sustaining. Politics, as has long been known, is not necessarily a zero sum game (Gidden, 1975). Far from giving anything away to gain desired policy outcomes, success in doing so increases actors' power in future policy contests.

I see Dame Carol rather as a particularly skilled savvy social power player. She brought together – with a determined grace, charm and persistence – various forms of power. These included the epistemic power that she herself had from her esteemed medical background, bolstered by the distinguished 'men of science' that she brought into the process (for example, Keith Humphreys, John Strang and Ed Day). Keith Humphreys was rewarded with the Order of the British Empire in Queen Elizabeth's last honours list, partly for this work. Dame Carol has served as chair of the health committee which recommends people for such honours. John Strang had already been knighted in 2016. Ed Day's honour for his service as National Recovery Champion cannot be far behind.

Dame Carol may also have engaged in her own form of policy cornering. A civil servant reminded me that she had appeared on *Desert Island Discs*[3] in 2016 and had taken the opportunity to mention the report she had written on addictions and employment (Black, 2016). At the time, it seemed unlikely that the government would publish her report, as it did not recommend what ministers had hoped it would. Mentioning the report in public put them in a position which made it harder not to publish. At this distance, it is difficult to say whether this was mere coincidence or another exercise of Dame Carol's savvy social power.

In 2021, she used the institutional power that she was lent by her government appointments, ministerial connections and personal reputation to bring members of influential policy constellations together to agree common solutions to the policy problem in the dominant policy narrative: drug-related crime. She used her own affective skills to ensure that policy makers felt comfortable with the process and solutions she presented. She sits in a long tradition of distinguished women who have effected change as savvy social power players in British health and social policy, including Lucy Faithfull (Niechcial, 2010), Barbara Wootton (Oakley, 2011), Cicely Saunders (Richmond, 2005) and Ruth Runciman (MacGregor, 2017).

The exclusion of challenging proposals and people

A striking feature of the 2021 drug strategy was the closed nature of the discussions that led up to it. There was far less public debate than I observed in the Scottish response to drug-related deaths. In contrast with some previous strategies, there was no formal process of public consultation. Those of us who were not directly involved heard rumours about it coming, but we were not invited to contribute. The latest strategy had only come out in 2017 (HM Government, 2017). But several interviewees told me that the Johnson administration saw itself as a completely new government, not a continuation of the previous nine years of Conservative rule.

Sajid Javid, the then Home Secretary, announced the review of drugs, to be done in two parts, in the wake of the medical cannabis kerfuffle that is described in Chapter 9. Dame Carol Black told me that she was not at all confident when she submitted the critical first part of her review (Black, 2020b) that ministers would still want her to continue with the second. But by that time, the process had developed a momentum of its own. Through her skills and connections, Black was able to keep ministers and senior civil servants on board. None of my interviewees could tell me who made the decision that there would then be a new drug strategy. It emerged from the process that Javid had kicked off and Black took on.

In writing her review, Black had consulted widely, but mostly by invitation. There was a 'call for evidence', but it only ran for a month in the usual holiday period (July/August) in summer 2020. I was invited into one of the 11 'roundtables' that were held with stakeholder groups. Some other of my interviewees – including Keith Humphreys, Ed Day and John Strang – worked closely with Dame Carol, giving her the benefit of their many years of experience in the field.

Other policy actors from constellations that usually challenge government policy were not invited into such discussions. The scope of Dame Carol's work was drawn tightly. It explicitly excluded consideration of drug legislation. This, and the absence of open consultation for the new drug strategy, meant that members of the progressive social justice and libertarian constellations were not able to use it as a 'policy window' through which to insert their preferences into the policy process. Indeed, the people who most consistently support commercial as well as individual freedom were almost completely absent from the process of consultation that Dame Carol instigated. They may have had some influence through the presence in Number 10 Downing Street of special advisers like Blair Gibbs, who had contacts with the emerging cannabis industry. But he had left Downing Street by the time the strategy was published, and any such influence had been erased in the document's multiple re-writes.

Dame Carol was able to bring some ideas from the social justice policy constellation into her report. Her two reports and the strategy document mention the regional and socio-economic disparity in drug-related deaths. This is a factoid that was congruent with the Johnson government's narrative on 'levelling up'. Other factoids and narratives were excluded from the Black review process.

For example, her reviews did not refer to the ethnic disparities in drug policing that actors like Release and StopWatch have campaigned on. The second part of the Black review provides a list of consultees. Neither Release nor StopWatch appears on it. Indeed, there is no organisation listed that specifically represents members of ethnic minorities, even in the section of this list that is headed 'lived experience' (Black, 2021, pp 61–64). I was able to mention these ethnic disparities in the roundtable that I attended, but they did not make it into her report. The drug strategy document does mention these disparities, but from a different source. In the drug strategy, they are referenced to the report of the Commission on Race and Ethnic Disparities (CRED), led by Tony Sewell (CRED, 2021). This report has been criticised as an attempt to mask the existence of institutional racism rather than to eliminate it (Tikly, 2022). It presents these disparities in a very different way from Release, StopWatch and me. Its proposed remedy to the ethnic disparity in stop and search is to increase monitoring and the use of body-worn cameras, not to reduce stops and decriminalise drug possession

(Shiner et al, 2018; Stevens et al, 2022). In other words, the findings of the Sewell report and its use in the drug strategy were consistent with the beliefs of both traditionalists and paternalists in the medico-penal constellation. It confirmed the views of traditionalists that racism is not a big problem and those of paternalists that any solution should involve more central control of state agencies. The socially progressive belief in reducing state control of disadvantaged communities did not make it into the drug strategy.

There is a notable skew in the list of consultees for the Black report towards more socially conservative visions of what drug policy should be. The only non-specialist think tank that appears in the list is Rory Geoghegan's former employer. The CSJ has long campaigned for a more abstinence-focused drug treatment system (Gyngell, 2007) and has also campaigned against cannabis legalisation (CSJ, 2018a).[4] It is joined in the list of Black's consultees by other people and groups who share these views, including Noreen Oliver and the Recovery Group UK. The Scottish Recovery Consortium was invited, but the Scottish Drugs Forum, which tends more to support harm reduction, was not. There are treatment organisations on the list who do support harm reduction, such as the Westminster Drugs Project and multiple members of the National Addiction Centre. But the forms of harm reduction they tend to support are those that are within the paternalist mainstream of the public health policy constellation. No prominent supporters of decriminalisation, overdose prevention centres or drug checking services are on the list. Significant drug policy reform was kept out of the process by not inviting in people who support it, as well as by the terms of reference which Sajid Javid set for the Black review. They were excluded from the making as well as the taking of these decisions.

This was an exercise in both institutional and epistemic power, based on the forces of ethico-political attraction and repulsion between policy constellations. Repulsion between traditionalists and social justice progressives meant that Conservative politicians were not likely to accept drug policy reformers into the process of creating the drug strategy. As a savvy operator, Carol Black knew that inviting them into the process would risk her prospects for using the familiarity and trust she had built with powerful policy actors to win the policy changes she wanted. There was enough compatibility between the ethico-political bases of the traditionalist and public health constellations for them to work together in creating the strategy. This enhanced the chances of the strategy favouring the moral preferences and material interests of the most powerful policy constellations. Institutional and epistemic power are held collectively. There were particularly significant wielders of it. Sajid Javid set the terms of the discussion. Kit Malthouse orchestrated the process from within government. Carol Black marshalled its main ideas. But they could not do this on their own. Boris Johnson, or people close to him with his blessing, used institutional power to lever money for treatment out of the

Treasury. They worked with the most influential actors, people who were already on the inside of the policy "zoo" that surrounded the drug strategy, not those who were kept outside in the policy wilderness. The mechanisms of exclusion and inclusion in the policy process are based on socially structured inequalities in power as well as culturally structured normative commitments.

Conclusion: explaining a contradictory and surprising strategy

In 2021, the policy constellations which had formed around previous policy disputes – including those around medical cannabis and drug-related deaths – also operated to produce the new drug strategy. In contrast to the medical cannabis debate, no policy actors from outside the usual sites of institutional power were able to force their policy positions onto the agenda. Instead of policy cornering by a challenger constellation, we observe the deployment of savvy social power inside the medico-penal constellation. Back-and-forth negotiations – but not necessarily transactions – between policy actors with different institutional bases produced the final outcome, in the form of a self-contradictory policy document that repeated old policy tropes around cutting supply and preventing use but surprisingly included new money for drug treatment.

The contradictions in the drug strategy do not just arise from the combined total of the individual preferences of policy makers. They reflect the culturally structured contrasts between the main ethico-political bases of the two policy constellations involved in its creation. There are sections which express the paternalism of the public health establishment. And there are also sections which reflect the traditionalism of the constellation that favours use of drug policy for social control. The policy constellations that favour progressive racial and social justice, as well as individual and commercial freedom, lacked the institutional power to get their policy preferences into the strategy. The affective power of the drugs death narrative was reflected in the strategy's subtitle on saving lives but was not – according to my interviewees – decisive in influencing its content.

The contingency of two contributory factors helps explain the more surprising element of the strategy: its new funding for drug treatment. If the UK had not voted for Brexit in 2016, it is less likely that its cheerleader Boris Johnson would have been in power in 2021. He plumped for the winning side in the referendum and surfed that turbulent wave to the premiership. If the referendum had gone the other way, it is more likely that the 2021 Prime Minister would have been one of David Cameron, his closest lieutenant and Chancellor George Osborne or Theresa May, who won the Conservative leadership contest which followed Cameron's resignation. None of these three showed any generosity towards drug treatment in the drug strategies of 2010 and 2017, which they oversaw. The decisive institutional power of Number 10 in securing money from the Treasury would likely have been absent. And if Dame Carol Black had not so skilfully used her savvy social power to promote the convincing narrative that drug treatment cuts crime (and so saves money), the drug strategy would have been different.

Boris Johnson himself was a key actor in both setting the prohibitionist and moralistic tone of some parts of the drug strategy and in deciding that substantial funding would be devoted to drug treatment. His position on drugs has been confusing and hypocritical, as a former user of illicit drugs who now condemns people who do the same. Johnson has displayed double standards, sexual infidelity and dishonesty throughout his career (Bower, 2020). The fact that this did not prevent him from reaching high office is an example of the structured privileges of class and race that cling to a White man who was born wealthy, attended one of the country's most expensive private schools and has spent his life cultivating powerful acquaintances (Younge, 2018). Such privilege does not just arise from the personal charisma of a man who has persuaded millions of Britons to vote for him. It is socially structured by intergenerationally reproduced patterns of advantage. It is advantages of this type that some policy actors can bring to particular policy constellations, so increasing the prospects of its members of achieving their desired policy goals.

So, as one interviewee told me when I asked what influences policy, "people matter". But people and their ideas do not emerge fully formed as sole operators. Their preferences are shaped by their connections to moral ideas and material interests. Their power to influence policy is itself amplified by the structures through which they achieve their powerful positions. It is the operation of this emergent interplay of people and ideas through the policy constellations they form that explains the content of the 2021 drug strategy.

12

A Retroductive Conclusion

The final stage of a critical realist analysis is retroduction and contextualisation (Danermark, Ekstrom and Karlsson, 2019). Retroduction explains the underlying mechanisms and causal conditions of the observed phenomena; in this case, the outcomes of drug policy processes in the UK. Contextualisation highlights areas where potential theoretical explanations compete or complement each other. These alternatives complement a sociological analysis which aims to trace the specificities of the links between structure and agency in particular policies, times and places (Stevens, 2011d).

This chapter carries out retroduction by proposing ten tendencies that I found in the making of drug policy in the UK, tendencies which may also apply to other policy fields in other places. The chapter contextualises these conclusions by comparing the policy constellations approach to the advocacy coalition framework (ACF; Jenkins-Smith et al, 2018), with which it shares several features but two crucial differences. One difference is that the policy constellations approach rejects the methodological individualism on which the ACF is built. The other is that coalitions are characterised by their coordination strategies, whereas constellations are not necessarily coordinated. The chapter will then consider some limitations and trade-offs in my choice of methods for studying drug policy. In the end, the analysis presented in this book should be judged by its practical adequacy. How does the knowledge it creates and shares help us to reduce human suffering and promote collective thriving? The chapter and the book close by considering these questions.

Retroduction: the propositions of the policy constellations approach

To help understand how constellations of actors, ideas, power, interests and moralities combine to produce policy outcomes, I present here some propositions for understanding this process. I created these propositions abductively by combining theories of power, morality and policy making with my observations of the UK drug policy field (Danermark et al, 2019). I present them here alongside my retroductive reflections on how they throw light on some interesting aspects of the cases I observed.

Policy making is not a process that is governed by immutable causal laws, as if 'social reality consists of a ubiquity of closed systems of isolated atoms' (Lawson, 2019, p 6). These propositions rather reflect commonly observed tendencies that are consistent with the complex and contingent forms of causation that are expected by critical realism (Byrne, 2011).

1. The policy preferences of policy actors will be deeply shaped by the ethico-political bases that they adhere to. Which ethico-political bases they adhere to will in turn be influenced by their positions in society, place and time.

For both the UK and Scottish level of drug policy making, the methods that I adopted for studying policy constellations were able to reveal some deeply underlying ethico-political bases that motivated policy actors to form connections with each other and to work in concert towards more specific policy goals. These ethico-political bases form different kinds of 'background consensus' (Habermas, 1976) and are fundamentally constitutive of drug policy fields in the UK. My mixed methods also helped me to trace the connections between the preferences and powers of policy actors and the social and cultural structures which enable their actions in policy making. For example, I showed in Chapter 8 how the politics of familiarity reinforce the divide between institutional insiders and outsiders, and so who gets to make policy and who does not. The specifics of these processes are contingent on the specific places and times at which they occurred, but they are influenced by deeper and longer-lasting generative mechanisms. These include the long accretion of moral preferences through religious and other processes by which societies develop and reproduce moral hierarchies; in other words, their cultural structures. It also involves the social structures of class, race and gender, which affect who gets to be included and excluded in the networks of sympathies that form policy constellations.

2. The policy preferences of the most structurally advantaged policy actors will tend to be those that are institutionalised in policy decisions.

In contrast to the naïve ideals of 'evidence-based policy', this book has consistently found that it is power – not knowledge – which determines the outcome of policy debates. In each of the cases I examined in Chapters 9, 10 and 11, the most structurally advantaged policy actors were able – at least – to modify policy outcomes in ways that suited their moral preferences and material interests. In the case of medical cannabis, the economic, media and affective power that was mobilised by a structurally advantaged group of challengers to the ongoing prohibition of cannabis-based medicines was able to force a change in policy. But members of the medico-penal constellation were able to reassert their institutional power by placing strict limits on who could access these medicines via an NHS prescription. The resulting situation favours wealthy people who can afford expensive private prescriptions over poorer people who cannot, while enabling medical professionals and conservative state officials to retain control of the licit market. The convergence of the material and ethical interests of the libertarian policy constellation are balanced by the preference of paternalist public health professionals to limit the freedom of others to use and trade in cannabis, a preference that also serves their interest in maintaining their own professional power and prestige.

3. Strong rational justifications and empirical evidence for a particular policy preference may be useful in the effort to institutionalise that policy outcome, but it is neither necessary nor sufficient for a policy idea to be rational and well-evidenced for it to become or remain the policy outcome.

A common mistake is to assume that 'evidence-based policy' offers a path to a neutral, impartial, depoliticised form of decision-making. This is a mistake because it ignores the role of power and morality in deciding what gets researched and which findings will make it into policy. This book has presented many examples of the effort to use rational arguments and research evidence to create change. But it has found no examples where that has – on its own – been effective in actually changing policy. Even in the case of the recent reduction of Friday prison releases that I discussed in Chapter 8, it required the institutional power of ministers and civil servants to implement the recommendation that had been made by the ACMD (2019c). There were few such examples of direct use of evidence. In most cases, evidence was used as ammunition to support pre-existing positions rather than being the base on which these positions were built. There were also policy proposals – such as the call for 'tough consequences' for recreational drug use in the 2021 UK drug strategy – for which research evidence was not present, suggesting again that evidence is not necessary as a base for drug policy. Note the difference here between this conclusion and Kothari and Smith's (2022, p 62) finding that 'evidence is necessary but not sufficient in public-health decision making'. This may be explained by differences between the field that they examined and the other parts of the drug policy field. Public health professionals have a strong commitment to the norms of the scientific method. Judging by the widespread, unevidenced use of long prison sentences as a purported solution to drug problems in the US and UK, evidence is far less necessary in the penal policy field (Tonry, 2007).

4. How a policy problem or proposal is perceived by policy actors and publics will affect the outcome of policy processes. So members of policy constellations who can define the problem or proposed solution in line with dominant ideas will be more likely to attain their desired policy goals.

Efforts to frame the drug problem in particular ways ran through all the data I analysed for this book. Every description of what the problem is and what solutions should be adopted can be seen as an attempt to gain control of the agenda for policy making. In the UK, I found two particular narrative tropes to be particularly effective in doing so. At the UK level, the narrative that drugs cause a large proportion of crime has been resurrected in the 2021 drug strategy. This narrative was first honed by Mike Trace and others for use in justifying investment in drug treatment in the 2000s. Its persuasive efficacy has been demonstrated again by its successful deployment by Carol Black and others to extract substantial funding for drug treatment from the Treasury for the 2021 UK drug strategy. In Scotland, the narrative that won out in creating a more substantial response to drug-related deaths was that failure to do so was a national shame. This successful combination of affective compassion and nationalist pride created a faster and fuller response to drug-related deaths in Scotland than in England.

5. These dominant ideas are deeply rooted in affective sentiment and emotion, as well as moral preferences. Whether policy changes or remains the same will be heavily influenced by the mobilisation of affective power.

These affective narratives do not just operate at the surface level of policy making as instrumentally developed stories to meet short-term goals. They reflect much deeper ethico-political positions on who we are and who should receive the compassion that is deserved by the people we see as fully human counterparts to ourselves. Different visions of who and what is deserving of compassion may lead to accusations of hypocrisy, as people who value different forms of compassion accuse their opponents of failing to back up their claims of being compassionate with action. For example, the drugs–crime narrative reflects the idea that drug use is inherently criminal. The presentation of treatment as the solution reflects the idea that drug use is inherently pathological. These complementary ideas are easily shared by traditionalist and paternalist members of the medico-penal constellation. In Scotland, the narrative of drug deaths being nationally shameful and state action being the solution was compatible with the moral precepts of both nationalism and ethical socialism, which continues to influence the Scottish polity. In neither case did the libertarian idea that state control is the problem that needs fixing have supporters with enough power to institutionalise their preference for legalisation of drugs. In both cases, the influence of these narratives was boosted by the mobilisation of affective power, using stories that elicited emotional responses as well as facts built rationally on evidence. For people with different ethico-political bases, the failure of others to act on the basis of their preferred narratives of who is being harmed by drugs and how – while claiming to be compassionate – may look hypocritical. But from the inside these narratives may seem perfectly consistent with the goal of preventing the suffering of fellow human beings.

6. Change in policy is hard to achieve when the desired change also: requires changes to the moral preferences of structurally advantaged social groups; diminishes the power of these groups; conflicts with previously institutionalised policies in the policy field at issue; or is discordant with currently institutionalised policy preferences in other fields.

I started this book by asking why zombie ideas which had long been discredited are still so influential in drug policy. The cases I have presented show why it is so difficult to achieve change. People's ethico-political beliefs are deeply held. Cultural structures usually change quite slowly, over generations (Archer, 2000). Both paternalist and traditionalist policy actors favour policies which maintain their ability to control the actions and consumption practices of less powerful social groups. Even when reformers attain power and are persuaded – as they have been in Scotland – of the case for decriminalisation and harm reduction, existing institutional structures prevent change from occurring. As I write this conclusion, for example, there is still no actually operating overdose prevention centre in the UK, and the possession of even small amounts of controlled drugs is still a criminal offence. Some English police forces and the Scottish government have taken steps to divert people from prosecution towards educative or therapeutic responses (Bain, 2021; Shaw et al, 2022; Spyt and Kew, 2023). But we should remember that diverting rather than decriminalising people who use drugs is still consistent with the idea that drug use is pathological, even if it is not criminal. Diversion to education or treatment still suggests that there is something wrong with the use of some drugs that needs to be fixed.

7. Policy change can occur when the preferences, powers and/or contexts of policy actors change. Making these changes occur is how policy constellations succeed in changing policy. Preventing them from occurring is how policy constellations ensure stability in policy. So policy arguments are not just aimed at changing preferences; they also

address the power that other actors can deploy and the contexts in which they operate.

Several of my interviewees told me how policy making is not just a case of marshalling the best evidence, considering the options and selecting the optimal solution. They told me about efforts to reinterpret the organisational contexts and ideational frames in which drug policy is made. The ubiquitous attempts to present actors' preferred policy as the one that was both compassionate and 'evidence-based' demonstrates the importance of the contest for affective and epistemic power. As some previous theories of the policy process have suggested, policy can change when the real external context changes. Policy actors attempt, in concert with fellow members of their constellations, to interpret these changes in ways that strengthen their power to have influence on the immediate policy response. The structures of social position and moral preference emerge from the accumulation of these continually erupting debates. In the UK, decades of intellectual sparring between the Home Office and challengers for dominance of the drug policy agenda continue to the present day. The balance of power between the medical and penal sides of the medico-penal constellation shifts as different policy constellations respond to the external environment in attempts to fulfil their moral preferences and entrench their own influence. One of the ways they can effect change is by changing the policy context in which competing constellations have to operate, not just changing their preferences. The use of political cornering in the legalisation of cannabis for medical use, as described in Chapter 9, provides an example of successful manipulation of the political environment in order to force policy change.

8. External changes to the policy context can change the relative balance of existing preferences, powers and contexts. This does not lead directly to policy change unless a policy constellation that desires change can use these changes to affect the preferences and powers of other actors in the field. There may therefore be a substantial lag between external contexts changing and policies changing.

In the UK, this tendency was most clearly visible with the increase in drug-related deaths. The delayed response to this change in the external environment of drug policy making showed how such changes are contingent on the powers and preferences of the policy actors who identify, interpret and respond to these external contexts. It also showed how the negotiation of these powers and preferences takes time. There is no automatic, direct process by which changes in the phenomena of illicit drug use transform themselves into policy responses. These changes are filtered through the epistemologically relative constructions that policy actors place upon these ontologically real, actual developments. As suggested by Schneider and Ingram (1993), the nature and urgency of responses to external changes will depend on the levels of power held by the people who are most directly affected, and on the value that is placed on them by people who have the power to make change happen. This process of identification and framing of policy problems, alongside the development and negotiation of proposed solutions, takes time. It took about seven years in Scotland and nine years in England for the rise in deaths that started in 2012 to be met with a substantial policy response.

9. Policy actors tend to come together in concerted action when there is convergence around policy preferences but will be less likely to work in concert where they disagree on moral issues or their material interests diverge.

My interviews with policy actors gave me lots of examples of people choosing to work alongside people who shared their ethico-political commitments, while expressing their difference and distance from people who did not. There were close inter-personal connections between groups of people who: favoured the legalisation of both cannabis and psilocybin for commercial sale; saw drug policy as a problem of racial injustice; favoured state-funded drug treatment as the solution to the UK's drug problem; or saw a need for more punishment of drug users and dealers in order to protect children, families and communities from harm. There were fewer personal links of friendship and mutual esteem that jumped across these constellations. The politics of familiarity tend to operate within morally congruent constellations but not across them. This has hampered the ability of the UK-level drug policy reform movement to achieve desired changes to drug laws because it is split between libertarians and social progressives who lack close personal connections and a shared ethico-political base. The institutional structures of the UK drug policy field create connections of necessity between members of the conservative and public health constellations who have to collaborate with each other and so create relationships of familiarity, trust and mutual esteem along the way. Savvy social power players, like Steve Moore and Carol Black, are highly skilled at using these constellations, and the knowledge and power that flow through them, to achieve their desired policy goals.

10. Policy actors can act in concert to change the preferences, powers and contexts of their own and other constellations. This does not necessarily require active coordination of policy actors. They can act simultaneously without deliberately coordinating their actions.

Drug policy is fundamentally an *emergent* process. I found no examples of policy decisions that solely reflected the power of one policy actor to impose their will on the field. This may explain the reluctance of David Best's interviewees to claim any responsibility for drug policy making; their claims that they wasnae there and didnae do it. It is always a process that happens elsewhere. It is contingent on the contributions of multiple people and organisations across the policy field. There are many people who are attempting to pull policy levers and coordinate others' actions, but nobody who can pull the strings as if leading all these actors in a skilfully orchestrated puppet show. Indeed, I found an absence of central coordination of drug policy making. Nominally, it is the Home Office that coordinates this process. When she was Home Secretary, Amber Rudd set up a central board to coordinate drug policy implementation. More recently, this task has been delegated to the Joint Combating Drugs Unit. But the field is too various and fissiparous to respond well to central coordination. Policy actors operate in relations of mutual dependence and antagonism. The ACMD, for example, is dependent on the institutional power of the Home Office and other departments to implement its advice. But the Home Office is also partially dependent on the ACMD to provide the epistemic power to legitimise its decrees. There is a similar process of mutual interdependence between institutionally powerful policy actors in Westminster and Edinburgh. The former cannot reach around the Scottish government and impose its will on the Scottish ground. The latter has to negotiate with the powers that be in London on the legal aspects of drug policy. The ardent desire of Scottish nationalists to be split from the UK is just one example of the fissiparousness of the drug policy field. But if and when Scotland achieves independence, its newly empowered government will still have to work in concert with the various parts of civil society, with their overlapping and conflicting desires for abstinence and reform. Remember that when I suggested to Angela Constance that, as drugs minister, she was in control, her first response was ironic laughter.

These ten tendencies build on previous policy theories with a critical realist view of the importance of socially and culturally structured power and morality. They create an explanatory critique of the UK drug policy field which both explains how policy outcomes occur and shows why these policies often do not meet the needs of the people who are most directly affected, including people who have problems with drugs.

Contextualisation: a competing and complementary theory of the policy process

There are many different ways of analysing public policies, as presented in various compendia (Sabatier and Weible, 2018; Cairney, 2021; Ritter,

2022). Rather than attempting a similarly compendious overview of all the ways in which the policy constellations approach differs from and builds on previous policy theories, I will focus on the one that I see as its strongest complement and competitor. This is the neo-pluralist ACF (Jenkins-Smith et al, 2018), which remains one of the most widely used and discussed approaches for the analysis of policy processes. It is the epitome of 'the empiricist project in contemporary policy studies' (Fischer, 2003, p 95). I also discuss the ACF in Online Appendix 1.1. In Online Appendix 1.2, I critically examine some post-structuralist approaches to the policy process, including Bacchi's (2009). I learnt much from the discourse coalition approach, even though I disagree with some of its constructionist assumptions (Hajer, 1993; Fischer, 2003).

The policy constellations approach shares many features of the ACF. The two most important are the common focus on networks of policy actors, inside and outside official government structures, and the observation that surface-level policy preferences are motivated by underlying normative beliefs. The ACF calls the conflicting networks involved in policy making 'advocacy coalitions'. This term focuses attention on its two parts: the advocacy and the coalition. I generally prefer not to use either of these terms. This is because not all the people who are involved in policy making see themselves as advocates. This term would be shrugged off, for example, by many of the clinicians and scientists who operate in the public health policy constellation. For them, being labelled as an advocate threatens their reputation and self-image as morally neutral, objective observers and caregivers (Baumberg-Geiger, 2021). As one of the public health experts interviewed by Smith and Stewart (2017, p 41) put it, 'there is probably a need to not only be independent but also be perceived to be very independent'.

The reason I usually avoid the term coalition is because the ACF builds in a defining feature of a coalition which was often absent from the policy constellations I observed: coordination. The ACF places actors into coalitions 'on the basis of their shared beliefs *and coordination strategies*' (Jenkins-Smith et al, 2018, p 141, my italics). In contrast, my placement of policy actors into constellations does not depend on the presence of joint, coordinated action. In policy constellations, concerted action can emerge from collective processes of shared beliefs and recognition without the need for deliberate coordination.

This reflects another crucial difference between the ACF and the policy constellations approach. The role of individualism in the ACF has been modified over time (Sabatier and Weible, 2007). The ACF retains, however, the influence of its original methodological individualism, seeing social action as the sum of individuals' actions. I argue that such individualism is not apt for describing or explaining processes which emerge at the level of the group.

While the ACF acknowledges that individuals' actions are affected by their social contexts, it does not go as far as accepting the critical realist notion that there are underlying structures that generate collective action through the interplay of agency and structure (Archer, 2000; Elder-Vass, 2012). The valuable range of concepts that the ACF provides can be enhanced by using an approach which acknowledges the enduring features of our social worlds that enable and constrain our actions.

I suggest that my addition of critical realism to the conceptual framing of policy making will help us understand some of the questions that Sabatier and Weible (2007, p 209) listed as unanswered by the ACF. These included: what are the properties of the networks involved in policy making; how inclusive or exclusive are they; what are the causal processes that lead to policy change; what is the role of power and resource in explaining the actions and outcomes of policy actors; and to what extent do policy participants frame events? I have provided answers to each of these questions using the policy constellations approach. This can be seen as a critical realist complement to – rather than a replacement of – the ACF. Based on the work of Haidt, Schwartz and others, my analysis adds a greater range of moral bases to the discussion of underlying normative belief groups than the four which Jenkins-Smith et al (2018) take from Douglas and Wildavsky (1982): hierarchs, egalitarians, individualists and fatalists. More recent work on the social and psychological distribution of policy beliefs offers a greater range of moral bases to which to compare the narratives, tropes, factoids and commitments of policy actors in various policy fields.

The list I provided of ten tendencies that help to explain policy processes was partly inspired by the 12 hypotheses that the ACF provides, but there is a major difference between hypotheses and tendencies. Hypotheses are part of the positivist, hypothetico-deductive model. This suggests that we can make statements about the world that are like general laws: fixed successions of event X followed by event Y in a Humean constant conjunction which can be taken as causal. This successionist view of causation is rejected by critical realism (Bhaskar, 1975; Byrne, 2011). By focusing on contingency, complexity and emergence, critical realist analysis refrains from proposing its findings as eternal and testable laws. Rather, it hopes to identify demi-regularities that can act as provisional guides for understanding and action as we carry on the never-ending quest for better knowledge of the underlying generative mechanisms of the social world (Lawson, 2019). I hope, nevertheless, that the tendencies I propose here are 'clear enough to be wrong' (Sabatier and Weible, 2007; Jones and McBeth, 2010). My analysis is falsifiable, in that it could be contradicted by other empirical findings. If, for example, more research found cases of policies where a challenging constellation with few resources of economic or media power were able to force policy change on a more institutionally powerful constellation through the use of research evidence alone, this would disconfirm part of the policy constellations approach.

Some limitations and trade-offs of this analysis

Every study has shortcomings, and critical realists in particular must be humble about the limits of our inevitably partial attempts to comprehend the complex social worlds we study. One set of limitations is imposed by the inability of the human brain (or at least my brain) to take in the full range of complex motivations that underlie human actions. In thinking about the ethico-political bases of drug policy, for example, I have focused on the basic values proposed by Schwartz (1992) and the moral foundations identified by Haidt and various collaborators (Haidt, Graham and Joseph, 2009; Haidt, 2012). I used these in constructing the modified circumplex of ethico-political bases of UK drug policy that is displayed in Figure 6.1. I paid less attention to alternative frameworks for thinking about underlying moralities. Such alternatives include: the cultural theory of Douglas and Wildavsky (1982), as used by Jenkins-Smith et al (2018) and by Zampini (2022); Lyotard's meta-narratives (Malpas, 2003), as used by Adams et al (2012); and Boltanski and Thévenot's (2006) orders of worth, as used by Ylä-Anttila and Luhtakallio (2016) and by Lerkkanen and Storbjörk (2023). A comparative analysis of these different ethical bases would be very useful. It could build on the work of Miles and Vaisey (2015) on Schwartz's basic values, Haidt's moral foundations, Lakoff's (2002) primordial family metaphor and Hunter's (1992) approach to culture wars. My neglect of these other approaches is partly explained by my limited mental bandwidth, as well as by the fact that I found Schwartz's and Haidt's approaches to be the most practically adequate for analysing drug policy making in the UK.

Some aspects of my analysis will be seen as limitations by readers who want replicability as an indicator of rigour. I have tried to make the methods of my analysis transparent, but it is not fully replicable. It relies heavily on my close knowledge of the field. If I had had the money to employ someone to carry out double coding of the data, I doubt we would have achieved a very high level of inter-rater reliability. That second analyst would have had different pre-existing knowledge of the field, which would have swayed them towards highlighting different aspects of the discourse.

There is a trade-off here between the validity of deep, intimate knowledge of empirical cases and the reliability of replicable analysis. This is equivalent to the choice that Dunn (2017, p 18) identified between methods that maximise 'interpretive understanding' and those which focus on 'precision of measurement'. I chose the former over the latter. From a critical realist perspective, such interpretive validity is more important than a less intimate but more replicable study. After all, critical realists do not strive to create uniform reproductions of general laws and fixed properties. We seek to get deep into the complexities and contingencies of particular cases and so to get closer to understanding the underlying mechanisms which combine to produce them.

This lack of replicability is also consistent with the essentially reflexive nature of policy constellations. As I stated in Chapter 4, policy constellations will look different depending on the observer's position in the policy field. There is no 'view from nowhere' (Nagel, 1989) to be had when it comes to policy making, as we all have some pre-existing assumptions and moral positions which will influence our epistemologically relative perspective of the policy process. I have tried to be explicit about my positions and perspectives so that readers can make their own judgements about how these may have affected the analysis presented in this book. Some may criticise me for being biased by my own ethico-political commitments. That is possible, but I would ask them to point to the evidence that I have overlooked that would lead to a different interpretation, rather than just assuming that I did not look for evidence which would challenge my argument. I did look for such aberrant cases and contradictory facts. Others may accuse me of being too generous to their opponents. They may question why, for example, I have attributed compassion as a motivation behind policy positions that they see as actively harmful. I invite them to reflect on whether they have fallen for the 'devil's shift'. This is the tendency of policy actors 'to exaggerate the power and maleficence of their opponents' (Jenkins-Smith et al, 2018, p 141). Instead, I have tried to follow Dunn's (2017, p 380) advice to use 'hermeneutic charity'. This means trying to understand why somebody holds a particular position before condemning them for holding it.

Those who want a more quantitative and replicable analysis of policy constellations might want to use technical developments such as natural language processing to test the idea that there are discernible constellations which share ethico-political bases. Such research could, for example, use standard lists of 'moral words' from the 'moral foundations dictionary'. This would enable the quantitative analysis of policy discourses, including narratives and news cycles (Frimer et al, 2019; Hopp et al, 2020b; Hopp et al, 2021). Such techniques will also enable more sophisticated use of the mathematical properties of social networks, including various measures of network centrality and alternative ways of identifying clusters and constellations within policy fields.

More sophisticated techniques of social network analysis (SNA) could more closely follow the theoretical suppositions of the policy constellations approach. I have used the modularity statistic in Gephi to identify the modules of nodes (policy actors and positions) that are most connected to each other. This has the limitation of creating discrete, crisp sets of membership of different modules (as Louvain communities; Blondel et al, 2008). In this form of modularity, nodes are either in or out of a particular module and can only be a member of one module. Theoretically, policy constellations overlap, and policy actors can be members of more than one constellation. I used qualitative judgement alongside the Gephi modularity statistics reported in Online Appendix 5.1 to place nodes in the constellations shown in Figures 7.2 and 10.2. It would be possible to use more recent SNA techniques for overlapping cluster generation (Becker et al, 2012; Kalinka, 2020) to give each node a fuzzy set score (somewhere between 0 and 1) for its membership in multiple clusters of nodes. This would also have the advantage of enabling fuzzy set qualitative comparative analysis (QCA; Ragin, 2008) of the necessary and sufficient conditions for particular types of nodes to be members of particular clusters/constellations.

Future analysts of policy constellations will have to deal, as I have, with another trade-off. This is the devilishly difficult bargain between clarity and complexity. A clear analysis risks misrepresenting the nuanced and multifaceted nature of social reality. A more sophisticated analysis risks the analysis becoming too complex to be understood. The sociograms I have presented in this book provide a case in point. Constellations could be organised along more dimensions than the two imposed by the ForceAtlas 2 layout of these sociograms on a flat page. Other approaches, such as fuzzy set theory and the multi-dimensional vector spaces used in QCA (Ragin, 2008), may offer a less reductive description of sets of policy actors. For this book, I have chosen to limit myself to the methods that I thought I was capable of using to balance clarity with sophistication, and to just the two dimensions of the sociograms I have used to map UK drug policy constellations.

I acknowledge a highly problematic limitation of my analysis. This is the relative absence of the perspectives of disempowered, marginalised and minoritised people. The gender balance of my interviewees and of the individual policy actors included in my SNA is unequal. The data I used came largely from men, despite the prominent presence of powerful women – Charlotte Caldwell, Angela Constance and Carol Black – in the policy cases I analysed. I have discussed the absence of people who use drugs from these policy debates. Another problematic exclusion is of members of communities that are racialised as Black, or from other ethnic categories than White British. In the UK, the harms of drug law enforcement have long been targeted on Black communities (Shiner et al, 2018; Akintoye et al, 2022). But Black people, as well as women and people who use drugs, are relatively under-represented in this book, as they are in policy discussions. My purposive sampling of people and documents led me to include the most influential actors. In the policy debates I analysed, people who use drugs and Black people have been accorded relatively marginal roles by the structures of power that shape these debates. The 'colour line' identified by Kojo Koram (2019) continues to shape drug policy and its analysis. Much existing drug policy research is institutionally racist. It excludes the perspectives of marginalised communities by focusing on the privileged positions and discourses of White policy actors. This book cannot escape that criticism. Decolonisation of both drug policy and research on it is an urgent task (Daniels et al, 2021; Lasco, 2022).

Conclusion: the practical adequacy of the policy constellations approach

The policy constellations approach provides conceptual tools for thinking about the complex processes involved in the making of policy. Policy making is, as Bernard Crick (2013, p 39) wrote of politics, 'a messy, mundane, inconclusive, tangled business, far removed from the passion for certainty'. We are unlikely to produce explanations that come with the precision and regularity that some researchers, following in the positivist footsteps of Auguste Comte (1988 [1830]), desire. But we can use theoretical concepts that are practically adequate in that they help us not only to understand policy processes but to work with others to improve them (Sayer, 2010). These tools include the concepts of the policy constellation itself, as well as related concepts such as epistemic, affective and savvy social power. It combines these in explaining one significant, if limited, change in UK drug policy – the legalisation of cannabis-based medical products – as an act of political cornering. These concepts also help to explain the lag between the emergence of 'ill-structured' problems and efforts to resolve them that Dunn (2017) also observed. Discursive and political struggle over drug policy making continues, for example, in the form of the ongoing attempts to open enhanced harm reduction services (Stevens, 2022) and take serious steps against the socio-economic determinants of drug-related death (McPhee and Sheridan, 2023).

In contrast to neo-pluralist approaches that try to explain policy making as the result of individual actions in policy cycles as short as 'ten years' (Jenkins-Smith et al, 2018, p 142), we need to take account of much more deeply rooted and long-standing cultural and social structures that can be abductively inferred from the observable actions and words of policy actors. This is what I have tried to do by taking a close look, from multiple perspectives and methods, at drug policy making in the UK from 2015 to 2021. A close examination of policy action even in such a short period has shown the influence of the deeper structures that motivate, enable and constrain collective action. It has, for example, explained why it has proved so difficult to change drug policy with the rational argument that it should be 'evidence-based'. Evidence in this and other fields develops relatively rapidly, but it is rarely accepted quickly. I have been able to trace the reasons why policies have not changed that much from the prohibitionist stance enshrined in UK drug laws since their inception back to the deeply rooted cultural structures: the ethico-political bases of policy constellations. The reason that some moralities have been more powerfully expressed in British drug policy than others is not because there is equilibrium between interests, as suggested by some neo-pluralist policy theories. It is that there are asymmetrical relations of various forms of power, based on deeper social structures of privilege and disadvantage.

I have argued that academic accounts of policy processes should be judged on the grounds of their practical adequacy. Do they help us to understand the world in ways that enable us to improve it by reducing suffering and promoting human flourishing? The ultimate test of the policy constellations approach is whether it is found to be adequate in this way. So I want to suggest one distinctive way in which the understanding of the drug policy processes that I have presented here may help us to improve them: network rewiring via connections to policy positions.

This is inspired by the complementary work of Moira Faul (2016) on analysing the social networks of policy actors. Faul suggested an interesting way of using knowledge of how such networks operate to challenge the inequalities they reinforce by 'network rewiring'. This involves the deliberate attempt to engineer new connections and information flows through the network in order to diffuse the power that tends to accrue to well-connected, institutionally central policy actors. This is already a deliberate strategy of some policy actors. During my data collection, two people – one from a campaign group and one from a think tank – told me that they started their work by drawing up lists of who were the most influential policy actors. They then deliberately sought to create connections with those actors. This is a well-known feature of networks, that new nodes in the network seek to form connections with already well-connected nodes (Faul, 2016). In this case, it resulted from deliberate attempts to rewire the policy field. My incorporation of policy positions into the analysis of these networks suggests a second mode of network rewiring. As well as seeking to create connections between policy actors directly, people who want to amplify the power of their own constellation may wish to form connections to policy positions which offer greater opportunities for creating connections with other, more powerful policy actors. My analysis of the networked drug policy fields – at both UK and Scottish levels – suggests that diversion of people who use drugs from criminal prosecution would be a particularly useful policy to work on for these purposes. In both fields, this policy is close to centrally connected policy actors and has a high degree of 'betweenness centrality' (it is included in short paths between other nodes in the network). This means that this could be a particularly fruitful policy to work on in building usefully powerful connections. To build connections in reformist constellations, it may be useful to know that support for overdose prevention centres has a high degree of centrality in these constellations, while support for the provision of recovery services is central to conservative and abstentionist constellations.

Despite my frustrations with the many times my recommendations have been ignored, there has been some good news along the way. My time in the drug policy field started by working with organisations and individuals, including Mike Trace at Cranstoun, who wanted to improve the services that were available to people in prison. For several years, we argued that opioid substitution treatment (OST) should be provided inside as well as outside prisons (O'Brien and Stevens, 1997). Eventually, this preference was enacted, and OST was rolled out across prisons in England and Wales. This was not because of any institutional power that we in Cranstoun had. The more proximal causes of this policy change were the legal power of a group of prisoners who sued the UK government under the European Convention on Human Rights (Silverman, 2006) and the epistemic power of academics at the National Addiction Centre who showed the extraordinarily high rates of death among people who used illicit opiates in the first two weeks after release (Farrell and Marsden, 2008). The introduction of OST into prisons was later shown to have reduced such deaths (Marsden et al, 2017). These are examples of the kinds of power that policy constellations – even those in challenger rather than dominant positions – can use to achieve policy goals that reduce suffering and death and promote flourishing communities of mutual respect and dignity. I hope this book will prove practically adequate in inspiring others to use various forms of power in concerted actions to achieve better drug policies.

In studying the messy business of drug policy making, I have pursued Harry Shapiro's (2021, p 10) suggestion that, 'perhaps underlying the whole scramble for the moral high ground is the idea that the drug war is a proxy war, a fight against some of society's deepest fears'. Or perhaps even a struggle to achieve our highest ideals, to bring about in the real world the values we hold most dear. I offer the policy constellations approach as a way to understand the dynamics and complexities of this struggle. I hope there are facts, quotes and concepts in this book that others can use to enhance their understandings and actions on drug policy. In particular, I hope that the concept of the policy constellation itself is useful. Its emphasis on how networks of policy actors are embedded in social and cultural structures of power and morality moves us beyond the individualistic, overly rationalised vision of policy making that is offered in many mainstream policy analyses. Along the way, the book has provided some other tools for thinking critically about policy making. These include the interplay of epistemic power with the other forms of power that constellations bring to the process. To put it simply, there is no such thing as evidence-*based* policy. Policy making is often informed by research evidence, but it is based in ethico-political commitments and material interests, not research evidence.

The power of any individual actor is constrained by the dense network of connections that create competing constellations. Medical cannabis is nowhere near as widely available as Steve Moore would have hoped when he placed Sajid Javid in the corner from which the only way out was the placement of cannabis-based medical products in schedule 2 of the Misuse of Drugs Regulations. Dame Carol Black told me of her fears that her surprising victory in extracting over half a billion pounds from the Treasury could easily be reversed if the drug treatment sector fails to demonstrate value for money. Angela Constance similarly acknowledged how dependent she was on other actors in the Scottish drug policy field to achieve the grand, egalitarian ideals of the 'rights-based approach'.

I developed the policy constellations approach by studying drug policy fields in the UK. Greg Los (2023a) has started the effort to apply it in other places. I hope others will join that effort. Schwartz (1992, p 2) argued that internationally, 'the differences in value priorities account for differences among the societies in other domains, such as educational policies, political involvement, health, law'. The policy constellations approach provides a method for this observation to be operationalised in explaining cross-national as well as in-country differences in drug and other policies. I have shown how these differences in ethico-political bases play out through policy constellations at the UK and Scottish levels of drug policy making. I hope, in future, to see other studies using the policy constellations approach in other countries and for other policies. For now, dear reader, I leave it to you to judge the practical adequacy of this attempt to explain the roles of power and morality in drug policy making in the UK.

Notes

Chapter 1
1. Ethics 'refers to the reflective study of moral choices'. Meta-ethics 'refers to the reflective study of ethics itself' (Dunn, 2017, p 324).
2. As Dunn (2017) also argues, policy decisions emerge from the complex interactions between individuals, organisations and groups rather than from any individual decision, or even the simple sum of multiple individuals' decisions. Policy constellations and outcomes are 'emergent phenomena' (Archer, 1982) that are not created by the conscious decision of any individual policy actor.

Chapter 2
1. Calculated by subtracting 5,793 Penalty Notices for Disorder for cannabis (https://www.gov.uk/government/statistics/criminal-justice-system-statistics-quarterly-june-2021) from the 25,019 formal out of court disposals for drug offences reported by Home Office (2021).
2. A caution still counts as a criminal record, even though it is immediately spent under the Rehabilitation of Offenders Act 1974. A conviction or caution that is spent under this Act does not need to be disclosed to potential employers, or on checks by the Disclosure and Barring Service. They can still be used as evidence of 'bad character' in subsequent court cases.
3. For 16–24-year-olds, these proportions were 89 per cent and 39 per cent, respectively.
4. On the concept of practical adequacy, see Sayer (2010) and Online Appendix 4.1.

Chapter 3
1. The making and taking of decisions are distinct processes. The people who develop the content and reasoning for a policy are often not the people who ultimately decide on it (Lockwood, 1960; cited by Gidden, 1975).
2. Technically, Schwartz's model is a 'quasi-circumplex' as the value positions are not equally spaced around its rim (Schwartz and Boehnke, 2004). Hedonism appears twice in the lists I give here because it straddles self-enhancement and openness to change.
3. Parkhurst (2017) provides useful descriptions of the multiple mechanisms, biases and heuristics by which we manage to maintain belief in the facts that support our values. For a helpful list, see page 87 of his book. Paul Cairney (2021, pp 50–51) also provides a similar list.

Chapter 4
1. Here is Bhaskar's (1998, p 57) phrasing on epistemological relativism: 'all beliefs are socially produced, so that all knowledge is transient, and neither truth-values nor criteria exist outside historical time'.

2. As Bhaskar (2009, p 125) puts it, 'science itself presupposes or embodies commitment to certain values such as objectivity, openness, integrity, honesty, veracity, responsibility, consistency, coherence, comprehensibility, explanatory power, etc'.
3. The difference between an advocacy coalition and a discourse coalition – apart from their different theoretical bases – is that analysis using the advocacy coalition framework tends to focus on the particular policies for which coalition members advocate, while Hajer's approach focuses more on the tropes that are shared across discourses that are at play in a particular policy field (Leifeld, 2017).

Chapter 5

1. In qualitative data analysis, coding means highlighting selected segments of the data and assigning them to codes, categories that the researcher uses to collate the segments of the data that share a common feature; for example, in the research for this book they relate to a particular morality, form of power, narrative, trope, factoid or policy position. It does not mean, as it would in some usages, writing instructions for computers to follow.
2. For lengthy reports, I only coded the summary section. This was partly to save time, but also because their authors will have packed the most important points into the summary, suggesting that these were their priorities. There were some long reports which I coded in their entirety, such as the 2017 and 2021 UK drug strategies, as I wanted to capture the full range of concepts that they covered.
3. Later in that meeting, Superintendent Norman Conway was able to read out the actual number of police warnings that had been given for drug possession by the Scottish police; 5,735 in 2020/2021. This was a rarer instance of a more securely based factoid, with a reference, being used in a parliamentary discussion.
4. For people not familiar with UK parliamentary procedure: while a politician is speaking in a parliamentary debate, another may indicate – by standing up – that they wish to ask a question. It is up to the person who is speaking whether they 'give way' to such interventions. The front bench of each house of Parliament is where the people who are appointed to speak for a party on a particular issue will sit during debates.

Chapter 7

1. Not all members assigned to each constellation support all the positions that are generally supported by its members. And members of some constellations may also support a few of the policy positions that are more closely clustered in other constellations. For example, I appear in Table 7.2 on the same row as the policy position of being opposed to putting cannabis in schedule 4. This is despite the fact that I support putting cannabis in this part of the Misuse of Drugs Regulations 2001 (Stevens, 2018). My assignment to the public health constellation is caused by my support for a number of other positions supported by several other of its members. My presence on the row alongside opposition to putting cannabis in schedule 4 is an accidental result of ordering these columns alphabetically and of my name starting with the same letter as the label used for that policy position. In addition to my support of several of the policy positions that cluster in the public health constellation, I also support some of the positions assigned to the reform constellation, especially those associated with progressive social justice.
2. 'ForceAtlas2 is a force directed layout: it simulates a physical system in order to spatialize a network. Nodes repulse each other like charged particles, while edges attract their nodes, like springs. These forces create a movement that converges to a balanced state' (Jacomy et al, 2014, p 2).
3. Using lower values for the resolution parameter in Gephi identifies a larger number of modules in the network.

⁴ A column in the *Morning Star* accused the IEA of breaking charity rules – which ban party political activity – by hosting FREER, as it was wholly aligned with Conservative Party politicians (Hughes, 2018).

Chapter 8

1. Full disclosure: as a board member of the International Society for the Study of Drug Policy (ISSDP), I negotiated a small amount of funding from the OSF drug policy programme in order to support scholars from low- and middle-income countries to attend some of the annual conferences of the ISSDP.
2. See https://quoteinvestigator.com/2014/01/15/stats-drunk/ for a description of the origins of that saying.
3. An example is the tragic case of Clair Copeland, who died in Consett in June 2021. She had been on a methadone prescription in prison and was released on a Friday. There was a mix-up with sending her prescription to the chemist, so she could not pick it up on the Saturday. As the prescribing agency was closed for the weekend, this could not be sorted out. Ms Copeland returned to street heroin use and died the following week (Gouldsbrough, 2022).

Chapter 9

1. I use the word 'coalition' here because this group of MPs fits Sabatier's (1988) definition of an advocacy coalition as a group that is deliberately coordinated over time.
2. Notwithstanding his research on the link between cannabis use and psychosis, Sir Robin has been quoted as being in support of decriminalising possession (Ellson and Smyth, 2018).

Chapter 10

1. 12 steps is a reference to the model initially described in the 'Big Book' of Alcoholics Anonymous (Wilson, 1939). This is a movement that has its origins in Christian evangelism, although many current members of the various anonymous fellowships forswear a Christian god.
2. This is a claim that is not as easy to sustain from a close examination of the data as it is from a quick read of annual reports from the European Monitoring Centre for Drugs and Drug Addiction, due to differences in the ways that deaths are investigated and recorded (Millar and McAuley, 2017).
3. 'From the cradle to the grave' was the phrase that Winston Churchill used to describe the system of social insurance that was recommended by Sir William Beveridge (1942). It came to symbolise the universalist social support developed by Atlee's Labour government of 1945 to 1951 which was, according to Keith Humphreys and many others, so influential in shaping the UK's polity.

Chapter 11

1. Counting words cannot tell us much without looking at the context and content, as is done in the social network analysis in this book. But such counts can provide a useful initial indication of the relative priority that a document's authors place on different concepts.
2. Dame Carol herself told me that this was not true, although she did have ways that she could get in touch with him.
3. *Desert Island Discs* is a long-running BBC radio programme, conceived by Roy Plumley in 1942, in which prominent people are invited to tell their life story and play their eight favourite pieces of music.
4. Intriguingly, the 2020 report of the Commission on Race and Ethnic Disparities contains a footnote to a report on 'the virtue of decriminalising cannabis' by the CSJ. But this is not a publicly available document, and the CSJ did not respond to my request to see it.

References

ACMD (2002) *The Classification of Cannabis under the Misuse of Drugs Act 1971*. London: Home Office.
ACMD (2008) *Cannabis: Classification and Public Health*. London: Home Office.
ACMD (2015a) *How Can Opioid Substitution Therapy Be Optimised to Maximise Recovery Outcomes for Service Users?* London: Home Office.
ACMD (2015b) *Press Release: Quality of Treatment for Heroin Users under Threat*. London: Home Office.
ACMD (2016a) *ACMD Response to Drug Strategy*. London: Home Office.
ACMD (2016b) *Interactions and relationships between the Misuse of Drugs Act 1971 and the Psychoactive Substances Act 2016*. Unpublished.
ACMD (2016c) *Phytocannabinoids: a review of the generic definition*. London: Home Office.
ACMD (2016d) *Press release: ACMD tells ministers drug-related deaths will continue to rise if treatment programmes are not maintained*. London: Home Office. Available at: https://www.gov.uk/government/news/acmd-tells-ministers-drug-related-deaths-will-continue-to-rise-if-treatment-programmes-are-not-maintained (Accessed: 30 March 2022).
ACMD (2016e) *Reducing opioid-related deaths in the UK*. London: Home Office.
ACMD (2016f) *The extent to which commissioning structures, the financial environment and wider changes to health and social welfare impact on recovery outcomes for individuals and communities*. London: Advisory Council on the Misuse of Drugs.
ACMD (2018a) *Further advice on scheduling of cannabis-derived medicinal products*. London: Home Office.
ACMD (2018b) *Response to consultation on cannabis-based medicinal products*. London: Home Office.
ACMD (2018c) *Scheduling of Cannabis-derived medicinal products*. London: Home Office.
ACMD (2018d) *Vulnerabilities and substance use*. London: Home Office.
ACMD (2019a) *ACMD framework for the assessment of the various impacts of rescheduling Cannabis-based Products for Medicinal use in humans (CBPMs) to Schedule 2 under the Misuse of Drugs Regulations 2001*. London: Home Office.
ACMD (2019b) *Advice on 2,4-Dinitrophenol*. London: Home Office.

REFERENCES

ACMD (2019c) *Custody-Community Transitions*. London: Home Office.

ACMD (2019d) *Future use and purpose of Temporary Class Drug Orders (TCDOs)*. London: Home Office.

ACMD (2019e) *Misuse of fentanyl and fentanyl analogues*. London: Home Office.

ACMD (2019f) *Press release: avoid Friday prison release to prevent drug relapse and deaths*. London: Home Office.

ACMD (2019g) *Self-commissioned workstreams for 2020*. London: Home Office.

ACMD (2020a) *Advice on Epidyolex*. London: Home Office.

ACMD (2020b) *Assessment of the harms of gamma-hydroxybutyric acid, gamma-butyrolactone, and closely related compounds*. London: Home Office.

ACMD (2020c) *Standard Operating Procedure for Using Evidence in ACMD reports*. London: Home Office.

ACMD (2020d) *Synthetic Cannabinoid Receptor Agonists*. London: Home Office.

ACMD (2021) *ACMD Advice on Consumer Cannabidiol (CBD) Products*. London: Home Office.

ACMD Recovery Committee (2017) *Commissioning Impact on Drug Treatment: The Extent to which Commissioning Structures, the Financial Environment and Wider Changes to Health and Social Welfare Impact on Drug Misuse Treatment and Recovery*. London: Home Office.

Adams, P.J., Prescott, A. and Dixon, R. (2012) 'Strange bedfellows: Meta-narrative traditions in the alcohol and other drug field', *Drug and Alcohol Review*, 31(4): 591–597.

Agley, J., Xiao, Y., Eldridge, L., Meyerson, B. and Golzarri-Arroyo, L. (2022) 'Beliefs and misperceptions about naloxone and overdose among U.S. laypersons: A cross-sectional study', *BMC Public Health*, 22: 924.

Ahmun, V., Jasper, L. and Dale-Perera, A. (2016) *Structural Racism as UK Drugs Policy*. London: Blacksox.

Akintoye, B., Ali, A. and Stevens, A. (2022) 'The Ongoing Impact on the Racialised Policing of Black Communities', in I. Crome, D. Nutt and A. Stevens (eds), *Drug Science and British Drug Policy: Critical Analysis of the Misuse of Drugs Act 1971*. Sherfield-on-Loddon: Waterside Press, pp 193–208.

ALBA (2021) *Shake Things Up*. Edinburgh: ALBA.

Aldridge, J., Measham, F. and Williams, L. (2011) *Illegal Leisure Revisited*. Abingdon: Routledge.

Allen, A. (1998) 'Rethinking Power', *Hypatia*, 13(1): 21–40.

APPGDPR (2016) *Access to Medicinal Cannabis: Meeting Patient Needs*. London: All-Party Parliamentary Group on Drug Policy Reform.

Archer, A., Cawston, A., Matheson, B. and Geuskens, M. (2020) 'Celebrity, democracy, and epistemic power', *Perspectives on Politics*, 18(1): 27–42.

Archer, M.S., Decoteau, C., Gorski, P., Little, D., Porpora, D., Rutzou, T. et al (2017) 'What is critical realism?', *Perspectives: A Newsletter of the ASA Theory Section* [Online]. Available from: http://www.asatheory.org/current-newsletter-online/what-is-critical-realism [Accessed 22 June 2023].

Archer, M.S. (1982) 'Morphogenesis versus structuration: On combining structure and action', *The British Journal of Sociology*, 33(4): 455–483.

Archer, M.S. (2000) *Being Human: The Problem of Agency*. Cambridge: Cambridge University Press.

Archer, M.S. (2010) 'Routine, reflexivity, and realism', *Sociological Theory*, 28(3): 272–303.

Arendt, H. (1970) *On Violence*. New York: Harcourt Brace & Co.

Ashton, M. (2008) 'The new abstentionists', *Druglink*, special insert (Dec/Jan): 1–16.

Askew, R. and Bone, M. (2019) 'Deconstructing prohibitionist ideology: A sociocognitive approach to understand opinions on UK drug policy and the law', *International Journal of Drug Policy*, 74: 33–40.

Askew, R., Griffiths, B. and Bone, M. (2022) 'The importance of PEOPLE who use drugs within drug policy reform debates: Findings from the UK Drug Policy Voices online survey', *International Journal of Drug Policy*, 105: 103711.

Atari, M., Haidt, J., Graham, J., Koleva, S., Stevens, S.T. and Dehghani, M. (2022) 'Morality beyond the WEIRD: How the nomological network of morality varies across cultures', preprint. PsyArXiv. doi: 10.31234/osf.io/q6c9r.

Atkins, V. (2018) *Reducing Opioid-Related Deaths in the UK: Further Response on Drug Consumption Rooms*. London: Home Office.

Atkinson, A.B. (2010) 'Progressive social justice and responding to the crisis', *Journal of Poverty and Social Justice*, 18(3): 221–228.

Atkinson, A.M., McAuley, A., Trayner, K.M.A. and Sumnall, H.R. (2019) '"We are still obsessed by this idea of abstinence": A critical analysis of UK news media representations of proposals to introduce drug consumption rooms in Glasgow, UK', *International Journal of Drug Policy*, 68: 62–74. doi: 10.1016/j.drugpo.2019.03.010.

Audit Scotland (2019) 'Drug and alcohol services: An update' *Audit Scotland* [Online]. Available from: https://www.audit-scotland.gov.uk/uploads/docs/report/2019/briefing_190521_drugs_alcohol.pdf. [Accessed 23 June 2023].

Bacchi, C. (2009) *Analysing Policy: What's the Problem Represented to Be?* Frenchs Forest, Australia: Pearson Education.

Bachrach, P. and Baratz, M.S. (1962) 'Decisions and nondecisions: An analytical framework', *American Political Science Review*, 57: 947–952.

Bain, D. (2021) 'Lord Advocate statement on Diversion from Prosecution', *COPFS* [Online]. Available from: https://www.copfs.gov.uk/about-copfs/news/lord-advocate-statement-on-diversion-from-prosecution/ [Accessed 12 March 2023].

Barnett, E. (2017) 'With ecstasy coming back, we need more campaigners like Leah Betts's parents', *The Guardian* [Online], 26 January. Available from: https://www.theguardian.com/commentisfree/2017/jan/26/ecsasy-comeback-brave-parents-leah-betts-drugs [Accessed 14 January 2023].

Bartle, J. (2019) *Room for Improvement: How Drug Consumption Rooms Save Lives*. London: Adam Smith Institute.

Baumberg-Geiger, B. (2021) 'Performing trustworthiness: The "credibility work" of prominent social scientists', *Sociology*, 55(4): 785–802.

Baumgartner, F. and Jones, B. (1993) *Agendas and Instability in American Politics*. Chicago: University of Chicago Press.

Baumgartner, F. and Jones, B. (2009) *Agendas and Instability in American Politics*, 2nd edition. Chicago: University of Chicago Press.

BBC News (2018) 'Billy Caldwell suffers seizure after cannabis oil confiscated', *BBC News* [Online], 12 June. Available from: https://www.bbc.com/news/uk-northern-ireland-44458807 [Accessed 20 January 2023].

BBC News (2019) 'SNP formally backs decriminalisation of drugs', *BBC News* [Online], 13 October. Available from: https://www.bbc.com/news/uk-scotland-scotland-politics-50036173 [Accessed 14 February 2023].

BBC News (2020) 'Drug deaths in Scotland: Minister Joe FitzPatrick loses job', *BBC News* [Online], 18 December. Available from: https://www.bbc.com/news/uk-scotland-scotland-politics-55368574 [Accessed 4 February 2023].

BBC News (2021a) 'Charlie Hughes: Parents of boy with epilepsy drop NICE high court challenge', *BBC News* [Online], 27 March. Available from: https://www.bbc.com/news/uk-england-norfolk-56550061 [Accessed 18 January 2023].

BBC News (2021b) 'New Kirk moderator supports decriminalisation of drug possession', BBC News [Online], 25 October. Available from: https://www.bbc.com/news/uk-scotland-59037524 [Accessed 14 February 2023].

Becker, E., Robisson, B., Chapple, C.E., Guénoche, A. and Brun, C. (2012) 'Multifunctional proteins revealed by overlapping clustering in protein interaction network', *Bioinformatics*, 28(1): 84–90.

Bell, D.A. (1980) 'Brown v. Board of Education and the interest-convergence dilemma', *Harvard Law Review*, 93(3): 518.

Berg, M. and Hudson, P. (2023) *Slavery, Capitalism and the Industrial Revolution*. Medford: Polity Press.

Berridge, V. (2013) *Demons: Our Changing Attitudes to Alcohol, Tobacco, and Drugs*. Oxford: Oxford University Press.

Berridge, V. (2012) 'The rise, fall, and revival of recovery in drug policy', *The Lancet*, 379(9810): 22–23.

Beveridge, W. (1942) *Social Insurance and Allied Services*. London: His Majesty's Stationery Office.

Bewley-Taylor, D.R. (2012) *International Drug Control: Consensus Fractured*. Cambridge: Cambridge University Press.

Bhaskar, R. (1975) *A Realist Theory of Science*. Leeds: Leeds Books.

Bhaskar, R. (1998) *The Possibility of Naturalism: A Philosophical Critique of the Contemporary Human Sciences*, 3rd edition. Abingdon: Routledge.

Bhaskar, R. (2009) *Scientific Realism and Human Emancipation*. London: Routledge.

Bhatarah, P., Duffy, P., Yates, A. and O'Sullivan, S. (2021) *Response to the ACMD on CBD from ACI and CMC*. London: Association for the Cannabis Industry and Centre for Medical Cannabis.

Birrell, I. (2018) 'Leave us alone or arrest me: Ian Birrell', *Mail on Sunday* [Online]. Available from: https://www.ianbirrell.com/leave-us-alone-or-arrest-me/ [Accessed 20 January 2023].

Black, C. (2016) *An Independent Review into the Impact on Employment Outcomes of Drug or Alcohol Addiction, and Obesity*. London: HMSO.

Black, C. (2020a) *Review of Drugs: Evidence Pack*. London: Home Office.

Black, C. (2020b) *Review of Drugs: Executive Summary*. London: Home Office.

Black, C. (2021) *Review of Drugs, Part 2: Prevention, Treatment, and Recovery*. London: Home Office.

Black, J. and Pettifor, T. (2017) 'Crime lord offered to kill drug dealers who sold ecstasy to teenager Leah Betts', Mirror [Online]. Available from: http://www.mirror.co.uk/news/uk-news/crime-lord-offered-kill-drug-9846203 [Accessed 14 January 2023].

Blondel, V.D., Guillaume, J.L., Lambiotte, R. and Lefebvre, E. (2008) 'Fast unfolding of communities in large networks', *Journal of Statistical Mechanics: Theory and Experiment*, 2008(10): P10008.

Boltanski, L. and Thévenot, L. (2006) *On Justification: Economies of Worth*, translated by C. Porter. Princeton: Princeton University Press.

Borges, J.L. (1999 [1927]) 'Literary Pleasures', in E. Weinberg (ed.), *Jorge Luis Borges: The Total Library. Non-Fiction 1922–1986*. London: Penguin, pp 28–31.

Boswell, C., Geddes, A. and Scholten, P. (2011) 'The role of narratives in migration policy-making: A research framework', *The British Journal of Politics and International Relations*, 13(1): 1–11.

Bourdieu, P. (1977) *Outline of a Theory of Practice*. Cambridge: Cambridge University Press.

Bourdieu, P. (1984) *Distinction: A Social Critique of the Judgment of Taste*. Boston: Harvard University Press.

Bourdieu, P. (1998) *Practical Reason: On the Theory of Action*. Cambridge: Polity Press.

Bower, T. (2020) *Boris Johnson: The Gambler*. London: WH Allen.

Brewster, D. (2023) *Cultures of Cannabis Control: An International Comparison of Policy Making*. Bristol: Bristol University Press.

Brine, S. and Newton, S. (2017) *Government Response to Four Reports from the Advisory Council on the Misuse of Drugs. Appendix: How can Opioid Substitution Therapy (and Drug Treatment and Recovery Systems) Be Optimised to Maximise Recovery Outcomes for Service Users?* London: Home Office.

Bruce, J.R. (2013) 'Uniting theories of morality, religion, and social interaction: Grid-Group Cultural Theory, the "Big Three" Ethics, and Moral Foundations Theory', *Psychology and Society*, 5(1): 37–50.

Buchanan, J. and Young, L. (2000) 'The war on drugs – a war on drug users?', *Drugs: Education, Prevention and Policy*, 7(4): 409–422.

Busby, M. (2018) 'Mother of epileptic boy will not get confiscated cannabis oil back', *The Guardian* [Online], 11 June. Available from: https://www.theguardian.com/society/2018/jun/11/epileptic-boys-mother-barred-from-bringing-cannabis-oil-into-uk [Accessed 20 January 2023].

Butler, I. and Drakeford, M. (2005) *Scandal, Social Policy, and Social Welfare*, revised 2nd edition. Bristol: Policy Press.

Butler, J. (2016) *Frames of War: When is Life Grievable?* New York: Verso.

Byrne, D. (2011) *Applying Social Science: The Role of Social Research in Politics, Policy and Practice*. Bristol: Policy Press.

Byrne, D.S. (2009) 'Case-Based Methods: Why We Need Them; What They Are; How to Do Them', in D.S. Byrne and C.C. Ragin (eds), *The SAGE Handbook of Case-Based Methods*. London: SAGE, pp 1–10.

Cairney, P. (2017) 'Evidence-based best practice is more political than it looks: A case study of the "Scottish Approach"', *Evidence & Policy*, 13(3): 499–515.

Cairney, P. (2019) *Understanding Public Policy: Theories and Issues*, 2nd edition. London: Red Glass Press.

Cairney, P. (2020) 'The UK government's COVID-19 policy: Assessing evidence-informed policy analysis in real time', *British Politics*. 16(1): 90–116.

Cairney, P. (2021) *The Politics of Policy Analysis*. London: Palgrave Macmillan.

Cairney, P. and Kwiatkowski, R. (2017) 'How to communicate effectively with policymakers: Combine insights from psychology and policy studies', *Palgrave Communications 2017*, 3(1): 37.

Campbell, A. (2017) *Treating Scotland's changing drug problem*. http://www.gov.scot/news/treating-scotlands-changing-drug-problem/

Carre, Z. and Ali, A. (2019) *Finding a Needle in a Haystack: Take-Home Naloxone in England 2017/18*. London: Release.

Caulkins, J.P. and Kilborn, M.L. (2019) 'Cannabis legalization, regulation, & control: A review of key challenges for local, state, and provincial officials', *The American Journal of Drug and Alcohol Abuse*, 45(6): 689–697.

Chomsky, N. and Herman, E.S. (1988) *Manufacturing Consent: The Political Economy of the Mass Media*. New York: Pantheon Books.

Christie, N. (1986a) 'Suitable Enemies', in H. Bianchi and R. van Swaaningen (eds), *Abolitionism: Towards a Non-repressive Approach to Crime*. Amsterdam: Free University Press, pp 42–54.

Christie, N. (1986b) 'The Ideal Victim', in E.A. Fattah (ed.), *From Crime Policy to Victim Policy*. Basingstoke: Macmillan, pp 17–30.

Christie, N.C., Hse, E., Iskiwitch, C., Iyer, R., Graham, J., Schwartz, B. et al (2019) 'The moral foundations of needle exchange attitudes', *Social Cognition*, 37(3): 229–246.

Churchill, J. (2019) *ACMD Ageing Cohort of Drug Users Report: Government Response*. London: Department of Health and Social Care.

Colebatch, H.K. (2009) *Policy*, 3rd edition. Maidenhead: Open University Press.

Colebatch, H.K. (2018) 'Linkage and the policy process', in H.K. Colebatch and R. Hoppe (eds), *Handbook on Policy, Process and Governing*. Cheltenham: Edward Elgar Publishing, pp 204–219.

Colebatch, H. K. and Hoppe, R. (eds) (2018) *Handbook on Policy, Process and Governing*. Cheltenham: Edward Elgar Publishing.

Collier, A. (1994) *Critical Realism: An Introduction to Roy Bhaskar's Philosophy*. London, New York: Verso.

Collins, J. (2017) 'Breaking the monopoly system: American influence on the British decision to prohibit opium smoking and end its Asian monopolies, 1939–1945', *The International History Review*, 39(5): 770–790.

Comte, A. (1988 [1830]) *Introduction to Positivist Philosophy*. Cambridge: Hackett Publishing Company.

Conservative Party (2019) *Get Brexit Done. Unleash Britain's Potential*. London: Conservative Party.

Couch, D. (2020) *Left Behind: The Scale of Illegal Cannabis Use for Medicinal Intent in the UK*. London: Centre for Medical Cannabis.

Cowburn, A. (2017) 'MPs join medical marijuana protest outside Parliament, with activists smoking joints and demanding legalisation', *The Independent* [Online]. Available from: https://www.independent.co.uk/news/uk/politics/mps-join-activists-at-cannabis-tea-party-outside-parliament-medicine-a7992996.html [Accessed 15 January 2023].

CRED (2021) *Commission on Race and Ethnic Disparities: The Report*. London: Cabinet Office.

Crick, B. (2013) *In Defence of Politics*. London: Bloomsbury.

Crippa, J.A.S., Derenusson, G.N., Ferrari, T.B., Wichert-Ana, L., Duran, F.L., Martin-Santos, R. et al (2011) 'Neural basis of anxiolytic effects of cannabidiol (CBD) in generalized social anxiety disorder: A preliminary report', *Journal of Psychopharmacology*, 25(1): 121–130.

Crow, D. and Jones, M. (2018) 'Narratives as tools for influencing policy change', 46(2): 217–234.

CSJ (2018a) *Cannabis: The Case against Legalisation*. London: Centre for Social Justice.

CSJ (2018b) *Desperate for a Fix: Using Shop Theft and a Second Chance Programme to Get Tough on Prolific Drug-Addicted Offenders*. London: The Centre for Social Justice.

CSJ (2023) 'About the CSJ', The Centre for Social Justice [Online]. Available from: https://www.centreforsocialjustice.org.uk/about [Accessed 15 May 2023].

Curchin, K., Weight, T. and Ritter, A. (2022) 'Moral framings in the Australian parliamentary debate on drug testing of welfare recipients', *Social Policy & Administration*, 56(3): 409–422.

Daily Record (2019) 'It's time to decriminalise drug use to beat Scotland's crippling death crisis', *Daily Record* [Online]. Available from: https://www.dailyrecord.co.uk/news/scottish-news/its-time-decriminalise-drug-use-17386758 [Accessed 21 December 2022].

Danermark, B., Ekstrom, M. and Karlsson, J.C. (2019) *Explaining Society: An Introduction to Critical Realism in the Social Sciences*. London: Routledge.

Daniels, C., Aluso, A., Shyne, N.B., Koram, K., Rajagopalan, S., Robinson, I. et al (2021) 'Decolonizing drug policy', *Harm Reduction Journal*, 18(120).

Davidson, R. (2021) 'Sturgeon's drugs shame' *UnHerd* [Online]. Available from: https://unherd.com/2021/08/sturgeons-drugs-shame/ [Accessed 4 February 2023].

De Saxe Zerden, L., O'Quinn, E. and Davis, C. (2015) 'Evidence-based policy versus morality policy: The case of syringe access programs', *Journal of Evidence-Informed Social Work*, 12(4): 425–437.

Debbaut, S. and Kammersgaard, T. (2022) 'The "public health" approach to illicit drugs: An eradicative drug discourse in a sanitorial disguise?', *Drugs, Habits and Social Policy*, 24(1): 1–13.

Decorte, T., Lenton, S. and Wilkins, C. (eds) (2021) *Legalizing Cannabis: Experiences, Lessons and Scenarios*. London, New York: Routledge.

Departmental Committee on Morphine and Heroin Addiction (1926) *The Rolleston Report*. London: HMSO.

DHSC (2018) *Commissioning Impact on Drug Treatment: Government Response*. London: Department of Health and Social Care.

Di Forti, M., Marconi, A., Carra, E., Fraietta, S., Trotta, A., Bonomo, M. et al (2015) 'Proportion of patients in south London with first-episode psychosis attributable to use of high potency cannabis: A case-control study', *The Lancet Psychiatry*, 2(3): 233–238.

Di Forti, M., Quattrone, D., Freeman, T.P., Tripoli, G., Gayer-Anderson, C., Quigley, H. et al (2019) 'The contribution of cannabis use to variation in the incidence of psychotic disorder across Europe (EU-GEI): A multicentre case-control study', *The Lancet Psychiatry*, 6(5): 427–436.

Douglas, M. and Wildavsky, A. (1982) *Risk and Culture: An Essay on the Selection of Technological and Environmental Dangers*. Berkeley: University of California Press.

Douse, K., Eastwood, N. and Stevens, A. (2022) 'A modest proposal to decriminalise the simple possession of drugs', in I. Crome, D. Nutt, and A. Stevens (eds), *Drug Science and British Drug Policy: Critical Analysis of the Misuse of Drugs Act 1971*. Sherfield-on-Loddon: Waterside Press, pp 293–302.

Drug Science (2016) *Cannabis and Cannabis Resin: Pre-Review Report*. London: Drug Science.

Drug Science (2019a) *Drug Science Launches Working Group on Medical Cannabis*. London: Drug Science.

Drug Science (2019b) *Press Release: Government Decision on Cannabis-Related Medicinal Products Draws Criticism from Independent Scientific Body, Drug Science*. London: Drug Science.

Drug Science (2023) 'Latest T21 data', *Drug Science* [Online]. Available from: https://www.drugscience.org.uk/t21data/ [Accessed 20 January 2023].

Dunn, W.N. (2017) *Public Policy Analysis: An Integrated Approach*, 6th edition. New York: Routledge.

Easton, M. (2008) 'Drug Treatment – Success or Failure?' *BBC* [Online] Available from: http://www.bbc.co.uk/blogs/thereporters/markeaston/2008/10/drug_treatment_officials_were.html [Accessed 11 August 2023].

Edwards, G. (2004) *Matters of Substance: Drugs – and Why Everyone's a User*. London: Allen Lane.

Elder-Vass, D. (2007) 'For emergence: Refining Archer's account of social structure', *Journal for the Theory of Social Behaviour*, 37(1): 25–44.

Elder-Vass, D. (2012) *The Reality of Social Construction*. Cambridge: Cambridge University Press.

Ellersgaard, C.H., Ditlevsen, K. and Larsen, A.G. (2022) 'Say my name? Anonymity or not in elite interviewing', *International Journal of Social Research Methodology*, 25(5): 673–686.

Ellis, C., Adams, T.E. and Bochner, A.P. (2011) 'Autoethnography: An overview', *Forum: Qualitative Social Research*, 12(1): 345–357.

Ellson, A. and Smyth, C. (2018) 'Decriminalise cannabis, urges psychosis expert Sir Robin Murray', *The Times* [Online], 11 October. Available from: https://www.thetimes.co.uk/article/decriminalise-cannabis-urges-psychosis-expert-sir-robin-murray-z6zjrcsqm [Accessed 18 February 2023].

English, R. and Doughty, S. (2017) 'Prince William branded 'naive' over legalising drugs remark', *Mail Online*. Available at: http://www.dailymail.co.uk/~/article-4904944/index.html [Accessed 1 April 2022].

Euchner, E.M., Heichel, S., Nebel, K. and Raschzok, A. (2013) 'From "morality" policy to "normal" policy: Framing of drug consumption and gambling in Germany and the Netherlands and their regulatory consequences', *Journal of European Public Policy*, 20(3): 372–389.

Evans-Brown, M. and Sedefov, R. (2017) 'New psychoactive substances: Driving greater complexity into the drug problem', *Addiction*, 112(1): 36–38.

Fadlallah, R., El-Jardali, F., Nomier, M., Hemadi, N., Arif, K., Langlois, E.V. et al (2019) 'Using narratives to impact health policy-making: A systematic review', *Health Research Policy and Systems*, 17(26).

Farrell, M. and Marsden, J. (2008) 'Acute risk of drug-related death among newly released prisoners in England and Wales', *Addiction*, 103(2): 251–255.

Faul, M.V. (2016) 'Networks and power: Why networks are hierarchical not flat and what can be done about it', *Global Policy*, 7(2): 185–197.

FAVOR UK (2021) *Summary of Residential Rehabilitation in Scotland*. Glasgow: Faces and Voices of Recovery UK. Available from: https://www.facesandvoicesofrecoveryuk.org/wp-content/uploads/2021/06/Summary-of-Residential-Rehabiltation-in-Scotlandv3.pdf [Accessed 11 August 2023].

Feldman, G. (2011) 'Illuminating the Apparatus: Steps toward a Nonlocal Ethnography of Global Governance', in C. Shore, S. Wright and D. Però (eds), *Policy Worlds: Anthropology and the Analysis of Contemporary Power*. New York: Berghahn Books, pp 32–49.

Ferguson, J. and Grant, R. (2015) 'Thousands of Scots call for cannabis to be legalised', *Daily Record* [Online]. Available from: http://www.dailyrecord.co.uk/news/scottish-news/thousands-scots-call-cannabis-legalised-6608375 [Accessed 15 January 2023].

Ferraiolo, K. (2014) 'Morality framing in US drug control policy: An example from marijuana decriminalization', *World Medical & Health Policy*, 6(4): 347–374.

Finnigan, K., Daly, A.J., Caduff, A. and Leal, C.C. (2021) 'Broken Bridges: The Role of Brokers in Connecting Educational Leaders Around Research Evidence', in M.S. Weber and I. Yanovitzky (eds), *Networks, Knowledge Brokers, and the Public Policymaking Process*. Cham: Palgrave Macmillan, pp 71–100.

Fischer, F. (2003) *Reframing Public Policy: Discursive Politics and Deliberative Practices*. Oxford, New York: Oxford University Press.

Fisher, H. and Measham, F. (2018) *Night Lives: Reducing Drug-Related Harm in the Night Time Economy*. London: Volteface.

Flanigan, J. (2012) 'Three arguments against prescription requirements', *Journal of Medical Ethics*, 38(10): 579–586.

Flatschart, E. (2016) 'Critical realist critical discourse analysis: A necessary alternative to Post-Marxist discourse theory', *Journal of Critical Realism*, 15(1): 21–52.

Fortson, R. (2017) 'Setting up a drug consumption room: Legal issues' London: Rudi Fortson QC. Available from: https://www.rudifortson4law.co.uk/legaltexts/Rudi-Fortson-DCR-legal-issues-17thOct2017-v1.pdf [Accessed 13 February 2023].

Foster, A. (2019) 'Disappointment for campaigners and investors as NICE pours cold water on cannabis', *Memery Crystal* [Online]. Available from: https://www.memerycrystal.com/disappointment-for-campaigners-and-investors-as-nice-pours-cold-water-on-cannabis/ [Accessed 20 January 2023].

Fotopoulou, M. and Aston, L. (2023) 'Policing of Drugs in Scotland: Moving beyond the Stalemate to Redesigning the Chess Board', in J. Spicer and M. Bacon (eds), *Drug Law Enforcement, Policing and Harm Reduction: Ending the Stalemate*. Abingdon: Routledge, pp 151–173.

Fox, S., Armentano, P. and Tvert, M. (2013) *Marijuana is Safer: So Why Are We Driving People to Drink?* Updated and expanded edition. White River Junction, VT: Chelsea Green Publishing.

Friedman, S.R. (1998) 'The political economy of drug-user scapegoating – and the philosophy and politics of resistance', *Drugs: Education Prevention and Policy*, 5(1): 15–32.

Frimer, J., Boghrati, R., Haidt, J., Graham, J. and Dehghani, M. (2019) *Moral Foundations Dictionary 2.0* [Online]. Available from: https://osf.io/ezn37/ [Accessed 20 January 2023].

Fuhse, J.A. (2009) 'The meaning structure of social networks', *Sociological Theory*, 27(1): 51–73.

Garavelli, D. (2020) 'Drug deaths in Scotland are an epidemic – yet Westminster is blocking reform', *The Guardian*. Available at: https://www.theguardian.com/commentisfree/2020/sep/11/drug-deaths-scotland-epidemic-scottish-independence [Accessed 21 December 2022].

Garius, L. and Ali, A. (2022) *'Regulating Right, Repairing Wrongs: Exploring Equity and Social Justice Initiatives within UK Cannabis Reform'*. London: Release [Online]. Available from: https://www.release.org.uk/publications/cannabis-regulating-right [Accessed 12 January 2022].

Gerstein, D.R. and Harwood, H.J. (1990) 'Ideas Governing Drug Policy', in D.R. Gerstein and H.J. Harwood (eds), *Treating Drug Problems, Volume 1: A Study of the Evolution, Effectiveness, and Financing of Public and Private Drug Treatment Systems*. Washington, DC: National Academies Press. Available from: https://www.ncbi.nlm.nih.gov/books/NBK235507/ [Accessed 7 January 2023].

Gibbs, B., Reed, T. and Wride, S. (2021) *Cannabis Legalisation – Canada's Experience*. London: Public First.

Gidden, A. (1975) 'Elites in the British Class Structure', in P. Stanworth and A. Giddens (eds), *Elites and Power in British Society*. Cambridge: Cambridge University Press, pp 1–21.

Giddens, A. (1984) *The Constitution of Society: Outline of the Theory of Structuration*. Cambridge: Polity Press.

Glasgow City Council (2019) 'Scotland's first heroin assisted treatment unveiled'. Glasgow: Glasgow City Council [Online] Available from: https://www.glasgow.gov.uk/article/25326/Scotlands-First-Heroin-Assisted-Treatment-Unveiled [Accessed 9 February 2023].

Gornall, J. (2019) 'Big tobacco, the new politics, and the threat to public health', *BMJ*, 365: 12164.

Gouldsbrough, P. (2022) 'Consett mother of four died of a drug overdose shortly after her release from prison', *The Northern Echo* [Online]. Available from: https://www.thenorthernecho.co.uk/news/19970858.consett-mother-four-died-drug-overdose-shortly-release-prison/ [Accessed 7 March 2023].

Graham, J., Haidt, J. and Nosek, B.A. (2009) 'Liberals and conservatives rely on different sets of moral foundations.', *Journal of Personality and Social Psychology*, 96(5): 1029–1046.

Granovetter, M.S. (1973) 'The strength of weak ties', *American Journal of Sociology*, 78(6): 1360.

Green Party of England (2019) *If Not Now, When? Green Party General Election Manifesto*. London.

Gyngell, K. (2007) *Breakthrough Britain: Ending the Costs of Social Breakdown, Volume 4: Addictions*. London: The Centre for Social Justice.

Habermas, J. (1976) *Legitimation Crisis*. London: Heinemann.

Habermas, J. (1977) 'Hannah Arendt's communication concept of power', *Social Research*, 44(1): 3–24.

Habermas, J. (1986) *Law and Morality: The Tanner Lectures on Human Values*. Delivered 1 and 2 October 1986. Boston. https://www.pravo.unizg.hr/_download/repository/habermas88.pdf.

Habermas, J. (1995) *The Structural Transformation of the Public Sphere: An Inquiry into a Category of Bourgeois Society*. Cambridge, MA: MIT Press.

Habermas, J. (1996) *Between Facts and Norms: Contributions to a Discourse Theory of Law and Democracy*. Cambridge, MA: MIT Press.

Habermas, J. (2006) 'Political communication in media society: Does democracy still enjoy an epistemic dimension? The impact of normative theory on empirical research', *Communication Theory*, 16(4): 411–426.

Haidt, J. (2012) *The Righteous Mind: Why Good People are Divided by Politics and Religion*. London: Allen Lane.

Haidt, J., Graham, J. and Joseph, C. (2009) 'Above and below left–right: Ideological narratives and moral foundations', *Psychological Inquiry*, 20(2–3): 110–119.

Haidt, J. and Joseph, C. (2004) 'Intuitive ethics: How innately prepared intuitions generate culturally variable virtues', *Daedalus*, 133(4): 55–66.

Hajer, M.A. (1989) *City Politics: Hegemonic Projects and Discourse*. Aldershot: Avebury.

Hajer, M.A. (1993) 'Discourse coalitions and the institutionalisation of practice: The case of acid rain in Britain', in F. Fischer and J. Forester (eds), *The Argumentative Turn in Policy Analysis and Planning*. Durham, NC: Duke University Press, pp 43–76.

Hajer, M.A. (1995) *The Politics of Environmental Discourse: Environmental Modernization and the Policy Process*. Oxford: Oxford University Press.

Hammersley, M. and Atkinson, P. (2007) *Ethnography: Principles in Practice*, 3rd edition. London: Routledge.

Handler, J.F. (2007) *Blame Welfare, Ignore Poverty and Inequality*. Cambridge: Cambridge University Press.

Hansard (2015) [HC] volume 600, column 1WH, Available from: https://hansard.parliament.uk//commons/2015-10-12/debates/15101213000001/Cannabis [Accessed 11 August 2023].

Hansard (2017a) [HC] volume 627, column 725, Available from: https://hansard.parliament.uk/commons/2017-07-18/debates/733C6229-49D0-4559-8F59-5F1244C2DE13/DrugsPolicy [Accessed 11 August 2023].

Hansard (2017b) [HC] volume 633, column 1054, Available from: https://hansard.parliament.uk/commons/2017-12-20/debates/9B501034-E35A-45F8-8834-18BAA9EFF507/Engagements [Accessed 11 August 2023].

Hansard (2018a) [HC] volume 643, column 192, Available from: https://hansard.parliament.uk/commons/2018-06-19/debates/6889E197-AF00-4F77-99C8-25ADC469528F/Cannabis-BasedMedicines [Accessed 11 August 2023].

Hansard (2018b) [HC] volume 636, column 23, Available from: https://hansard.parliament.uk/Commons/2018-02-20/debates/5C18DA05-4AF4-408A-A7C2-67F3E84133CC/MedicalCannabis [Accessed 11 August 2023].

Hansard (2019a) [HC] volume 627, column 725, Available from: https://hansard.parliament.uk/commons/2017-07-18/debates/733C6229-49D0-4559-8F59-5F1244C2DE13/DrugsPolicy [Accessed 11 August 2023].

Hansard (2019b) [HC] volume 660, column 527, Available from: https://hansard.parliament.uk/commons/2019-05-20/debates/8231D857-B2DF-47EA-86F4-E7CF7068A6CE/MedicalCannabisUnderPrescription

Hansard (2021a) [HC] volume 702, column 182 WH, Available from: https://hansard.parliament.uk/Commons/2021-10-27/debates/DF66F50C-F9FA-4AD9-911B-AE4344079853/DameCarolBlack%E2%80%99SIndependentReviewOfDrugsReport [Accessed 11 August 2023].

Hansard (2021b) [HC] volume 700, column 102, Available from: https://hansard.parliament.uk/commons/2021-09-06/debates/42F4200B-2D42-4A91-A40D-9E22A1FA0D44/MedicinalCannabis [Accessed 11 August 2023].

Hansard (2021c) [HC] volume 705, column 676, Available from: https://hansard.parliament.uk/commons/2021-12-10/debates/3412378D-471C-4ED8-A315-73CA97C9A6DB/MedicalCannabis(Access)Bill [Accessed 11 August 2023].

Hansard (2021d) [HC] volume 702, column 1096, Available from: https://hansard.parliament.uk/Commons/2021-11-04/debates/6C5A1651-2C7D-4C85-95D0-31ADAAD56098/MedicalCannabisAlleviationOfHealthConditions [Accessed 11 August 2023].

Hansard (2021e) [HC] volume 705, column 73, Available from: https://hansard.parliament.uk/Commons/2021-12-06/debates/54065168-8B45-47B1-BEEB-1BA4B49DB4AF/Ten-YearDrugsStrategy [Accessed 24 June 2022].

Hansen, D.L., Shneiderman, B. and Smith, M.A. (2011) *Analyzing Social Media Networks with NodeXL: Insights from a Connected World*. Boston: Morgan Kaufmann.

Harper, C.A. and Rhodes, D. (2021) 'Reanalysing the factor structure of the moral foundations questionnaire', *British Journal of Social Psychology*, 60(4): 1303–1329.

Hastings, M. and Jenkins, S. (2010) *The Battle for the Falklands*, new edition. Pan Military Classics. London: Pan Macmillan.

Haugaard, M. (2020) *The Four Dimensions of Power*. Manchester: Manchester University Press.

Hawkins, B. and Oliver, K. (2022) 'Select Committee Governance and the Production of Evidence: The Case of UK E-cigarettes Policy', in F. Fafard, A. Cassola and E. de Leeuw (eds), *Integrating Science and Politics for Public Health*. Palgrave Studies in Public Health Policy Research. Cham: Springer International Publishing, pp 187–208.

Health and Social Care Committee (2019) *Drug Policy: First Report of Session 2019*. London: House of Commons.

Heclo, H. (1978) 'Issue networks and the executive establishment', in A. King (ed.), *The Political System*. Washington DC: The American Institute for Public Policy.

Hickman, M., Steer, C., Tilling, K., Lim, A.G., Marsden, J., Millar, T. et al (2018) 'The impact of buprenorphine and methadone on mortality: A primary care cohort study in the United Kingdom', *Addiction*, 113(8): 1461–1476. doi: 10.1111/add.14188.

Hill, M. (2009) *The Public Policy Process*, 5th edition. Harlow: Pearson.

Hitchens, P. (2012) *The War We Never Fought*. London: Bloomsbury Continuum.

HM Government (2010) *Drug Strategy 2010: Reducing Demand, Restricting Supply, Building Recovery: Supporting People to Live a Drug Free Life*. London: Home Office.

HM Government (2017) *2017 Drug Strategy*. London: Home Office. Available from: https://www.gov.uk/government/publications/drug-strategy-2017 [Accessed 11 August 2023].

HM Government (2020) *Faster Access to Cannabis-Based Medicines as Import Restrictions Are Changed*. Available from: https://www.gov.uk/government/news/faster-access-to-cannabis-based-medicines-as-import-restrictions-are-changed [Accessed 20 January 2023].

HM Government (2021) *From Harm to Hope: A 10-Year Drugs Plan to Cut Crime and Save Lives*. London: HM Government.

Hoeh, N.R. (2022) 'An evidential rather than moral imperative', *BMJ*, 376: n3114.

Home Office (1985) *Tackling Drug Misuse: A Summary of the Government's Strategy*. London: Home Office.

Home Office (2021) *Crime Outcomes in England and Wales 2020 to 2021*. Available from: https://www.gov.uk/government/statistics/crime-outcomes-in-england-and-wales-2020-to-2021 [Accessed 10 January 2022].

Home Office (2022) *Government Response to the ACMD on CBPMs in Humans*. London: Home Office.

Hope, D. and Limberg, J. (2022) 'The economic consequences of major tax cuts for the rich', *Socio-Economic Review*, 20(2): 539–559.

Hopp, F.R., Fisher, J.T., Cornell, D., Huskey, R. and Weber, R. (2021) 'The extended Moral Foundations Dictionary (eMFD): Development and applications of a crowd-sourced approach to extracting moral intuitions from text', *Behaviour Research Methods*, 53(1): 232–246.

Hopp, F.R., Fisher, J.T. and Weber, R. (2020a) 'A graph-learning approach for detecting moral conflict in movie scripts', *Media and Communication*, 8(3): 164–179.

Hopp, F.R., Fisher, J.T. and Weber, R. (2020b) 'Dynamic transactions between news frames and sociopolitical events: An integrative, Hidden Markov Model approach', *Journal of Communication*, 70(3): 335–355.

Howarth, D. (2000) *Discourse*. Buckingham: Open University Press.

HRI (2022) *Global State of Harm Reduction 2022*. London: Harm Reduction International.

Hughes, S. (2018) 'Making the IEA "Freer" to espouse Tory ideology', *Morning Star* [Online]. Available from: https://morningstaronline.co.uk/article/freer-espose-tory-ideology [Accessed 29 December 2022].

Humphreys, K., Shover, C.L., Andrews, C.M., Bohnert, A.S.B., Brandeau, M.L., Caulkins, J.P. et al (2022) 'Responding to the opioid crisis in North America and beyond: Recommendations of the Stanford–Lancet Commission', *The Lancet* 399(10324): 495–604. doi: 10.1016/S0140-6736(21)02252-2.

Hunter, J. (1992) *Culture Wars: The Struggle to Control the Family, Art, Education, Law, and Politics in America*. New York: Basic Books.

Hutcheon, P. (2019) *Critic of SNP Government Anti-Drugs Strategy in Row Over Tobacco Industry Funding, Herald*. Available at: https://www.heraldscotland.com/news/17539768.critic-snp-government-anti-drugs-strategy-row-tobacco-industry-funding/ [Accessed 22 December 2022].

IEA (2022) 'About Us', Institute of Economic Affairs [Online]. Available from: https://iea.org.uk/about-us/ [Accessed 7 December 2022].

IfG (2021) *Transcript, Nick Hurd, 11 January 2021, Ministers Reflect Archive*. Institute for Government [Online]. Available from: https://www.instituteforgovernment.org.uk/sites/default/files/2022-11/nick-hurd-ministers-reflect.pdf [Accessed 20 January 2023].

Inglehart, R. and Welzel, C. (2005) *Modernization, Cultural Change, and Democracy: The Human Development Sequence*. Cambridge: Cambridge University Press.

Ingram, H., Schneider, A.L. and Deleon, P. (2007) 'Social Construction and Policy Design', in P.A. Sabatier (ed), *Theories of the Policy Process*, 2nd edition. Boulder, CO: Westview Press.

Jacomy, M., Venturini, T., Heymann, S. and Bastian, M. (2014) 'ForceAtlas2, a continuous graph layout algorithm for handy network visualization designed for the Gephi software', *PLoS ONE*, 9(6): e98679.

Jasanoff, S. (2003) 'Breaking the waves in science studies: Comment on H.M. Collins and Robert Evans, "The Third Wave of Science Studies"', *Social Studies of Science*, 33(3): 389–400.

Javid, S. (2018a) *Commission to the ACMD: Scheduling under the Misuse of Drugs Regulations 2001*. London: Home Office.

Javid, S. (2018b) *Government Response to the ACMD: Cannabis Derived Medicinal Products*. London: Home Office.

Javid, S. (2021) 'Dame Carol Black's Independent Review of Drugs: Publication of Part 2', *Hansard*, 698 (8 July 2021).

Javid, S. and Hancock, M. (2018) *Response to ACMD: Cannabis-Derived Medicinal Products, 21 September 2018*. London: Home Office and Department of Health and Social Care.

Jenkins, W.I. (1978) *Policy Analysis: A Political and Organisational Perspective*. Oxford: Martin Robertson.

Jenkins-Smith, H.C., Nohrstedt, D., Weible, C.M. and Ingold, K. (2018) 'The Advocacy Coalition Framework: An Overview of the Research Program', in C.M. Weible and P.A. Sabatier, (eds), *Theories of the Policy Process*, 4th edition. New York: Routledge, pp 146–171.

Jenkins-Smith, H.C. and Sabatier, P.A. (1993) 'The Study of Public Policy Processes', in P.A. Sabatier and H. Jenkins-Smith (eds), *Policy Change and Learning: An Advocacy Coalition Approach*. Boulder, CO: Westview Press, pp 1–9.

Johnson, B. (2021) 'Foreword', in HM Government, *From Harm to Hope: A 10-Year Drugs Plan to Cut Crime and Save Lives*. London: HM Government, pp 3–4.

Johnson, M. (2007) *Wasted: Violence, Addiction – and Hope*. London: Sphere.

Jones, H.E., Harris, R.J., Downing, B.C., Pierce, M., Millar, T., Ades, A.E. et al (2020) 'Estimating the prevalence of problem drug use from drug-related mortality data', *Addiction*, 115(12): 2393–2404.

Jones, A., Jamieson, D. and Hogg, R. (2018) *Statement on 'Reducing Opioid-Related Deaths in the UK: Further Response on Drug Consumption Rooms'*. Durham: Offices of the Police and Crime Commissioners for North Wales, West Midlands and Durham.

Jones, M.D. and McBeth, M.K. (2010) 'A narrative policy framework: Clear enough to be wrong?', *The Policy Studies Journal*, 38(2): 329–354.

Kalinka, A.T. (2020) 'The generation, visualization, and analysis of link communities in arbitrary networks with the R package linkcomm', *The Comprehensive R Archive Network* [Online]. Available from: https://cran.r-project.org/web/packages/linkcomm/vignettes/linkcomm.pdf [Accessed 18 March 2023].

Keane, H. (2003) 'Critiques of harm reduction, morality and the promise of human rights', *International Journal of Drug Policy*, 14(3): 227–232.

Keeling, P. (2021a) *A Joint Response to the New Drug Strategy*. London: Collective Voice.

Keeling, P. (2021b) *If Not Now, When?* London: Collective Voice.

Keen, S. (2001) *Debunking Economics: The Naked Emperor of the Social Sciences*. Annandale NSW: Pluto Press.

Khurana, D., Koli, A., Khatter, K. and Singh, S. (2023) 'Natural language processing: State of the art, current trends and challenges', *Multimedia Tools and Applications*, 82(3): 3713–3744.

Kimber, J., Hickman, M., Strang, J., Thomas, K. and Hutchinson, S. (2019) 'Rising opioid-related deaths in England and Scotland must be recognised as a public health crisis', *The Lancet Psychiatry*, 6(8): 639–640.

King, D. and Moore, A. (2020) *The UK Review of the Medical Cannabis: The Needs of a Nation*. London: Conservative Drug Policy Reform Group.

King, D., Bhatarah, P., Duffy, P., Yates, A. and O'Sullivan, S. (2021) *A Step-by-Step Approach: Establishing the Zero Threshold in CBD Products*. London: Conservative Drug Policy Reform Group and Association for the Cannabis Industry.

Kingdon, J.W. (1984) *Agendas, Alternatives, and Public Policies*. Boston: Little, Brown.

Kingdon, J.W. (2013) *Agendas, Alternatives, and Public Policies, Updated Edition, with an Epilogue on Health Care*. Harlow: Pearson.

Kirman, A. (1989) 'Intrinsic limits of modern economic theory: The emperor has no clothes', *The Economics Journal*, 395(1): 126–139.

Klein, A. (2008) *Drugs and the World*. London: Reaktion Books.

Knox, W.W. (1988) 'Religion and the Scottish labour movement c. 1900–39', *Journal of Contemporary History*, 23(4): 609–630.

Koleva, S.P., Graham, J., Iyer, R., Ditto, P.H. and Haidt, J. (2012) 'Tracing the threads: How five moral concerns (especially purity) help explain culture war attitudes', *Journal of Research in Personality*, 46(2): 184–194.

Koram, K. (ed.) (2019) *The War on Drugs and the Global Colour Line*. London: Pluto Press.

Kothari, A. and Smith, M.J. (2022) 'Public Health Policymaking, Politics, and Evidence', in F. Fafard, A. Cassola, and E. de Leeuw (eds), *Integrating Science and Politics for Public Health*. Cham: Springer International Publishing, pp 59–74.

Kübler, D. (2001) 'Understanding policy change with the advocacy coalition framework: An application to Swiss drug policy', *Journal of European Public Policy*, 8(4): 623–641.

Labour Party (2019) *It's Time for a Real Change. The Labour Party Manifesto 2019*. London.

Lakoff, G. (2002) *Moral Politics: How Liberals and Conservatives Think*, 2nd edition. Chicago: The University of Chicago Press.

Lammy, D. (2017) *The Lammy Review: An Independent Review into the Treatment of, and Outcomes for, Black, Asian and Minority Ethnic Individuals in the Criminal Justice System*. London: Cabinet Office.

Lasco, G. (2022) 'Decolonizing harm reduction', *Harm Reduction Journal*, 19(1): 8. doi: 10.1186/s12954-022-00593-w.

Latour, B. (2005) *Reassembling the Social: An Introduction to Actor-Network-Theory*. Oxford: Oxford University Press.

Laurie, P. (1967) *Drugs: Medical, Psychological, and Social Facts*. Harmondsworth: Penguin.

Law, J. (2004) *After Method: Mess in Social Science Research*. London: Routledge.

Lawson, T. (1997) *Economics and Reality*. London: Routledge.

Lawson, T. (2019) *The Nature of Social Reality*. London, New York: Routledge.

Layder, D. (1998) *Sociological Practice: Linking Theory and Social Research*. London: Sage.

LCDPR (2018) *Labour Members Launch New Campaign Calling for Changes in UK Drug Policy*. London: Labour Campaign for Drugh Policy Reform. Available at: https://www.labourdrugpolicy.com/new-blog/2018/7/17/labour-members-launch-new-campaign-calling-for-change-in-uk-drug-policy.

Leifeld, P. (2017) 'Discourse Network Analysis: Policy Debates as Dynamic Networks', in J.N. Victoria, M.N. Lubell and A.H. Montgomery (eds), *The Oxford Handbook of Political Networks*. Oxford: Oxford University Press, pp 301–326.

Lerkkanen, T. and Storbjörk, J. (2023) 'Debating the drug policy in Sweden: Stakeholders' moral justifications in media 2015–2021', *Contemporary Drug Problems*, 50(2): 269–293.

Lerner, J.S., Li, Y., Valdesolo, P. and Kassam, K.S. (2015) 'Emotion and decision making', *Annual Review of Psychology*, 66(1): 799–823.

Liberal Democrats (n.d.) 'Let's legalise and regulate cannabis', *Liberal Democrats* [Online]. Available from: https://www.libdems.org.uk/cannabis [Accessed 4 June 2022].

Lloyd, B., Zahnow, R., Barratt, M.J., Best, D., Lubman, D.I. and Ferris, J. (2017) 'Exploring mortality among drug treatment clients: The relationship between treatment type and mortality', *Journal of Substance Abuse Treatment*, 82: 22–28.

Lloyd, C. (2009) 'How we got to where we are now', in J. Barlow (ed.), *Substance Misuse: The Implications of Research, Policy and Practice.* London: Jessica Kingsley Publishers, pp 19–35.

Lockwood, D. (1960) '"The distribution of power in industrial society": A comment by D. Lockwood', *The Sociological Review*, 8(1_suppl): 35–41.

Lord Kamall (2022) 'Cannabis: Prescriptions. Written answer', *UK Parliament* [Online]. Available from: https://questions-statements.parliament.uk/written-questions/detail/2022-07-08/hl1593 [Accessed 7 March 2023].

Los, G. (2023a) 'Application of the policy constellations framework to the Polish drug policy over the past twenty-five years. *Archiwum Kryminologii*: 44(2): 65–86.

Los, G. (2023b) 'Critically explaining British policy responses to novel psychoactive substances using the policy constellations framework', *Drugs: Education, Prevention and Policy*. doi: 10.1080/09687637.2023.2218536.

Lowe, R. (ed.) (2019) *On Social Freedom: A Collection of Essays.* London: FREER.

Lukes, S. (1974) *Power, a Radical View.* London: Macmillan.

Lukes, S. (2013) 'The Social Construction of Morality?', in S. Hitlin and S. Vaisey (eds), *Handbook of the Sociology of Morality.* New York: Springer, pp 549–560.

Lupton, D. (1995) *The Imperative of Health: Public Health and the Regulated Body.* London: Sage.

MacCoun, R.J. and Reuter, P. (2001) *Drug War Heresies: Learning from Other Vices, Times, & Places.* Cambridge: Cambridge University Press.

MacGregor, S. (2017) *The Politics of Drugs: Perceptions, Power and Policies.* Basingstoke: Palgrave Macmillan UK.

Madden, A., Tanguay, P. and Chang, J. (2021) *Drug Decriminalisation: Progress or Political Red Herring?* London: INPUD.

Malpas, S. (2003) *Jean-Francois Lyotard.* London, New York: Routledge.

Malthouse, K. (2020a) *Response to the ACMD Recommendation: Epidyolex.* London: Home Office.

Malthouse, K. (2020b) *Response to the ACMD Report on the Misuse of Fentanyl and Fentanyl Analogues.* London: Home Office.

Malthouse, K. (2021) *Letter to ACMD Chair on Drug Misuse Prevention Review.* London: Home Office.

Manning, P. (2016) 'There's no glamour in glue: News and the symbolic framing of substance misuse:' *Crime, Media, Culture.* 2(1): 49–66.

Marsden, J., Stillwell, G., Jones, H., Cooper, A., Eastwood, B., Farrell, M. et al (2017) 'Does exposure to opioid substitution treatment in prison reduce the risk of death after release? A national prospective observational study in England', *Addiction*, 112(8): 1408–1418.

Marsh, S. and Badshah, N. (2018) 'Mother of boy whose cannabis oil was seized pushes for legalisation', *The Guardian* [Online], 17 June. Available from: https://www.theguardian.com/society/2018/jun/17/mother-of-boy-whose-cannabis-oil-was-seized-pushes-for-legalisation [Accessed 20 January 2023].

Marx, K. and Engels, F. (1998 [1845]) *The German Ideology: Including Theses on Feuerbach and Introduction to The Critique of Political Economy*. Amherst, NY: Prometheus Books.

McAuley, A., Fraser, R., Glancy, M., Yeung, A., Jones, H.E., Vickerman, P. et al (2023) 'Mortality among individuals prescribed opioid-agonist therapy in Scotland, UK, 2011–20: A national retrospective cohort study', *The Lancet Public Health*. 8(7): e484-e493. doi: 10.1016/S2468-2667(23)00082-8.

McCambridge, J., Hawkins, B. and Holden, C. (2014) 'Vested interests in addiction research and policy: The challenge corporate lobbying poses to reducing society's alcohol problems: Insights from UK evidence on minimum unit pricing', *Addiction*, 109(2): 199–205.

McCann, K. (2018) 'Theresa May admits "running through fields of wheat" is the naughtiest thing she ever did', *The Telegraph* [Online], 11 January. Available from: https://www.telegraph.co.uk/politics/2017/06/05/theresa-may-admits-running-fields-wheat-naughtiest-thing-ever/ [Accessed 12 May 2023].

MCCS and Drug Science (2021) *Commentary and Critique on the BNPA Publication: Guidance on the Use of Cannabis-Based Products for Medicinal Use in Children and Young People with Epilepsy*. London: Medical Cannabis Clinical Society and Drug Science.

McCulloch, L. (2017) *Back Yard: An Investigation into the Feasibility of Establishing Drug Consumption Rooms*. London: Volteface.

McCulloch, L. and Furlong, S. (n.d.) *Making the Grade: School Prevention, Identification and Responses to Drug-Related Harm*. London: Volteface and Mentor UK. Available at: https://volteface.me/app/uploads/2019/04/Volteface-Making-the-Grade-Full-Report.pdf [Accessed 31 March 2022].

McCulloch, L., Matharu, H. and North, P. (2018) *The Children's Inquiry*. London: Volteface.

McGarvey, D. (2020) 'Joe FitzPatrick must carry can for grim toll of drug deaths', *Daily Record* [Online]. Available from: https://www.dailyrecord.co.uk/news/scottish-news/scots-drug-deaths-scandal-public-23185701 [Accessed 4 February 2023].

McGarvey, D. (2019) 'Scotland's drug shame', *UnHerd* [Online]. Available from: https://unherd.com/2019/07/scotlands-drug-shame/ [Accessed 4 February 2023].

McGivern, M. (2019) 'It's time to decriminalise drugs and to treat problem as a health issue', *Daily Record* [Online]. Available from: https://www.dailyrecord.co.uk/news/scottish-news/its-time-decriminalise-drugs-scotland-14981588 [Accessed 4 February 2023].

McKeganey, N. (2010) *Controversies in Drugs Policy and Practice*. Basingstoke: Palgrave.

McKeganey, N. (2017) 'A different way'. Available at: https://www.drinkanddrugsnews.com/a-different-way/ [Accessed 22 December 2022].

McPhee, I. and Sheridan, B. (2023) 'Policy traps and policy placebos: Assessing drug policy network responses to drug related deaths', *Drugs, Habits and Social Policy*, 24(1): 39–52. doi: 10.1108/DHS-06-2022-0023.

Measham, F. and Shiner, M. (2009) 'The legacy of "normalisation": The role of classical and contemporary criminological theory in understanding young people's drug use', *International Journal of Drug Policy*, 20(6): 502–508.

MHCLG (2019) *Drug Related Harms in Homeless Populations: Government Response*. London: Ministry of Housing, Communities and Local Government.

Miles, A. and Vaisey, S. (2015) 'Morality and politics: Comparing alternate theories', *Social Science Research*, 53(September): 252–269.

Millar, T. and McAuley, A. (2017) *EMCDDA Assessment of Drug-Induced Death Data and Contextual Information in Selected Countries*. Lisbon: European Monitoring Centre for Drugs and Drug Addiction.

Miller, D., Gilmore, A.B., Sheron, N., Britton, J. and Babor, T.F. (2014) 'Re: Costs of minimum alcohol pricing would outweigh benefits', *BMJ*, 348: g1572.

Miller, D. and Harkins, C. (2010) 'Corporate strategy, corporate capture: Food and alcohol industry lobbying and public health', *Critical Social Policy*, 30(4): 564–589.

Miller, D., Harkins, C., Schlögl, M. and Montague, B. (2018) *Impact of Market Forces on Addictive Substances and Behaviours: The Web of Influence of the Addictive Industries*, 1st edition. New York: Oxford University Press.

Mintrom, M. (2019) 'So you want to be a policy entrepreneur?', *Policy Design and Practice*, 2(4): 307–323.

MoJ (2019) *ACMD Custody-Community Transitions Report: Government Response*. London: Ministry of Justice.

MoJ (2021a) 'Criminal justice system statistics publication: Outcomes by offence 2010 to 2020: Pivot table analytical tool for England and Wales'. GOV.UK [Online] Available from: https://assets.publishing.service.gov.uk/government/uploads/system/uploads/attachment_data/file/987715/outcomes-by-offence-2020.xlsx [Accessed 6 January 2022].

MoJ (2021b) 'Offender management statistics quarterly: April to June 2021', GOV.UK [Online]. Available from: https://www.gov.uk/government/statistics/offender-management-statistics-quarterly-april-to-june-2021 [Accessed 9 January 2022].

MoJ (2022) 'End to Friday releases to cut crime and make streets safer', GOV. UK [Online]. Available from: https://www.gov.uk/government/news/end-to-friday-releases-to-cut-crime-and-make-streets-safer [Accessed 6 March 2023].

Mol, A. (2002) *The Body Multiple: Ontology in Medical Practice*. Durham, NC: Duke University Press.

Monaghan, M., Wincup, E. and Hamilton, I. (2020) 'Scandalous decisions: Explaining shifts in UK medicinal cannabis policy', *Addiction*, 116: 1925–1933.

Moore, A. (2019) *Public Attitudes to Drugs in the UK: Is the UK Ready for Drug Policy Reform?* London: Conservative Drug Policy Reform Group.

Moore, A., Webster, T., Atkins, D. and Stone, R. (2021) *Making UK Drug Policy a Success: Reforming the Policymaking Process*. London: Conservative Drug Policy Reform Group.

Moore, S. (2016) 'RIP Big Society – here's to Life Chances', *Medium* [Online], 15 January. Available from: https://steve4good.medium.com/rip-big-society-here-s-to-life-chances-d7ca856cc074 [Accessed 16 January 2023].

Moreno, J.L. and Jennings, H.H. (1938) 'Statistics of social configurations', *Sociometry*, 1(3/4): 342–374.

Morgan, P. (2019) Boris Johnson on using cocaine: 'I tried it at university and I remember it vividly', *British GQ* [Online]. Available from: https://www.gq-magazine.co.uk/article/boris-johnson-drugs [Accessed 12 May 2023].

Munglani, R. (2018) Letter to *The Times*: 'Cannabis pain relief', *The Times*. 26 October, p 34.

Munro, J.F. (1993) 'California water politics: Explaining policy change in a cognitively polarized subsystem', in P.A. Sabatier and H.C. Jenkins-Smith (eds), *Policy Change and Learning: An Advocacy Coalition Approach*. Boulder, CO: Westview Press, pp 105–127.

Murphy, J. (2017) 'Addiction frameworks and support for expanding treatment for drug offenders', *Contemporary Drug Problems*, 44(3): 232–245.

Murphy, J. and Russell, B. (2020) 'Police officers' views of naloxone and drug treatment: Does greater overdose response lead to more negativity?', *Journal of Drug Issues*, 50(4): 455–471.

Murray, R.M., Quigley, H., Quattrone, D., Englund, A. and Di Forti, M. (2016) 'Traditional marijuana, high-potency cannabis and synthetic cannabinoids: Increasing risk for psychosis', *World Psychiatry*, 15(3): 195–204.

Musto, C. (2018) *Regulating Cannabis Markets: The Construction of an Innovative Drug Policy in Uruguay*. PhD thesis submitted to University of Kent and Utrecht University.

Mykkänen, M. and Freshwater, N. (2021) 'Typology of think tanks: A comparative study in Finland and Scotland', *Academicus International Scientific Journal*, 23: 72–90.

NACRO (2018) *Barriers to Effective Resettlement: Friday Prison Releases*. London: National Association for the Care and Resettlement of Offenders.

Nagel, T. (1989) *The View from Nowhere*. Oxford: Oxford University Press.

NCLCC (2021) *County Lines Strategic Assessment 2020/21*. London: National County Lines Coordination Centre.

NHS (2018) 'Medical cannabis (cannabis oil)'. NHS [Online] Available from: https://www.nhs.uk/conditions/medical-cannabis/ [Accessed 4 November 2018].

NICE (2007) *Naltrexone for the Management of Opioid Dependence. NICE Technology Appraisal 115*. London: National Institute for Health and Clinical Excellence.

NICE (2019a) *Cannabis-Based Medicinal Products. [C] Evidence Review for Spasticity*. London: National Institute for Health and Care Excellence.

NICE (2019b) *Cannabis-Based Medicinal Products: Guidance*. London: National Institute for Health and Care Excellence. Available at: https://www.nice.org.uk/guidance/ng144 [Accessed 18 January 2023].

NICE (2021) *Cannabis-Based Medicinal Products: Clarification of Guidance, National Institute for Health and Care Excellence*. NICE. Available from: https://www.nice.org.uk/guidance/ng144/resources/cannabisbased-medicinal-products-clarification-of-guidance-march-2021-9070302205 [Accessed 18 January 2023].

Nicholls, J., Cramer, S., Ryder, S., Gold, D., Priyadarshi, S., Millar, S. et al (2019) 'The UK Government must help end Scotland's drug-related death crisis', *The Lancet Psychiatry*, 6(10): P804.

Nicholls, J., Livingston, W., Perkins, A., Cairns, B., Foster, R., Trayner, K.M.A. et al (2022) 'Drug consumption rooms and public health policy: Perspectives of Scottish strategic decision-makers', *International Journal of Environmental Research and Public Health*, 19(11): 6575.

Nichols, N., Malenfant, J. and Schwan, K. (2020) 'Networks and evidence-based advocacy: Influencing a policy subsystem', *Evidence and Policy*, 16(4): 639–659.

Niechcial, J. (2010) *Lucy Faithfull: Mother to Hundreds*. London: Compositions by Carn.

Niesink, R.J.M. and van Laar, M.W. (2013) 'Does cannabidiol protect against adverse psychological effects of THC?', *Frontiers in Psychiatry*, 4: 130.

NIH (2022) 'Political savvy'. National Institutes of Health [Online]. Available from: https://hr.nih.gov/working-nih/competencies/competencies-dictionary/political-savvy [Accessed 4 November 2022].

NIHR (2018) 'Themed call: Cannabis-based products for medicinal use (2018)', National Institute for Health and Care Research, [Online]. Available from: https://www.nihr.ac.uk/documents/themed-call-cannabis-based-products-for-medicinal-use-2018/24043 [Accessed 20 January 2023].

North, P. (2017a) *Icelandic Youth*. London, Basingstoke: Volteface.

North, P. (2017b) *Street Lottery: Cannabis Potency and Mental Health*. London: Volteface.

NRS (2021) *Drug-Related Deaths in Scotland in 2020*. Edinburgh: National Records Scotland.

Nutt, D. (2020) 'New psychoactive substances: Pharmacology influencing UK practice, policy and the law', *British Journal of Clinical Pharmacology*, 86(3): 445–451.

Nutt, D. (2021) *Nutt Uncut*. Winchester: Waterside Press.

Nutt, D. (2022) *Why Doctors Have a Moral Imperative to Prescribe and Support Medical Cannabis*. London: Drug Science.

Oakley, A. (2011) *A Critical Woman: Barbara Wootton, Social Science and Public Policy in the Twentieth Century*. London: Bloomsbury.

O'Brien, O. and Stevens, A. (1997) *A Question of Equivalence: A Report on the Implementation of International Guidelines on HIV/AIDS in Prisons of the European Union*. London: Cranstoun Drug Services.

Oliver, K. and Faul, M.V. (2018) 'Networks and network analysis in evidence, policy and practice', *Evidence and Policy*, 14(3): 369–379.

ONS (2020) *Drug Misuse in England and Wales: Year Ending March 2020*. London: Office for National Statistics.

ONS (2021) *Deaths Related to Drug Poisoning in England and Wales*. London: Office for National Statistics.

Padley, M.E. and Gökarıksel, B. (2021) 'The affective politics of policy making spaces: Gendered and racial embodiments of neoliberal deservingness and power in a city council meeting', *Emotion, Space and Society*, 39: 100792. doi: 10.1016/j.emospa.2021.100792.

Pahl, R.E. and Winkler, J.T. (1974) 'The economic elite: Theory and practice', in P. Stanford and A.A. Giddens (eds), *Elites and Power in British Society*. Cambridge: Cambridge University Press, pp 102–122.

Palmer, C. (2022) 'How to cope with hangxiety', TRIP [Online]. Available from: https://drink-trip.com/blogs/news/how-to-cope-with-hangxiety [Accessed 27 January 2023].

Pamuk, K. (2021) *Politics and Expertise: How to Use Science in a Democratic Society*. Princeton: Princeton University Press.

Parker, H., Aldridge, J. and Measham, F. (1998) *Illegal Leisure. The Normalization of Adolescent Recreational Drug Use*. London: Routledge.

Parkhurst, J. (2017) *The Politics of Evidence: From Evidence- Based Policy to the Good Governance of Evidence*. Abingdon: Routledge.

Patel, P. (2020) *Home Secretary's Commissioning Letter to the Chair of the ACMD*. London: Home Office.

Patel, P. (2021) *Response to the ACMD on GHB, GBL and closely Related Compounds*. London: Home Office.

Pedwell, C. (2014) *Affective Relations: The Transnational Politics of Empathy*. New York: Palgrave Macmillan.

Peters, B.G. and Nagel, M.L. (2020) *Zombie Ideas: Why Failed Policy Ideas Persist*. Cambridge: Cambridge University Press.

PHE (2016) *Understanding and Preventing Drug-Related Deaths: The Report of a National Expert Working Group to Investigate Drug-Related Deaths in England*. London: Public Health England.

PHE (2019) *Principles for Engaging with Industry Stakeholders*. London: Public Health England. Available at: https://www.gov.uk/government/publications/principles-for-engaging-with-industry-stakeholders/principles-for-engaging-with-industry-stakeholders#commodity-specific-guidance.

Phillips, M. (2018) 'Drug liberalisation is a disastrous mistake', *MelaniePhillips.com*. Available at: https://www.melaniephillips.com/going-soft-drugs-disastrous-mistake/ [Accessed 14 December 2022].

PHS (2019) 'Drug deaths are preventable, not inevitable', Public Health Scotland [Online]. Available from: http://www.healthscotland.scot/news/2019/july/drug-deaths-are-preventable-not-inevitable [Accessed 1 February 2023].

Pierce, M., Bird, S.M., Hickman, M., Marsden, J., Dunn, G., Jones, A. et al (2015) 'Impact of treatment for opioid dependence on fatal drug-related poisoning: A national cohort study in England', *Addiction*, 111: 298–308.

Piurko, Y., Schwartz, S.H. and Davidov, E. (2011) 'Basic personal values and the meaning of left–right political orientations in 20 countries', *Political Psychology*, 32(4): 537–561.

Platt, L., Minozzi, S., Reed, J., Vickerman, P., Hagan, H., French, C. et al (2018) 'Needle and syringe programmes and opioid substitution therapy for preventing HCV transmission among people who inject drugs: Findings from a Cochrane Review and meta-analysis', *Addiction*, 113(3): 545–563.

Power, M. (2017) *Green Screen*. London: Volteface.

Pryor, D. (2018) 'Norway is aiming to decriminalise drugs. The UK should choose legalisation', *The Guardian*. Available at: https://www.theguardian.com/commentisfree/2018/jan/18/norway-decriminalised-drugs-uk-chose-legalisation-policy [Accessed 31 March 2022].

Pryor, D. (2020) *Britain's Drug Death Disgrace, Adam Smith Institute*. Available at: https://www.adamsmith.org/blog/britains-drug-death-disgrace [Accessed 31 March 2022].

Pryor, D. and McCulloch, L. (2019) *The Green Light: How Legalising and Regulating Cannabis Will Reduce Crime, Protect Children and Improve Safety*. London: Adam Smith Institute.

Quiggins, J. (2010) *Zombie Economics: How Dead Ideas Still Walk Among Us*. Princeton: Princeton University Press.

Rae, M., Howkins, J. and Holland, A. (2022) 'Escalating drug related deaths in the UK', *BMJ*, 378: o2005.

Ragin, C.C. (2008) *Redesigning Social Inquiry: Fuzzy Sets and Beyond*. Chicago: University of Chicago Press.

Ravndal, E. and Amundsen, E.J. (2010) 'Mortality among drug users after discharge from inpatient treatment: An 8-year prospective study.', *Drug and Alcohol Dependence*, 108(1–2): 65–69. doi: 10.1016/j.drugalcdep.2009.11.008.

Rayner, T. (2023) 'Westminster Accounts: Why a cannabis company invests in a group of MPs – and the unusual way it works', *Sky News* [Online]. Available from: https://news.sky.com/story/westminster-accounts-why-a-cannabis-company-invests-in-a-group-of-mps-and-the-unusual-way-it-works-12783288 [Accessed 13 January 2023].

Reiner, R. (1985) 'A watershed in policing', *The Political Quarterly*, 56(2): 122–131.

Release (2018) *Twitter Thread on Victoria Atkins Letter on Drug Consumption Rooms*. Available at: https://twitter.com/Release_drugs/status/984829019836297216 [Accessed 30 March 2022].

Release (2019) *Saving Lives: Best Practice Guidance on the Provision of Naloxone for People Who Might Experience or Witness an Opioid Overdose*. London: Release.

Reynolds, P. (2015) 'For all the hysteria about cannabis and psychosis, here are the facts.', *Peter Reynolds* [Online]. Available from: https://peter-reynolds.co.uk/2015/03/21/for-all-the-hysteria-about-cannabis-and-psychosis-here-are-the-facts/ [Accessed 14 June 2022].

Rhodes, R.A.W. (1990) 'Policy networks: A British perspective', *Journal of Theoretical Politics*, 2(3): 293–317.

Rhodes, R.A.W. (ed.) (2018) *Narrative Policy Analysis: Cases in Decentred Policy*. London: Palgrave Macmillan.

Rhodes, T. and Lancaster, K. (2019) 'Evidence-making interventions in health: A conceptual framing', *Social Science and Medicine*, 238: 112488.

Richardson, J. (2018) 'The changing British policy style: From governance to government?', *British Politics*, 13(2): 215–233.

Richmond, C. (2005) 'Dame Cicely Saunders, founder of the modern hospice movement, dies', *BMJ* [Online]. Available from: https://www.bmj.com/content/suppl/2005/07/18/331.7509.DC1 [Accessed 15 March 2023].

Ritter, A. (2022) *Drug Policy*. Abingdon: Routledge.

Roe, E. (1994) *Narrative Policy Analysis: Theory and Practice*. Durham, NC: Duke University Press.

Rogeberg, O. (2015) 'Drug policy, values and the public health approach – four lessons from drug policy reform movements', *NAD Nordic Studies on Alcohol and Drugs*, 32(4): 347–364.

Rolles, S. (2022) 'Twitter reply to Alex Stevens', *Twitter* [Online]. Available from: https://twitter.com/SteveTransform/status/1599011201454788608 [Accessed 28 December 2022].

Rolles, S., Barton, M., Eastwood, N., Lloyd, T., Measham, F., Nutt, D. et al (2016) *A Framework for a Regulated Market for Cannabis in the UK: Recommendations from an Expert Panel*. London: Liberal Democrats.

Ross, A., Potter, G.R., Barratt, M.J. and Aldridge, J.A. (2020) '"Coming out": Stigma, reflexivity and the drug researcher's drug use', *Contemporary Drug Problems*, 47(4): 268–285.

Ross, D. (2021) *Proposed Right to Addiction Recovery (Scotland) Bill*. Edinburgh: Scottish Parliament.

Rucker, J., Schnall, J., D'Hotman, D., King, D., Davis, T. and Joanne, N. (2020) *Medicinal Use of Psilocybin: Reducing Restrictions on Research and Treatment*. London: Adam Smith Institute and Conservative Drug Policy Reform Group.

Rudd, A. (2017) 'Our drugs strategy will tackle a corrosive, creeping threat destroying countless lives', *Huffington Post* [Online]. Available from: http://www.huffingtonpost.co.uk/amber-rudd/drug-strategy_b_17474964.html [Accessed 7 February 2018].

Sabatier, P.A. (1988) 'An advocacy coalition framework of policy change and the role of policy-oriented learning therein', *Policy Sciences*, 21: 129–168.

Sabatier, P.A. (1993) 'Policy change over a decade or more', in P.A. Sabatier and H.C. Jenkins-Smith (eds), *Policy Change and Learning: An Advocacy Coalition Approach*. Boulder, CO: Westview Press, pp 211–235.

Sabatier, P.A. and Jenkins-Smith, H.C. (1993) *Policy Change and Learning: An Advocacy Coalition Approach*. Boulder, CO: Westview Press.

Sabatier, P.A. and Weible, C.A. (2007) 'The advocacy coalition framework: Innovations and clarifications', in P.A. Sabatier (ed.), *Theories of the Policy Process*, 2nd edition. Boulder, CO: Westview Press, pp 189–222.

Sabatier, P.A. and Weible, C.M. (eds) (2018) *Theories of the Policy Process*, 4th edition. New York: Routledge.

Santo, T., Clark, B., Hickman, M., Grebely, J., Campbell, G., Sordo, L. et al (2021) 'Association of opioid agonist treatment with all-cause mortality and specific causes of death among people with opioid dependence: A systematic review and meta-analysis', *JAMA Psychiatry*, 78(9): 979–993.

Savage, M., Devine, F., Cunningham, N., Taylor, M., Li, Y., Hjellbrekke, J. et al (2013) 'A New model of social class: Findings from the BBC's Great British Class Survey Experiment', *Sociology*, 47(2): 219–250.

Sayer, A. (2000) *Realism and Social Science*. London: Sage.

Sayer, A. (2011) *Why Things Matter to People: Social Science, Values and Ethical Life*. Cambridge: Cambridge University Press.

Sayer, A. (2010) *Method in Social Science: A Realist Approach*, revised 2nd edition. London: Routledge.

Scheerer, S. (1993) 'Political ideology and drug policy', *European Journal on Criminal Policy and Research*, 1(1): 94–105.

Schmidt, V.A. (2008) 'Discursive institutionalism: The explanatory power of ideas and discourse', *Annual Review of Political Science*, 11(1): 303–326. doi: 10.1146/annurev.polisci.11.060606.135342.

Schneider, A. and Ingram, H. (1993) 'Social construction of target populations: Implications for politics and policy', *American Political Science Review*, 87(2): 334–347.

Schwartz, S.H. (1992) 'Universals in the Content and Structure of Values: Theoretical Advances and Empirical Tests in 20 Countries', in M.P. Zanna (ed.), *Advances in Experimental Social Psychology*. San Diego, London: Academic Press, pp 1–65.

Schwartz, S.H. (2012) 'An overview of the Schwartz theory of basic values', *Online Readings in Psychology and Culture*, 2(1). doi: 10.9707/2307-0919.1116.

Schwartz, S.H. and Boehnke, K. (2004) 'Evaluating the structure of human values with confirmatory factor analysis', *Journal of Research in Personality*, 38(3): 230–255.

Scott, J. and Marshall, G. (2009) *A Dictionary of Sociology*, 3rd edition. Oxford: Oxford University Press.

Scottish Affairs Committee (2019) 'Problem drug use in Scotland'. Parliament [Online]. Available from: https://publications.parliament.uk/pa/cm201919/cmselect/cmscotaf/44/4402.htm [Accessed 2 October 2021].

Scottish Conservatives and Unionists (2021) *Rebuilding Scotland*. Edinburgh: The Scottish Conservative and Unionist Party.

Scottish Government (2008) *The Road to Recovery: A New Approach to Tackling Scotland's Drug Problem*. Edinburgh: Scottish Government.

Scottish Government (2017) 'Treating Scotland's changing drug problem'. Scottish Government [Online]. Available from: http://www.gov.scot/news/treating-scotlands-changing-drug-problem/ [Accessed 5 February 2023].

Scottish Government (2018a) Fairer Scotland Duty: Interim guidance for public bodies. Scottish Government [Online]. Available from: http://www.gov.scot/publications/fairer-scotland-duty-interim-guidance-public-bodies/pages/2/ [Accessed 5 February 2023].

Scottish Government (2018b) *Rights, Respect, and Recovery: Scotland's Strategy to Improve Health by Preventing and Reducing Alcohol and Drug Use, Harm and Related Deaths*. Edinburgh: Scottish Government.

Scottish Government (2022a) *National Care Service*. Scottish Government [Online]. Available from: https://www.gov.scot/policies/social-care/national-care-service/ [Accessed 14 February 2023].

Scottish Government (2022b) *National Mission on Drugs – National Collaborative: March 2022 Progress Update*. Scottish Government [Online]. Available from: http://www.gov.scot/publications/national-collaborative-progress-update/ [Accessed 13 February 2023].

Scottish Government (2022c) *The Drug Deaths Taskforce*. Edinburgh: Scottish Government.

Scottish Greens (2021) *Our Common Future*. Edinburgh: Green Party of Scotland.

Scottish Labour (2021) *Scottish Labour's National Recovery Plan*. Edinburgh: Scottish Labour.

Scottish Liberal Democrats (2021) *Put Recovery First*. Edinburgh: Scottish Liberal Democrats.

Scottish Parliament (2021) *Criminal Justice Committee: 27th October 2021*. Edinburgh: Scottish Parliament.

Scottish Recovery Consortium (2022) 'Right to Recovery: Joint Statement Response'. Available at: https://scottishrecoveryconsortium.org/right-to-recovery-joint-statement-response/ [Accessed 20 December 2022].

SDDTF (2020) *Scottish Drug Deaths Taskforce: One Year Report*. Edinburgh: Scottish Drugs Deaths Taskforce.

SDDTF (2021a) *Medication Assisted Treatment (MAT) Standards for Scotland: Access, Choice, Support*. Edinburgh: Scottish Drugs Deaths Taskforce.

SDDTF (2021b) *Report on Drug Law Reform*. Edinburgh: Scottish Drugs Deaths Taskforce.

SDDTF (2022) *Changing Lives: Our Final Report*. Edinburgh: Scottish Drugs Deaths Taskforce.

SDF (Scottish Drugs Forum) (2018) *The Control of Drugs – Issues in Harm Reduction Series*. Glasgow: Scottish Drugs Forum.

SDF (2021) *Drug-related deaths in Scotland: MSP Briefing*. Glasgow: Scottish Drugs Forum.

SDF (2022) *Right to Recovery: Joint Statement, Scottish Drugs Forum*. Scottish Drugs Forum [Online]. Available from: https://www.sdf.org.uk/members-bill-response/ [Accessed 1 February 2023].

SDF and Scottish Government (2019) *Staying Alive in Scotland – 2019 Edition*. Glasgow: Scottish Drugs Forum.

Seddon, T. (2022) 'The Sixties, Barbara Wootton and the counter-culture: Revisiting the origins of the Misuse of Drugs Act 1971', in D. Nutt, I. Crome and A. Stevens (eds), *The Misuse of Drugs Act at 50*, Sherfield-on-Loddon: Waterside Press, pp 183–192.

Sen, A. (2009) *The Idea of Justice*. London: Allen Lane.

SFAAD (2022) *Consultation Response: Right to Addiction Recovery (Scotland) Bill*. Edinburgh: Scottish Families Affected by Alcohol and Drugs. Available at: https://www.sfad.org.uk/resources/policy-responses.

Shapiro, H. (2021) *Fierce Chemistry: A History of UK Drug Wars*. Stroud: Amberley.

Shaw, D., Stott, J., Kirk, E. and Adams, D. (2022) *The Use of Out-of-Court Disposals and Diversion at the 'Front End'*. London: Crest.

Shiner, M., Carre, Z., Delsol, R. and Eastwood, N. (2018) *The Colour of Injustice: 'Race', Drugs and Law Enforcement in England and Wales*. London: Release.

Shorter, G.W., Harris, M., McAuley, A., Trayner, K.M. and Stevens, A. (2022) 'The United Kingdom's first unsanctioned overdose prevention site: A proof-of-concept evaluation', *International Journal of Drug Policy*, 104: 103670.

Silke, J. (2021) 'Drug deaths: Scotland should press ahead with safe consumption rooms after failure of "prohibition"', *The Scotsman* [Online]. Available from: https://www.scotsman.com/drug-deaths-scotland-should-press-ahead-with-safe-consumption-rooms-after-failure-of-prohibition-joseph-silke-3356163 [Accessed 28 January 2023].

Silverman, J. (2006) 'Prisoners who take on the system', *BBC News* [Online], 14 November. Available from: http://news.bbc.co.uk/1/hi/uk/6146606.stm [Accessed 13 March 2023].

Smith, A. (1968 [1759]) *The Theory of Moral Sentiments*. London: Cass.

Smith, K.E. (2017) 'Beyond "evidence-based policy" in a "post-truth" world: The role of ideas in public health', in J. Hudson, C. Needham and E. Heins (eds), *Social Policy Review 29: Analysis and Debates in Social Policy, 2017*. Bristol: Policy Press, pp 151–176.

Smith, K.E. and Stewart, E.A. (2017) 'Academic advocacy in public health: Disciplinary "duty" or political "propaganda"?', *Social Science and Medicine*, 189: 35–43.

Snowdon, C. (2014) 'Re: Under the influence: 2. How industry captured the science on minimum unit pricing', *BMJ*, 348: f7531.

SNP (2019) *Stronger for Scotland*. Edinburgh: Scottish National Party.

SNP (2021) *Scotland's Future*. Edinburgh: Scottish National Party.

Sordo, L., Barrio, G., Bravo, M.J., Indave, B.I., Degenhardt, L., Wiessing, L. et al (2017) 'Mortality risk during and after opioid substitution treatment: Systematic review and meta-analysis of cohort studies', *BMJ*, 357: j1550.

South, N. (1998) 'Tackling Drug Control in Britain: From Sir Malcolm Delevingne to the New Drugs Strategy', in R. Coomber (ed.), *The Control of Drugs and Drug Users: Reason or Reaction?* London: CRC Press, pp 87–106.

Spear, H.B. (2002) *Heroin Addiction Care and Control: The British System*. Edited by J. Mott. London: DrugScope.

Spicer, J. (2020) 'Between gang talk and prohibition: The transfer of blame for county lines', *International Journal of Drug Policy*, 87: 102667.

Spilsbury, M. (2022) *Diversity in Journalism: An Update on the Characteristics of Journalists*. London: National Council for the Training of Journalists.

Spyt, W. and Kew, J. (2023) 'Treading the paths of drug diversion', in M. Bacon and J. Spicer (eds), *Drug Law Enforcement, Policing and Harm Reduction: Ending the Stalemate*. Abingdon: Routledge, pp 174–196.

Stanley, J. (2015) *How Propaganda Works*. Princeton: Princeton University Press.

Starling, B. (2016) *The Tide Effect: How the World Is Changing Its Mind on Cannabis Legalisation*. London: Volteface and the Adam Smith Institute.

Stevens, A. (2007) 'Survival of the ideas that fit: An evolutionary analogy for the use of evidence in policy', *Social Policy and Society*, 6(1): 25–35.

Stevens, A. (2011a) *Drugs, Crime and Public Health: The Political Economy of Drug Policy*. London: Routledge.

Stevens, A. (2011b) 'Recovery through contradiction?', *Criminal Justice Matters*, 84(1): 20–21.

Stevens, A. (2011c) 'Telling policy stories: An Ethnographic study of the use of evidence in policy-making in the UK', *Journal of Social Policy*, 40(2): 237–256.

Stevens, A. (2011d) 'Sociological approaches to the study of drug use and drug policy', *International Journal of Drug Policy*, 22: 399–403.

Stevens, A. (2017) 'Principles, pragmatism and prohibition: Explaining continuity and change in British drug policy', in A., Liebling, S. Maruna and L. McAra (eds), *Oxford Handbook of Criminology*, 6th edition. Oxford: Oxford University Press, pp 825–845.

Stevens, A. (2018) 'Medical cannabis in the UK', *BMJ*, 363: k4844.

Stevens, A. (2019) '"Being human" and the "moral sidestep" in drug policy: Explaining government inaction on opioid-related deaths in the UK', *Addictive Behaviors*, 90: 444–450.

Stevens, A. (2020a) 'Critical realism and the "ontological politics of drug policy"', *International Journal of Drug Policy*, 84: 102723.

Stevens, A. (2020b) 'Governments cannot just "follow the science" on COVID-19', *Nature Human Behaviour*, 4: 560.

Stevens, A. (2021) 'The politics of being an "expert": A Critical realist auto-ethnography of drug policy advisory panels in the UK', *Journal of Qualitative Criminal Justice & Criminology*, 10(2): 1–31.

Stevens, A. (2022) 'New prospects for harm reduction in the UK? A commentary on the new UK drug strategy', *International Journal of Drug Policy*, 109: 103844.

Stevens, A. and Measham, F. (2014) 'The "drug policy ratchet": Why do sanctions for new psychoactive drugs typically only go up?', *Addiction*, 109(8): 1226–1232.

Stevens, A. and Zampini, G.F. (2018) 'Drug policy constellations: A Habermasian approach for understanding English drug policy', *International Journal of Drug Policy*, 57(61–71): 61–71.

Stevens, B. (2022) 'New data suggests NHS licenced cannabis-based medicine prescriptions are on the rise this year', *BusinessCann* [Online]. Available from: https://businesscann.com/new-data-suggests-nhs-licenced-cannabis-based-medicine-prescriptions-are-on-the-rise-this-year/ [Accessed 7 March 2023].

Stewart, H. (2021) 'Boris Johnson admits he has six children', *The Guardian* [Online], 21 September. Available from: https://www.theguardian.com/politics/2021/sep/21/boris-johnson-admits-he-has-six-children [Accessed 12 May 2023].

Stewart, H. and Walker, P. (2021) 'Dominic Cummings says Boris Johnson "unfit for job" of PM amid Covid crisis', *The Guardian* [Online], 26 May. Available from: https://www.theguardian.com/politics/2021/may/26/dominic-cummings-covid-chaos-no-10-like-out-of-control-movie-boris-johnson [Accessed 12 May 2023].

Stewart, R. (2020) 'Book review. *Boris Johnson: The Gambler*, by Tom Bower', *TLS* [Online]. Available from: https://www.the-tls.co.uk/articles/boris-johnson-tom-bower-book-review-rory-stewart/ [Accessed 12 May 2023].

Sturgeon, N. (2021) *Drugs Policy – Update: Statement by the First Minister – 20 January 2021*. Edinburgh: Scottish Government.

Sumnall, H., Atkinson, A., Montgomery, C., Maynard, O. and Nicholls, J. (2023) 'Effects of media representations of drug related deaths on public stigma and support for harm reduction', *International Journal of Drug Policy*, 111: 103909.

Thompson, J.B. (1990) *Ideology and Modern Culture: Critical Social Theory in the Era of Mass Communication*. Cambridge: Polity Press.

Tikly, L. (2022) 'Racial formation and education: A critical analysis of the Sewell report', *Ethnicities*, 22(6): 857–881.

Tilly, C. (2003) 'Changing forms of inequality', *Sociological Theory*, 21(1): 31–36.

Tiratelli, M., Quinton, P. and Bradford, B. (2018) 'Does stop and search deter crime? Evidence from ten years of London-wide data', *British Journal of Criminology*, 58(5): 1212–1231.

Tonry, M. (2007) 'Determinants of Penal Policies', in M. Tory (ed.), *Crime, Punishment, and Politics in Comparative Perspective*. Chicago: Chicago University Press, pp 1–4.

Transform (2015) *The War on Drugs: Harming, not protecting, young people*. Bristol: Transform Drug Policy Foundation.

Transform (2017a) *Heroin Assisted Treatment (HAT): Saving lives, improving health, reducing crime*. Bristol: Transform Drug Policy Foundation.

Transform (2017b) *Scottish Drug Policy Reform: Keeping vulnerable people safer by putting health first*. Bristol: Transform Drug Policy Foundation.

Transform (2018a) *Drug Consumption Rooms: Saving lives, making communities safer*. Bristol: Transform Drug Policy Foundation.

Transform (2018b) *Drug Safety Testing: Saving lives, increasing awareness*. Bristol: Transform Drug Policy Foundation.

Transform (2018c) *Press Release: UK Drugs Minister Misled Parliament Say Canadian Lawyers and Scientists*. Available at: http://www.tdpf.org.uk/blog/press-release-uk-drugs-minister-misled-parliament-say-canadian-lawyers-scientists [Accessed 12 February 2018].

Transform (2020) *Reforming Drugs Policies to Reduce the Trafficking and Exploitation of Vulnerable People*. Bristol: Transform Drug Policy Foundation.

Transform (2022) *The Misuse of Drugs Act 1971: Counting the costs*. Bristol: Transform Drug Policy Foundation.

Trayner, K.M.A., Palmateer, N.E., Hutchinson, S.J., Goldberg, D.J., Shepherd, S.J., Gunson, R.N. et al (2020) 'High willingness to use drug consumption rooms among people who inject drugs in Scotland: Findings from a national bio-behavioural survey among people who inject drugs', *International Journal of Drug Policy*, 90: 102731.

Truss, L. (2019) 'On the nanny state', in R. Lowe (ed.), *On Social Freedom: A Collection of Essays*. London: FREER, pp 5–6.

Tyler, I. (2020) *Stigma: The Making of Inequality*. London: Zed Books.

valentine, k. (2009) 'Evidence, values and drug treatment policy', *Critical Social Policy*, 29(3): 443–464.

Vandenberghe, F. (2019) 'The normative foundations of critical realism: A comment on Dave Elder-Vass and Leigh Price', *Journal of Critical Realism*, 18(3): 319–336.

Varone, F., Ingold, K. and Joirdain, C. (2016) 'Symposium: Studying policy advocacy through social network analysis', *European Political Science*, 16: 322–336.

Volk, C. (2016) 'Towards a critical theory of the political: Hannah Arendt on power and critique', *Philosophy & Social Criticism*, 42(6): 549–575.

Vomfell, L. and Stewart, N. (2021) 'Officer bias, over-patrolling and ethnic disparities in stop and search', *Nature Human Behaviour*, 5(5): 556–575.

Walker, P. (2021) 'Which top UK politicians have admitted to drug use?', *The Guardian* [Online], 6 December. Available from: https://www.theguardian.com/society/2021/dec/06/which-top-uk-politicians-have-admitted-to-drug-use [Accessed 5 January 2023].

Walley, A.Y., Lodi, S., Li, Y., Bernson, D., Babakhanlou-Chase, H., Land, T. et al (2020) 'Association between mortality rates and medication and residential treatment after in-patient medically managed opioid withdrawal: A cohort analysis', *Addiction*, 115(8): 1496–1508.

Wang, Y. (2020) 'What is the role of emotions in educational leaders' decision making? Proposing an organizing framework', *Educational Administration Quarterly*, 57(3): 372–402.

REFERENCES

Ward, A. (2020) 'Effectiveness of residential rehab services & 12 steps'. Faces and Voices of Recovery UK [Online]. Available from: https://www.facesandvoicesofrecoveryuk.org/effectiveness-of-residential-rehab-services-12-steps/ [Accessed 10 February 2023].

Webster, R. (2017) 'Drugs, Alcohol & Justice: A charter for change'. Available at: https://www.russellwebster.com/charter-for-change/ [Accessed 10 June 2022].

Webster, L. (2021) 'FMQs: Nicola Sturgeon "open-minded" about support for Tories' right to recovery plan', *The National* [Online]. Available from: https://www.thenational.scot/news/19632241.fmqs-nicola-sturgeon-open-minded-support-tories-right-recovery-plan/ [Accessed 10 February 2023].

Wilkins, C., Tremewan, J., Rychert, M., Atkinson, Q., Fischer, K. and Forsyth, G.A.L. (2022) 'Predictors of voter support for the legalization of recreational cannabis use and supply via a national referendum', *International Journal of Drug Policy*, 99: 103442.

Williams, E. (1944) *Capitalism and Slavery*. Chapel Hill: The University of North Carolina Press.

Wilson, B. (1939) *Alcoholics Anonymous*. Newark, NJ: Works Publishing Co.

Wolton, L. and Crow, D.A. (2022) 'Politicking with evidence: Examining evidence-based issues in electoral policy narratives', *Policy Sciences*, 55: 661–691.

Wooding, D. (2021) 'Boris unleashes all-out war on drugs to clean up Britain's crime-plagued streets', *The Sun* [Online]. Available from: https://www.thesun.co.uk/news/16941848/boris-johnson-drugs-crackdown-war/ [Accessed 6 March 2023].

Worstall, T. (2019) 'Finally, a sensible drug policy', Adam Smith Institute [Online]. Available from: https://www.adamsmith.org/blog/finally-a-sensible-drug-policy [Accessed 31 March 2022].

Ylä-Anttila, T. and Luhtakallio, E. (2016) 'Justifications analysis: Understanding moral evaluations in public debates', *Sociological Research Online*, 21(4): 1–15.

Young, J. (1971) *The Drugtakers: The Social Meaning of Drug Use*. London: Paladin.

Younge, G. (2018) 'Boris Johnson's white privilege: Imagine he was a black woman', The Guardian [Online], 2 March. Available from: https://www.theguardian.com/commentisfree/2018/mar/02/boris-johnson-white-privilege-black-woman [Accessed 12 May 2023].

Zakimi, N., Greer, A., Bouchard, M., Dhillon, A. and Ritter, A. (2023) 'Sociometric network analysis in illicit drugs research: A scoping review', *PLoS ONE*, 18(2): e0282340.

Zampini, G.F. (2018) 'Evidence and morality in harm-reduction debates: Can we use value-neutral arguments to achieve value-driven goals?', *Palgrave Communications*, 4(62): 1–10.

Zampini, G.F. (2022) 'Combining insights from moral foundations theory and cultural theory to understand stakeholders' positions in the drug policy debate', Paper presented at the Conference of the International Society for the Study of Drug Policy, Lisbon.

Zembylas, M. (2022) 'Affective ideology and education policy: Implications for critical policy research and practice', *Journal of Education Policy*, 37(4): 511–526.

Index

References to figures appear in *italic* type. Those in **bold** refer to tables.

2017 drug strategy 8, 49, 63, 125, 128–129, 137, 145
2021 drug strategy
  Boris Johnson and 147, 151, 159
  Dame Carol Black and 44, 90, 105, 149, 152–153, 155, 156, 157, 159, 163
  development of 8, 23
  documentation 46
  drug-related deaths 125, 129
  drugs and crime 17, 98–99, 147, 163
  drugs and money 49
  ethico-political bases and 149
  funding for treatment 63, 145–146, 147, 148–149, 163
  Home Office 150
  inequalities and 67
  Kit Malthouse and 96
  media and 98–99
  morality and 146–147
  policy constellations and 150, 156, 157, 158–159
  Rory Geoghegan and 152
  Sajid Javid and 83, 155
  tough punishment 17, 162
  treatment 145, 147, 148, 158, 163

A

abduction/abductive 42, 160, 173
abstinence
  conservativism and 64, 84, 175
  England 17, 125
  funding for 127, 142
  harm reduction against 125, 142
  promotion of 17, 90, 125, 127, 157
  residential rehabilitation 140, 142
  Scotland 17, 23, 125–127, 132–133, *132*, 134–135, **134**, 137, 142–143, 167
  traditionalism and 35, 72, 84, 129
  see also policy constellations: abstentionism
Access to Medical Cannabis (APPGDPR) 111
ACMD (Advisory Council on the Misuse of Drugs)
  advice on drug-related deaths 2, 43, 128
  advice on drugs classes 14, 110, 113
  advice on Friday prison releases 102, 162
  advice on harm reduction 138–139
  advice on treatment 102, 137, 139, 141, 148, 149
  decriminalisation and 139
  government line and 2, 139
  Home Office and 167
  on cannabis 111–112, 113
  on medical cannabis 109–110, 117, 119–120, 121, 122, 123
advocacy coalition framework (ACF) 3, 5, 160, 168–169
Afghanistan 15
Aikin, Nickie 103–104
alcohol 5, 16, 70, 71, 73, 89, 99, 116, 134, 137
Anderson, Fleur 63, **80**
Antoniazzi, Tonia 111
APPGDPR (All-Party Parliamentary Group on Drug Policy Reform) 111, 112, 118, 120
Archer, Alfred 22
Archer, Margaret 7, 24, 34, 38
ASI (Adam Smith Institute) 22, 69, 70, 71, 72, **82**, 87, 88, 104
Askew, Rebecca 68
Atkins, Victoria 46, **80**
Atlee, Clement 12

B

Barnes, Dr Jennifer 112, 120
Barnes, Professor Mike 112, 120, 122
Beckley Foundation 86, 87
benzodiazepines 16
Berridge, Virginia 13, 17, 89
Best, David 11, 44, **45, 81**, 167
Betts, Leah 104
Bhaskar, Roy 7
Birch, Paul 115, 122, 123
Birrell, Ian 117

Black, Dame Carol
  2021 drug strategy and 44, 90, 105, 149, 152–153, 155–157, 159, 163
  favouring paternalism **81**, 84
  funding for treatment 176
  government and 95, 96, 155
  interviewee **45**
  on decriminalisation 50
  public health constellation 84
  savvy social power 105, 146, 152–157, 159, 166
Black, people who are racialised as 15, 30, 68, 86, 87, 172–173
Blair, Tony 16
Blunt, Crispin 99, 111
Borges, Jorge Luis 39
Bourdieu, Pierre 24, 25
Boyd, Deirdre 72, **80**, 83, 127
Braverman, Suella 88
Brewster, David 102
Brexit 12, 158
Brine, Steve 102
Britain 8

C

Cairney, Paul 3, 69
Caldwell, Billy 109, 114, 116–117, 118, 119, 120
Caldwell, Charlotte 109, 115, 116–118, 123, 124, 172
Cameron, David 70, 96, 105, 115, 152, 158
Canada 12, 70, 117
cannabinoids 87, 100
cannabis
  ACMD on 111–112, 113
  classification 14, 18, 113
  components 111–112
  'gateway drug' 11
  harms 14, 119
  home growing **82**, 88, 110
  industry 71, 73, **82**, 100
  legalisation
    medical
      backlash 119–122, 123, 162
      drug policy reform policy constellation 85, 110
      medico-penal policy constellation 110
      opposition to 82, 101, 111, 113
      public health policy constellation 81
      rare prescriptions 18, 120–121, 123, 162, 176
      support for 55, 63, 92, 96, 101, 104–105, 110–112, 114
      UK 8, 18, 23, 43, 46, 106, 113–119, 123, 161–162, 165, 173
    recreational
      calls for 22, 51, 62, 70, 114, 166
      Canada 12, 70
      difficult topic 64
      funding for 99
      liberty ethico-political base 70, 71, **82**, 116
      morality and 26
      New Zealand 26
      opposition to 62, 66, 101, 157
      progressive social justice ethico-political base **82**, 86–87
      Uruguay 53
      USA 116
  medical
    ACMD on 109–110, 117, 119–120, 121, 122, 123
    Home Office 109–110, 111, 117, 120, 121, 122
    research on 87
    treatment of anxiety 18, 112
    treatment of chronic pain 18, 112
    treatment of epilepsy 18, 104, 109, 112, 114, 116
    see also cannabis: legalisation: medical
  mental health and 14, 66, 111–113, 120
  policies on 102, 110–111
  recreational 12, 22, 51, 53, 62, 70, **82**, 86–87, 96, 99, 101, 104, 114, 116
  use of 18
Carmichael, Alistair 111
CBD (cannabidiol) 112
circumplex 29, *29*, 37, 61, *62*, 63, 70, 72, 84, 170
coca 15
cocaine 18, 19, 83
Colombia 15
compassion *see* ethico-political bases: compassion
Conservative Party
  drug policy 83, 118, 145, 157
  Drug Policy Reform Group (CDPRG) **82**, 87, 88, 99
  inequalities and 67, 146
  policy constellations and 94, 110
  Scotland 46, 132–133, **134**, 135
  traditionalism 64
conservativism
  drug policy and 157
  Home Office 110
  media 98
  medical cannabis and 123
  morality and 27
  small 'c' conservatism 63–64
  social 28
  social justice and 68
  traditionalism and 63–64, 137
  see also policy constellations: conservative
Constance, Angela **45**, 94, 103, *131*, 136–137, 140–141, 143–144, 167, 172, 176
contextualisation 160, 167
COVID-19 2, 12, 65, 121, 126

INDEX

Cowan, Ronnie 111, 129, **133**, 137
Cranstoun **82**, 87, 175
CRED (Commission on Race and Ethnic Disparities) 15, **80**, 156–157
critical realism
  causation and 161
  cautious ethical naturalism 7, 34, 40
  critical theory and 34
  data analysis 42
  definition 6–7
  drug policy making and 19
  epistemological relativism 7, 34, 39, 40
  ethnographic research and ix
  judgment rationality 7, 34
  morality and 25, 36, 52, 167
  ontological realism 7, 34, 40, 56
  policy constellations and viii, 4, 6–7, 8, 33, 34, 40, 169
  social structures and 24, 36, 167
critical theory 7, 20, 33, 34
CSEW (Crime Survey for England and Wales) 17
CSJ (Centre for Social Justice) 62, 68, **80**, 83, 152, 157
cultural structures
  changing slowly 164
  deeply rooted 173, 174
  differences in 73, 143
  drug policy and 97, 106, 110, 125, 145, 161
  ethico-political bases and 25, 40, 125, 158
  inequalities and 97
  morality and 7, 8, 33, 52, 161, 167, 175
  policy constellations and 5, 7, 8, 93, 106, 110, 158
  power and 8, 33, 36, 106, 123, 167, 175
  social networks and 53
culture wars 26, 72

D

Dale–Perera, Annette 2, 128
Davidson, Baroness Ruth **134**, 138
Day, Ed 1, **45**, 51–52, 64, **81**, 96, 104, 122, 154, 155, 156
decriminalisation
  abstentionist policy constellation and 134
  ACMD and 139
  conservative policy constellation and **80**, 83
  Dame Carol Black on 50
  difficult issue 64
  diversion against 164
  drug policy reform policy constellation and 77, **82**, 85
  liberty ethico-political base and 70, **82**
  of possession 68, 70, 77, 104, 139
  progressive social justice ethico-political base and 68
  public health policy constellation and 134
  reformist policy constellation and **133**, 136

Scotland *131*, **133**, 134, **134**, 136, 138, 139, 140, 164
  support for 38, 138, 139
Delevingne, Sir Malcolm 13, 110
Di Forti, Marta 101, 112
Dingley, Alfie 109, 114, 118, 119
discourse analysis 42, 46, **47**, 61
DNP (2,4-dinitrophenol) 46
drug policy
  cultural structures and 97, 106, 110, 125, 145, 161
  drug users and 69, 89–90, 172
  England 125
  ethico-political bases and 7–8, 20, 40, 52, 61–75, 77, *78*, 170
  evidence-based 51, 66, 69, 100–103, 141–142, 146, 151, 161–162, 165, 173, 175–176
  factoids 17, 49–50, 51, 52, 67, 70, 138, 148, 149, 156
  fields viii, 7, 28, 44, 161, 167, 174–175
  Home Office 89, 95, 145, 150–151, 165, 167
  interest convergence and 30
  literature on viii
  morality and
    circumplex 37
    controversies 31
    expression of 174
    influence on 2, 3, 7, 8, 20–21, 25–26, 146
    moving away from 26, 66, 148
    not discussed openly 52
    positions 61, 64, 73–74, 77, 80, 92, 123, 147, 149, 161, 171
    role in understanding ix, 7
    UK 28–29, 61, 160–161, 174
  narrative tropes 17, 49, 51, 52, 63, 70, 83, 84, 147, 148, 149, 151, 156, 163, 164
  power and 2–3, 7, 8, 20, 21, 22, 93–124, 127, 160–161, 165
  Scotland
    abstinence 17, 125, 134, 142
    differences to UK policies 6, 8, 143
    drug users and 89
    morality and 28–29
    response to drug-related deaths 124, 126, 130, 140, 142, 163
    social structures and 7, 8, 97, 145, 158
  UK
    analysis 42–44, 46, 54, 55, 170, 173
    approaches 12
    changes 12, 173
    compassion and 63
    conservativism 64, 166
    criminalisation 16
    definition 5
    ethico-political bases and 62–71, *62*, 73–75, *78*, 170
    factoids 49

217

fields viii, 7, 44, 161, 167, 174–175
  morality and 28–29, 61, 160–161, 174
  policy constellations and 4, 5, 13, 52, 61, 76–92, *91*, 161, 172, 176
  power and 20, 93–124, 127, 160–161, 165
  racism and 173
  see also 2021 drugs strategy
  see also policy constellations
drug–related deaths
  2021 drug strategy and 125, 129
  abstinence and 127–128
  ACMD and 43
  alcohol 16
  benzodiazepines 16
  compassion and 35, 74, 88, 126
  documents on 46
  England 8, 16, *16*, 43, 106, 128–129, 166
  harm reduction and 12, 126
  heroin 63
  inequalities and 67, 156
  opiates 175
  opioids 15, 43
  prevention of 63
  psychoactive substances 63
  rise in 2, 8, 12, 43, 125, 126, 128, 130, 165
  Scotland
    'national shame' 126, 138, 140
    numbers 16, *16*, 138
    response to 8, 43, 100, 106, 124, 125–126, 130, 138–140, 142–144, 163, 166
    rise in 125, 128, 137, 138
  socio-economic determinants of 173
  UK 8, 16, 63, 125, 128, 165
  Wales 16
  working class and 129
Drug Science **82**, 86, 87
drugs
  benefits ix, 87, 110, 112
  classes 14, 18, 113
  control 13, 19, 64, 65
  crime and 15, 16–17, 49–50, 51, 99, 147–149, 155, 159, 163
  dealing 63, 83
  harms ix, 1, 13, 14, 15, 22, 26, 27, 28, 37, 54–55, 62, 65, 70, 72
  illicit 1, 5, 11, 12, 13, 16, 17, 18, 19, 24–25, 26, 49, 50, 52, 53–54
  possession 14, 62, 68, 70, 77, 85, 104, 139, 156, 164
  poverty and 67
  psychedelic 73
  use 17, 19, 64, 129
  war on 1, 11, 14, 99
Duncan–Smith, Iain 68, **80**, 83–84, 96, 127

E

ecstasy *see* MDMA
Edwards, Professor Griffith 66

End Our Pain **82**, 87, 114, 115, 118
Engels, Friedrich 25
England
  abstinence 17, 125
  drug-related deaths 8, 16, *16*, 43, 106, 128–129, 166
  ethico-political bases 125
  funding for treatment 63, 84, 142, 146, 148, 149
  medical cannabis 120
  OST 175
  policy constellations 144
  sentences for drug possession 14
  treatment 63, 84, 125, 142, 146, 148, 149
equality 20, 28, 67, 69, 79, 97–98, 101, 133, 136, 143
ethical socialism 130, 133, 143, 163–164
ethico-political bases
  2021 drug strategy and 149
  analysis of 51, *74*, *78*, 79, 171–172
  compassion
    cannabis legalisation and 123
    circumplex of ethico-political bases *62*
    drug-related deaths and 35, 74, 88, 126
    interpretation of 62–63, 163, 171
    liberty and 29, **82**, 88, 110
    paternalism and 20, **81**
    policy making and 30, 51, 61, 62
    progressive social justice and **82**, 110
    shared by all actors 20, 29, 62, 63, 72, 73, **74**, 77, 79, 80, 136
    traditionalism and 27, 29, 35, 62, 72, **80**
  conflicting 37, 72–73, 85
  cultural structures and 25, 40, 125, 158
  drug policy and 7–8, 20, 40, 52, 61–75, 77, *78*, 170
  England 125
  liberty
    cannabis legalisation 72
    circumplex *62*
    definition 69–71, **74**
    free markets 79
    harm reduction 71
    progressive social justice and 79, **82**, 85, 88
    traditionalism and 62, 63, 92
  morality and 8, 30, 52
  overlaps 71–72, 76
  paternalism
    cannabis and 110
    circumplex 62
    default 65–67
    ideological narratives **74**
    legal 27, 65, **74**
    liberty and 73, 79
    medico-penal policy constellation and 149, 163
    positions **81**
    progressive social justice and 72, 87

INDEX

protection 65, 71
public health policy constellation and 84, 157, 158, 162
Scotland *131*, *132*, 134, 136, 143
state control 20
traditionalism and 67, 72, 76–77, 89, 110, 123, 146, 149, 157, 164
paternalist egalitarianism 131, 132, 136, 143
policy actors and 8, 37, 51–53, 62, 68, 71, 73, 77, 79, 85, 92, 146, 161
policy constellations and 8, 40, 56, 71, 76–86, 91–92, 161, 171, 174
progressive social justice
  beliefs 20, 28
  cannabis legalisation 71, 110, 136
  circumplex *62*
  compassion and 62, **82**, 116
  drug policy reform policy constellation and 79
  fairness and equality 67–68, 79
  harm reduction 69, 88, 136
  ideological narratives **74**
  lack of power 146, 149, 156, 157, 158
  liberty and 71, 79, 85, 86, 166
  paternalism and 72
  policy constellations and *91*
  positions **82**
  rising influence 74
  Scotland *131*, 136
  traditionalism and 62, 68, 72–73, 92, 157
Scotland 73, 133, 134, 136
shared 37, 53
traditionalism
  abstinence 35, 66, 72, 84
  authority and 20, 30, 69
  cannabis legalisation 110
  circumplex *62*
  compassion and 29, 62
  conservativism and 63–64, 88
  ideological narratives **74**
  liberty and 62, 92
  medico-penal policy constellation 129
  morality and 26, 64–65, 66
  paternalism and 67, 72, 76–77, 89, 110, 123, 146, 149, 157, 164
  positions **80**
  progressive social justice and 62, 68, 72–73, 92, 157
  Scotland *131*, 132, 133, 143
  values 79
UK drug policy and 62–71, *62*, 73–75, *78*, 170
underpinnings of preferences 7, 52, 74
ethics *see* morality
ethnography 42, 43, 50, 54, 56, 61, 80, 81
EU 12

F

Faul, Moira 3, 174
FAVOR UK 127, **134**, 135, 141

Fernback, Martha 104
Findlay, Russell 49–50
FitzPatrick, Joe **133**, 137, 140
Fletcher, Katherine 121–122
Flynn, Paul 51, 111, 116, 118, 123, 124
Foucault, Michel 25
Fox, Steve 116

G

Geoghegan, Rory 152, 157
German Ideology, The (Karl Marx, Friedrich Engels) 25
Gibbs, Blair 70, 156
Giddens, Anthony 24
Gove, Michael 117
Gramsci, Antonio 25
Green Party 62, 68, **82**, 86, 133, **133**, 140

H

Habermas, Jürgen 21, 23, 34–35
Haidt, Jonathan 27, 28, 62, 65, 67, 70, 74, 84, 170
Hamilton, Ian 113–114
Hancock, Matt 96, 121, 154
Hardy, Emma 63
harm reduction
  abstinence against 125, 142
  arguments against 101
  charities 86
  drug checking services 65, 77, 85, 86, 157
  drug-related deaths and 12
  funding for 54–55
  needle and syringe programmes 69
  opposition to 77, 101
  overdose prevention centres (OPCs)
    calls for in UK 65–66, 69, 71
    difficult topic 64
    drug policy reform policy constellation 77, 85, 87
    epistemic power and 100
    liberty ethico-political base 71, **82**, 88
    Scotland 126, 131, 134, 135, 136–137, 139–140
    social justice progressive ethico–political base 69, **82**
    UK not considering 129, 157, 164
    worldwide 12
  Scotland 22, 125, 126, 134–135, 136–137, 138–139, 141, 157, 164
  support for 69, 71, **74**, 77, **82**, 85, 87, 88, 125, *131*, 173
  UK 54–55, 65, 157
  USA 26, 28
heroin 13, 14, 16, 18, 63, 72, 83, 104, 125, 128, 136, 141
Hitchens, Peter 24, 98
HIV 35, 90, 103
Home Office
  2021 drug strategy 150

abstentionist policy constellation 134
ACMD and 167
CBD and 112
conservativism 110
'dragging things out' 116
drug policy 89, 95, 145, 150–151, 165, 167
institutional power 109–110, 151, 167
involvement in Scotland 54, 131
medical cannabis and 109–110, 111, 117, 120, 121, 122
medico-penal policy constellation 13, 89, 110
public health policy constellation and 110
traditionalism 80
homelessness 18
Hudson, Pat 104
Hughes, Charlie 120–121
human rights 68, 69, 86, 143
Humphreys, Professor Keith 11, 12, **45**, 66, **80**, 103, 154, 156
Hurd, Nick 100–101, 113, 117, 118, 119

I

Idea of Justice, The (Amartya Sen) 68
IEA (Institute of Economic Affairs) 70, 71, **82**, 87, 88, 99–100
inequalities 22, 25, 28, 30, 67–68, 97, 122, 134, 156, 162, 166, 174
interest convergence 30

J

Javid, Sajid **80**, 83, 96, 117–119, 121–123, 152, 153, 155, 157, 176
Johnson, Alan 96
Johnson, Boris 2, 12, 17, 64, 68, 70, **80**, 83, 96, 129, 147, 151, 157, 158–159
Johnson, Mark 90

K

Koram, Kojo 173
Krykant, Peter 126, **133**, 136–137, 139–140

L

Labour Party 17, 46, 64, 68, 86, 94, 96, 133, **133**
Lamb, Norman 46, **82**
Lancaster, Kari 3
Lane, Kevin 104
Layder, Derek 42
legalisation
 arguments for 17, 22, 70, 104, 139
 calls for in UK 77, 86, 96
 Canada 12, 70
 cannabis
  medical
   backlash 119–122, 123, 162
   drug policy reform policy constellation 85, 110
   medico-penal policy constellation 110

opposition to 82, 101, 111, 113
public health policy constellation 81
rare prescriptions 18, 120–121, 123, 162, 176
support for 55, 63, 92, 96, 101, 104–105, 110–112, 114
UK 8, 18, 23, 43, 46, 106, 113–119, 123, 161–162, 165, 173
recreational
 calls for 22, 51, 62, 70, 114, 166
 Canada 12, 70
 difficult topic 64
 funding for 99
 liberty ethico-political base 70, 71, **82**, 116
 morality and 26
 opposition to 62, 66, 101, 157
 New Zealand 26
 progressive social justice ethico-political base **82**, 86–87
 Uruguay 53
 USA 116
failed referendum in New Zealand 26
money-making and 70
opposition to 82–83
psilocybin 99, 166
risks of 85
Scotland 136
Uruguay 12, 53
ways of 68–69
Lesh, Matthew **45**, 70–71, **82**, 88
Liberal Democrats 46, **82**, 86, 133
liberalism
 drug policy and 37, 86, 87, 104
 free market 134
 Millian 27, 67, **74**
 practical 71
 progressive (secular) 27–28, 63, 67, **74**
 Scotland 134
libertarianism *see* ethico-political bases: liberty
liberty *see* ethico-political bases: liberty
Liddell, Dave **45**, 54, 68, 72–73, **81**, 124, 137, 138, 140, 141
limitations 170–173
Lucas, Caroline 111

M

MacCoun, Rob 25, 27, 64, 65, 67, 70, 72, 74–75
Malthouse, Kit 55, 66, **80**, 83, 84, 96, 103–104, 131, *131*, **134**, 139, 150, 157
Marks, Dr John 65
Marx, Karl 25
Matheson, Catriona 22, 127, 128, **133**, 141, 142
Matters of Substance (Griffith Edwards) 66
May, Theresa 12, **80**, 117, 129, 158
McCambridge, Jim 71
McCulloch, Liz 50

McGarvey, Darren 'Loki' 138, 140
McKeganey, Neil 24, 101, **134**
McKinlay, Craig 101
McLaughlin, Anne 66, 113
MDMA 18, 104
Measham, Fiona 14, **82**, 86
mental health 15, 51, 66, 111–112, 120, 123
methadone 102, 127, 135, 137, 142
Mill, John Stuart 67
Millar, Professor Alan 143
Millar, Tim 2
Miller, David 71
Millian ideas 27, 67, 72, **74**
Misuse of Drugs Act 1971 5, 13–14, 15, 16, 43, 65, 93, 130, 139
Misuse of Drugs Regulations 2001 5, 18, 81, 109, 176
Monaghan, Mark 109, 113–114
Moore, Steve
  adviser to David Cameron 99
  founder of Volteface 70, 109
  government and 95, 96
  interviewee **45**, 89
  legalisation of medical cannabis 96, 101, 105, 109, 115–116, 117, 118, 121–122, 176
  liberty ethico-political base **82**
  savvy social power 105, 123, 166
Moral Foundations Questionnaire 27, 56
morality
  2021 drug strategy and 146–147
  changes during 1960s 13
  contemporary 26
  critical realism and 25, 36, 52
  cultural structures and 7, 8, 33, 52, 161, 167, 175
  definition 6
  drug policy and
    circumplex 37
    controversies 31
    expression of 174
    influence on 2, 3, 7, 8, 20–21, 25–26, 146
    moving away from 26, 66, 148
    not discussed openly 52
    positions 61, 64, 73–74, 77, 80, 92, 123, 147, 149, 161, 171
    role in understanding ix, 7
    UK 28–29, 61, 160–161, 174
  morality policy 31
  moral sidestep 129
  policy constellations and 5, 7, 34, 35–36, 150
  political views and 29, 30
  politicians and 12
  power and 2, 7, 20, 21, 25, 33, 36
  research on 27–29
  social structures and 7, 8, 33, 175
Moran, Layla 111
morphogenesis 24

MSA (multiple streams approach) 3
Murray, Professor Sir Robin 101, 112
Musto, Clara 53

N

naloxone 28, 140, 142
naltrexone 142
neo-pluralism 3, 33, 40, 56, 168, 173
New Zealand 26
Newton, Sarah 49
NHS 11–12, 18, 85, 95, 120, 121, 122, 162
NICE (National Institute for Health and Care Excellence) 119, 120, 121–122, 123, 142
nitrous oxide, 93
North, Paul **45**, **82**, 114–115, 118
Northern Ireland 6, 116, 117, 124, 147
Nutt, David 2, **82**, 86, 112, 122

O

OHID (Office for Health Improvement and Disparities) **81**, 84, 85, 89, 95
Oliver, Kathryn 3
OPCs *see* harm reduction: overdose prevention centres
opiates 19, 69, 142, 175
opioids 11, 15, 17, 43, 90, 102, 119, 126–127
opium 15
Osborne, George 145, 158
OSF (Open Society Foundation) 99
OST (opioid substitution therapy) 102, 126–127, 128, 175

P

Parkhurst, Justin 31
Patel, Priti **80**, 83, 96, 154
paternalism *see* ethico-political bases: paternalism
paternalist egalitarianism *see* ethico-political bases: paternalist egalitarianism
Pedwell, Carolyn 30
PET (punctuated equilibrium theory) 3
police 21, 26, 35, 38, 68, 83, 85, 90, 164
policy constellations
  2021 drug strategy and 150, 156, 157, 158–159
  abstentionist (Scotland) 17, 126, 132, *132*, **134**, 135, 137, 140–141, 143, 175
  ACF and 168
  actors
    acting in concert 6, 97, 166–167
    attributes 50
    drug policy field 7, 15, 17, 46, 73, 77
    ethico-political bases and 8, 37, 51–53, 62, 68, 71, 73, 77, 79, 85, 92, 146, 161
    government and 36, 95
    interaction 34, 53
    legalisation of medical cannabis 109–110, 114, 118, 123
    morality and 92

positions 53–55, 71, 75, 76, 77, *78*, 79–81, 84, 89, 91, 93
power and 8, 21–23, 35–38, 64, 93, 94, 97–103, 105–106, 150, 154, 157–158, 176
previous decisions and 11
resources 33
Scotland 126, 130–134, 136–39
shared preferences 5, 8, 35–37, 38, 61, 88, 97, 122, 145, 161, 164–165
social networks and 7, 24, 36, 42, 52, 53, 55, 94, 96, 168, 174–175
Borges on 39
conservative 76, 80, 88–89, *91*, 92, 104, 129, 166, 175
critical realism and viii, 4, 6–7, 8, 33, 34, 40
critical theory and 34
cultural structures and 5, 7, 8, 93, 106, 110, 158
definition 5–6, 35
drug policy reform 80, 85–87, *91*, 92, 99, 104, 110–111, 126
England 144
ethico-political bases and 8, 40, 56, 71, 76–86, 91–92, 161, 171, 174
libertarian 87–88, 91
medico-penal
  conservative and public health 77, 88–89
  Home Office 13, 89, 110
  paternalism and 149, 163
  traditionalism and 129, 157, 163
morality and 5, 7, 34, 35–36, 150
overlaps 77, 79, 80, 88–89, 91, 172
paternalist egalitarian (Scotland) 132, 136
power and 8, 23, 34, 36, 37–39, 61, 93–98, 106, 174, 175
progressive (Scotland) 132, 136
progressive social justice 86–87, 91
public health 76, 80, 84–85, 88–89, *91*, 110, 126, 135, 157, 166, 168
reformist (Scotland) 126, 132, *132*, **133**, 135, 136, 137, 140–141, 142, 143, 175
Scotland 6, 125, 126, 130, 132, *132*, **133**, 135–136, 137–142, 143
shared mission 36–37
social networks and 4, 33, 35, 52–53, 93, 94, 136, 161, 169, 174, 175, 176
social reality and 39
social structures and 5, 7
treatment and 89
UK drug policy and 4, 5, 13, 52, 61, 76–92, *91*, 161, 172, 176
see also drug policy
policy narratives 11, 19, 40, 103, 155
  imperilled child narrative 63, 70, 103
  drugs–crime narrative 148–149, 163
  war on drugs narrative 1, 11, 14, 99
Politics of Policy Analysis, The (Paul Cairney) 3

post-structuralism ix, 3, 7, 168
poverty 17
power
  affective 22–23, 94, 103–105, 109–110, 118–119, 122–123, 141–142, 143, 158, 161–165
  constellations of 34–35
  cultural structures and 8, 33, 36, 106, 123, 167, 175
  definition 6
  distribution of 25
  drug policy and 2–3, 7, 8, 20, 21, 22, 93–124, 127, 160–161, 165
  economic 20, 21, 38, 94, 99–100, 109, 110, 123, 161–162, 169
  epistemic 19–23, 94, 100–105, 109, 110–113, 118–119, 123, 141–143, 150–151, 157, 165
  familiarity and 95–97, 115, 130, 157, 161
  institutional 20–21, 93, 94, 97, 105–106, 109, 110, 119, 122–123, 135, 151, 154–158, 162
  legal 20, 21, 38, 93, 175
  media 23, 38, 94, 98–99, 109, 110, 118, 122, 123, 161, 169
  morality and 2, 7, 20, 21, 25, 33, 36
  policy actors and 8, 21–23, 35–36, 38, 64, 93, 94, 97–103, 105–106, 150, 154, 157–158, 176
  policy constellations and 8, 23, 34, 36, 37–39, 61, 93–98, 106, 174, 175
  political 20, 21
  reproduction of 24
  savvy social 20, 23, 94, 97, 105–106, 109, 115–118, 122–123, 146, 152, 154–155, 157–159, 166
  social 19–23, 94, 97–98, 106
  social networks and 97
  social structures and 5, 7, 8, 24, 33, 35, 36, 106, 123, 161, 175
  stratification of 24, 32, 38
prisons 14–15, 18, 102–103, 162, 175
progressive social justice *see* ethico-political bases: progressive social justice
proportionality 28
Pryor, Daniel *45*, 70–71, **82**, 88
psilocybin ('magic' mushrooms) 70, 71, 87, 88, 99, 104, 166
psychoactive substances 19, 63
Psychoactive Substances Act 2016 93, 104, 112

R

Raab, Dominic **80**, 84, 127
racism 68, 156–157, 173
Rawlinson, Professor Sir Michael 113
recovery 17, 22, 71–72, 77, 83–84, 89, 90, 102
Reducing Opioid–Related Deaths in the UK (ACMD) 2, 43, 128, 137, 141, 148

INDEX

reflexivity 37, 39, 171
Release **82**, 86, 87, 118, 122, 131, **133**, 135, 156
religion 20, 26, 28, 52, 161
replicability 170–171
residential rehabilitation 45, **80**, 127–128, 134, **134**, 135, 141–142
retroduction 160
Reuter, Peter 11, 25, 27, 64, 65, 67, 70, 72, 74–75
Rhodes, Tim 3
Righteous Mind, The (Jonathan Haidt) 27, 28
Robertson, Dr Roy 128
Rolles, Steve 22, *45*, 49, 63, **82**, 85, 86, 98, 99, 114, 135–136
Rolleston, Sir Humphrey 13
Ross, Douglas **134**, 135
Rudd, Amber 96, 153–154, 167

S

Scheerer, Sebastian 65
Schwartz, Shalom 27, 28, 62, 63, 67, 70, 72, 77, 84, 170, 176
Scotland
  abstentionism 17, 126, 127, 132, *132*, 133, **134**, 135, 137, 139, 140–143, 167
  drug policy
    abstinence 17, 125, 134, 142
    differences to UK policies 6, 8, 143
    drug users and 89
    morality and 28–29
    response to drug-related deaths 124, 126, 130, 140, 142, 163
  drug-related deaths
    'national shame' 126, 138, 140
    numbers 16, *16*, 138
    response to 8, 43, 100, 106, 124, 125–126, 130, 138–140, 142–144, 163, 166
    rise in 125, 128, 137, 138
  ethical socialism 130, 133, 143, 163–164
  ethico-political bases 73, 133, 134, 136
  harm reduction 22, 126, 134–135, 136–137, 138–140, 141, 157, 164
  Home Office involvement 54, 131
  legalisation 136
  liberalism 134
  marginalisation 68
  policy constellations 6, 125, 126, 130, 132, *132*, **133**, 135–136, 137–142, 143
  reformism 126, 132, *132*, **133**, 135, 136, 137, 140–141, 142, 143, 167
  treatment 125, 126–127, 128, 135, 137, 14114–2, 143
SDDTF (Scottish Drug Deaths Taskforce) 138–139, 140–141, 142, 143
SDF (Scottish Drugs Forum) 135, 136, 137
self-enhancement *29*, 30, 65, 69–70
Sen, Amartya 68
Shapiro, Harry 175

Smith, Adam 72, 133–134
Smith, Jeff **82**, 111, 121
Snowdon, Chris *45*, 70–71, 73, **82**, 87, 97, 99–100, 101, 134
SNP (Scottish National Party) 46, **82**, 130, 133, **133**, 136, 137, 139, 140, 143–144
social groups 24
social networks
  drug policy and 7, 33, 35–36, 52–53, 76
  policy constellations and 4, 33, 35, 52–53, 93, 94, 136, 161, 174, 175, 176
  power and 97
  rewiring 174
  SNA (social network analysis) 4, 7, 42, 52–53, 54–56, 81, 85, 171–172
  social structures and 24
social structures
  advantage and 159, 174
  causal powers of 56
  class, race and gender 24, 25, 36, 97, 161
  deeply rooted 173
  drug policy and 7, 8, 97, 145, 158
  inequalities and 97, 174
  media and 98
  morality and 7, 8, 33, 175
  policy constellations and 5, 7
  power and 5, 7, 8, 24, 33, 35, 36, 106, 123, 161, 175
  social networks and 24
Soros, George 99, 100
Southwell, Mat 64–65, 67–68, **82**, 90
Starling, Boris 22
stigmatisation 6, 15, 17, 64
StopWatch **82**, 86, 156
Strang, John **45**, 81, 95, 96, 154–155, 156
Straw, Jack 64
Sturgeon, Nicola 54, 133, **133**, 136, 137, 141
Sumnall, Harry 18, **82**
Sweeney, Paul **133**, 139–140

T

Tenacious Labs 99
Thatcher, Margaret 12
Theory of Moral Sentiments (Adam Smith) 72
Throup, Maggie 46
tobacco 5, 71, 73, 89, 100
Trace, Mike **45**, 81, 95, 163, 175
traditionalism *see* ethico-political bases: traditionalism
Transform **82**, 86, 100, 115, 118, 131, **133**, 137
treatment
  2021 drug strategy 145, 147, 148, 158, 163
  access to 38, 135
  ACMD advice on 102, 137, 139, 141, 148, 149
  England 63, 84, 125, 142, 146, 148, 149
  funding 54, 62–3, 128, 137, 142, 145–146, 147, 148–149, 163, 176

cuts in 126, 128, 137
England 63, 84, 142, 146, 147, 148, 149, 157–158, 159, 163
Scotland 126, 137, 141
support for 54, 62–63, **81**, 84
heroin-assisted 72, 141–142
OST (opioid substitution treatment) 17, 83, 102, 126–127, 128, 175
policy constellations and 89
providers 84–85, 87, 95
Scotland 125, 126–127, 128, 135, 137, 141–142, 143
support for 80
system 84–85, 90, 149
USA 26
Truss, Liz 29, 88

U

UK
  drug policy
    analysis 42–44, 46, 54, 55, 170, 173
    approaches 12
    changes 12, 173
    compassion and 63
    conservativism 64, 166
    criminalisation 16
    definition 5
    ethico-political bases and 62–71, *62*, 73–75, *78*, 170
    factoids 49
    fields viii, 7, 44, 161, 167, 174–175
    morality and 28–29, 61, 160–161, 174
    policy constellations and 4, 5, 13, 52, 61, 76–92, *91*, 161, 172, 176
    power and 20, 93–124, 127, 160–161, 165
    racism and 173
    see also 2021 drugs strategy
  drug-related deaths 8, 16, 63, 125, 128, 165
  harm reduction 54–5, 65, 157
  legalisation of medical cannabis 8, 18, 23, 43, 46, 106, 113–119, 123, 161–162, 165, 173
  morality 27–29
  policy constellations 7, 8, 28, 76, 125
UN 12, 90
universalism 28–29, 30
UPA (United Patients Alliance) 111, 114, 118
Uruguay 12, 53
USA 12, 14, 23, 26–27, 28, 73–74, 116
User Voice 90

V

Volteface 50, 70, 71, **82**, 87, 88, 104, 109, 114, 115, 116, 117, 118, 123

W

Wales 6, 14, *16*, 17, 124, 147
Ward, Annemarie 127, **134**
Wasted (Mark Johnson) 90
Wincup, Emma 113–114
wokeness 26
Worstall, Tim 72

Z

'zombie ideas' 1, 164